Authority to Control the
School Program

Michael W. Kirst, Ed., *State, School, and Politics: Research Directions*

Joel S. Berke, Michael W. Kirst, *Federal Aid to Education: Who Benefits? Who Governs?*

Al J. Smith, Anthony Downs, M. Leanne Lachman, *Achieving Effective Desegretation*

Kern Alexander, K. Forbis Jordan, *Constitutional Reform of School Finance*

George R. LaNoue, Bruce L. R. Smith, *The Politics of School Decentralization*

David J. Kirby, T. Robert Harris, Robert L. Crain, Christine H. Rossell, *Political Strategies in Northern School Desegregation*

Philip K. Piele, John Stuart Hall, *Budgets, Bonds, and Ballots: Voting Behavior in School Financial Elections*

John C. Hogan, *The Schools, the Courts, and the Public Interest*

Jerome T. Murphy, *State Education Agencies and Discretionary Funds: Grease the Squeaky Wheel*

Howard Hamilton, Sylvan Cohen, *Policy-Making by Plebiscite: School Referenda*

Daniel J. Sullivan, *Public Aid to Nonpublic Schools*

James Hottois, Neal A. Milner, *The Sex Education Controversy: A Study of Politics, Education, and Morality*

Lauriston R. King, *The Washington Lobbyists for Higher Education*

Frederick M. Wirt, Ed., *The Polity of the School: New Research in Educational Politics*

Peter J. Cistone, Ed., *Understanding School Boards: Problems and Prospects*

Lawrence E. Gladieux, Thomas R. Wolanin, *Congress and the Colleges: The National Politics of Higher Education*

Dale Mann, *The Politics of Administrative Representation: School Administrators and Local Democracy*

Harrell R. Rodgers, Jr., Charles S. Bullock III, *Coercion to Compliance:*

Richard A. Dershimer, *The Federal Government and Educational R&D*

Tyll van Geel, *Authority to Control the School Program*

Authority to Control the School Program

Tyll van Geel
University of Rochester

Lexington Books
D.C. Heath and Company
Lexington, Massachusetts
Toronto

Library of Congress Cataloging in Publication Data

Van Geel, Tyll.
  Authority to control the school program.
  Bibliography: p.
  Includes index.
  1. Educational law and legislation—United States. 2. Education
and state—United States. 3. Teachers' unions—United States.
I. Title.
KF4119.V3   379.73   75-24656
ISBN 0-669-00228-3

This work was developed under a grant from the National Institute
of Education, Department of Health, Education, and Welfare. However, the content does not necessarily reflect the position or policy
of that agency, and no official endorsement of these materials should
be inferred.

Published simultaneously in Canada

Printed in the United States of America

International Standard Book Number: 0-669-00228-3

Library of Congress Catalog Card Number: 75-24656

To Katy, with love

Contents

Preface   xiii

Chapter 1   **Introduction**   1

The New Models   2
The System in Operation   4
Principles for the Allocation of Authority   7

Chapter 2   **The Federal Courts and the U.S. Constitution**   17

Allocating Authority between Public and Private
Decision Makers   18
Religion in the Public Schools   20
The School as a Marketplace for Political Ideas   22
The School as a Cultural Marketplace   29
The Minimally Adequate Education   35
Conclusions   41

Chapter 3   **The Federal Government**   43

The Constitutional Basis of Federal Involvement
in Education   44
Title I, ESEA   45
Title VI, Civil Rights Act of 1964   51
Title IX   57
Sex and Race Bias in Educational Materials   63
Curriculum Development and Dissemination   66
Conclusions   70

Chapter 4   **The Changing State Role**   73

Decentralized States   74
Moderately Decentralized States   75
Centralized States   77
Recent Developments   83
Educational Accountability   85
Children with Special Needs   88
Special Education   88
Bilingual Education   91
Experimentation and Innovation   93
Administering Grants-in-Aid   94
Conclusions   95

Chapter 5   **The State Courts**   97

Right to an Education   97

028981

	Other Constitutional Issues	108
	The Right to an Education and Statutory Interpretation	109
	The Abuse of Discretion	113
	Conclusions	115
Chapter 6	**Professionals and Their Unions**	**117**
	The Permissibility of Delegating Authority	117
	The Academic Freedom of Teachers	120
	Teachers' Unions and Control of the Curriculum	123
	Conclusions	135
Chapter 7	**The Public and Parents**	**137**
	Citizens and the School Board	137
	The Constitution and Parental Rights	139
	Other Exemption Cases	142
	Demanding That a Course Be Taught	143
	Selection of Books and Methods of Instruction	147
	Grading and Classification of Pupils	148
	Advisory Committees	150
	Conclusions	152
Chapter 8	**State Control of Private Schools**	**153**
	How States Regulate Private Schools	153
	Interpreting the Statutes	157
	Delegation, Due Process, and Prior Approval	163
	Prohibiting Home Instruction	165
	Private Teachers Must Be Certified	166
	The Imposition of Curriculum Requirements	167
Chapter 9	**Conclusions and Policy Recommendations**	**169**
	Sharing Control of the Curriculum	169
	The Professionals	173
	Parental Authority	173
	An Assessment	175
	Modifications of the System	177
	Educational Vouchers	184
	Notes	**187**
	Bibliography	**223**
	Index	**243**
	About the Author	**251**

Preface

Who *does* and who *should* control the curriculum of the public and private schools are ancient issues that still have the capacity for stirring angry debate. That this should be so is not surprising, as determining who controls the curriculum also determines what shall be taught in the schools, and the issue of what shall be taught has roots in such fundamental controversies as what kind of society and political system we are to live within. When we discuss who controls the curriculum, we discuss who has the authority to control one of the important instruments for shaping the future of the society and nation.

This book is an assessment of the question of who has legal authority to control the program in the public and private schools of the country. The authority of the federal government, the federal and state courts, state boards of education and chief state school officers, local boards of education, teachers and their unions, and parents is assessed through an analysis of statutes, regulations, and court cases. Also discussed is how that legal authority has been used. Trends in changes in the allocation of authority are discerned and analyzed, and an assessment is made of the present and emerging distribution of authority in light of ten principles that have in the past counted in debates over the allocation of authority. The book concludes with recommendations, based on those ten principles, on how authority over the control of the school program ought to be reallocated.

The terms *curriculum* and *school program* are used interchangeably in the book and are to be taken in their broadest sense. They are meant to refer to the purposes, intended outcomes, and methods of instruction; the courses and programs offered; the books and materials used, as well as their content and themes; and processes and experiences through which children are put. They even include such aspects of the so-called hidden curriculum as hair and dress codes. The terms *authority* or *legal authority* are used in their strict sense, meaning the legal, formal right to make choices, or at least to participate in the making of choices with regard to the school program to which children are exposed. Authority is a right created by legal rules which have been adopted by such legitimate lawmaking bodies as the legislature or courts. Those who have been given such legal authority by reason of the office they hold or the status they enjoy, such as that of parent, properly expect their decisions to be binding.

The book begins with an introductory chapter that sketches in nonlegal terms the present system for controlling the program of the public schools. This first chapter concludes with a discussion of the ten principles that have counted in shaping that system of governance. Chapter 2 discusses the basic legal principles arising from the U.S. Constitution that shape and determine the allocation of authority over the school program and the limits of that authority. In chapter 3, the authority (its limits and exercise) of the federal government is taken up. Chapter 4 turns to an assessment of the changing legal relationship between the state agencies charged with authority to control the state program and the local school boards. The emerging role of the state courts in interpreting state constitutions, shaping the relationship between state agencies and local boards, and in reviewing the exercise of authority by local boards is discussed in chapter 5. Chapter 6 examines the law as it bears on the delegation of authority by school boards to the professionals they have hired and as it bears on the right of teachers' unions to demand control over the school program. With chapter 7, we turn to an assessment of the rights of citizens in general, and parents in particular, to influence and control what is to be taught in the local district. The limits of state authority to control the program of private schools is taken up in chapter 8. The concluding chapter 9 returns to matters taken up in the first chapter by adding more details to the governance model outlined in chapter 1 and by assessing that model in light of the ten principles adumbrated in the first chapter. This chapter ends with recommendations for changes in how authority to control the schools' program should be reallocated.

This study began with and is in part based on a study completed under grant No. NE-G-00-3-0069 from the National Institute of Education and entitled: Authority to Control the School Curriculum: An Appraisal of Rights in Conflict, November, 1975, written by Tyll van Geel with the assistance of Arthur Block, who is currently clerk to the Honorable Clarence Newcomer, United States District Judge, U.S. District Court, Eastern District, Pennsylvania. Without Art's assistance, I doubt the N.I.E. project would have been completed with the rigor and richness of detail it now has, and, accordingly, I owe him a great debt in the writing of this book. Professor Frank I. Michelman, Harvard Law School, served as a consultant on the N.I.E. project with great critical acumen; his assistance in sharpening the analysis presented at various points in these pages also is greatly appreciated. My colleague at the University of Rochester, William Boyd, not only provided valuable comments as the work progressed but has been a constant source of ideas, references, and general support during the writing of the book. Jon Schaffarzick, my N.I.E. Project Officer, was most gracious and generous with his time during the completion of the project as well as being a source of ideas, references, and information of great usefulness. In addition, I am thankful for the steady, good humored, and most competent secretarial assistance provided by Muriel Parkin.

Finally, and most importantly, I thank my wife, Katharine Weinrich van Geel, for her helpful comments and astute editorial assistance, not to mention her unflagging support.

Authority to Control the School Program

1 INTRODUCTION

Thirty years ago the question of who has the authority to control the educational program to which children are exposed was easily answered. While state legislatures constitutionally retained ultimate control of the public school program, these legislatures generally acted with restraint in exercising their own authority. (The control of private schools is taken up in chapters 2 and 8.) When it came to imposing their own conceptions of a minimally adequate and sound educational program upon the state, the state legislatures imposed significant, but only general, requirements. That is, the legislatures of the country required only that students take courses dealing with American history, the U.S. and state constitutions, the principles of good citizenship, and basic subjects such as English and arithmetic. Religious exercises were prescribed by the legislatures, as were courses on the nature and effects of alcoholic drinks and road safety. As for allocating authority to enforce and implement these provisions, legislatures delegated significant authority to special educational agencies—a state board of education, chief state school officer, and local boards of education.

But the state legislatures did not all design the institutional arrangements in the same way, and there emerged roughly speaking, three patterns or models for school governance (see chap. 4 for more details). In some states, the state agencies were given only advisory authority with regard to the school program, thereby maintaining a considerable degree of local control over the educational program. In other states, state agencies were given somewhat more substantial powers, such as the opportunity to approve or disappove the offering by local districts of particular courses. The third pattern was the most centralized, with state agencies being given the authority to prescribe the school program and to control the selection of the textbooks to be used in all the public schools of the state. Associated with these three patterns were differences in the extent to which the state agencies were isolated from or involved in electoral politics. In the least centralized states, there was an increased tendency to make state officials appointive but, in the centralized states, it was very common to provide for the election of state officials, even in partisan elections. In all states, however, the state courts played only a small role in shaping the school program and the federal courts were almost totally uninvolved. Nor did the federal government, teachers' unions, or parents, as parents, play any significant role. Students had no recognized rights.

1

The New Models

In several important respects all this has changed in both the centralized and decentralized states. In all states, state involvement in the educational program has broadened and deepened, making the centralized states more centralized and the decentralized states less so. Thus, we can speak today of three newer models of centralization and decentralization. Furthermore, the courts, at both the federal and state level, have become involved and have limited the discretion of state and local officials to control the school program. The federal government's influence on the school program has now been felt (see chap. 3). Teachers' unions have come into existence and have had some success in making the school program a subject of collective negotiations (see chap. 6). The most obvious big loser under the new system for controlling the public school program is the local board of education—it must share its control with several new participants in the policy-formation process. A less obvious loser is the parent, for, as the state, the federal government, the courts, and the unions extend their control, the possibility of meaningful parental control at the local level diminishes. This is so despite the fact that parents have obtained in several states opportunities for encreased involvement in educational decision making.

Besides the expansion of the list of participants in the policymaking process for the school program, the new model is also marked by several additional features. First, control of the curriculum increasingly has become legalized, that is, subject to an ever-burgeoning body of judicially forged doctrine, to legislation, and state regulations. This development has had the effect of further eroding local control of the educataional program. Second, states that were once highly decentralized—meaning there was a minimum of state involvement in the control of the local program—have moved toward greater centralization. Third, the content of the school program has become more variegated and complex than heretofore, especially because now schools are expected to take into account a variety of special needs of students that in the past local school districts had tended to neglect.

Fourth, there is a new division of labor. Formulation and implementation of public school curriculum—about a dozen tasks in all—are now shared in new ways among those on the expanded list of participants in the curriculum policymaking system (see appendix 1A). Whereas, under the old models, many of these roles were occupied exclusively by the local board or perhaps were shared by the local board and state, under the new models, these roles are cooperatively executed not only by the state agencies and local boards but also by federal agencies, unions, and courts. For example, the establishment of minimum standards for the educational program traditionally has been the function of the state legislature and state educational agencies. Today these participants are still involved in this task (they are, in fact, carrying out their role in new ways), but, in addition, the federal government has begun to play a role, and there is every reason to believe that the courts will increasingly respond to requests to be involved.

Fifth, the larger number of participants, the legalization of the process, and the greater division of labor involve such further implications as an increase in the time it takes to make decisions with regard to the school program. Also, there are now more stages in the decision-making process at which proposals can be vetoed, and there is a more elaborate appeals system which can be used to seek review of decisions made by one of the participants in the decision process. For example, many decisions made at the local level can now be appealed not only to state agencies but also to a federal agency and the courts. A complex hierarchy of authority has thus emerged, involving the three levels of government (federal, state, and local) and the three branches of government (legislative, executive, and judicial). Complex procedures have emerged for meshing these parts of the government. For example, states have adopted what are termed administrative procedure acts which regulate the procedures educational agencies at the state and local levels must go through when adopting rules and reaching quasi-judicial decisions. These same acts lay down the conditions that must be met in order to appeal decisions to the judiciary and spell out the standards the judiciary must follow in rendering its decisions.

In short, the system that has emerged for making curriculum policy has all the characteristics of a vast bureaucracy that reaches from the schoolhouse to Washington, D.C. Whether these developments have improved the quality of the educational program of the public schools and whether student achievement is now higher than if the old system had remained unchanged is not possible to answer. It is possible to say, however, that the main substantive outcome of these changes seems to be that children who had before largely been neglected by the public schools (for example, the handicapped) now must be paid specific attention. But, in addition, it would not be surprising to uncover with further study that related to these changes are such additional aspects of the bureaucratic syndrome as an increase in the impersonality of teachers' treatment of students, a loosened sense of responsibility on the part of decision makers at the local level, alienation, anomie, and a sense of powerlessness on the part of officials at all levels of government.

The System in Operation

Our grasp of these changes can be strengthened by providing an almost true-to-life case study of the establishment of a new educational program in a district enrolling a significant proportion of non-English-speaking Mexican-American pupils. Until recently districts such as the fictional San Matador, under state law, could use only English as a medium of instruction, but, as a result of a recently passed law, districts in the state were given permission, if they chose, to provide bilingual instruction. At about the same time as this change in state law occurred, both the state and federal governments adopted new grant-in-aid programs to assist districts in mounting bilingual instruction. With seed money from a foundation, San Matador developed a limited-enrollment, elementary-level bilingual program in an abandoned old schoolhouse. Students from all over the district who met the entrance requirements (for example, students whose mother tongue was Spanish and who could not speak English) could apply for the program; but, since the program could only enroll three hundred pupils, it would be necessary to give admittance on a first-come-first-served basis. Those not admitted were placed on a waiting list. As originally conceived, the program was not only to be bilingual but also bicultural; thus the texts and supplementary materials to be used in the program would strongly reflect Spanish and Mexican cultures. A parent advisory group would also be established, as was required by the regulations accompanying the grants to be sought from the state and federal governments.

The project applications were approved in the spring by the respective state and federal agencies, and the doors of the new school were to open the next fall, but actual efforts in getting the building ready and selecting teachers and materials were hindered by the fact that Congress did not appropriate the money for the needed federal grant until August. (This problem of the uncertainties of when the appropriation would come through and of what its size would be plagued the project for its duration.) Once the project got rolling, other problems began to mount. First, state officials under political pressure changed their minds about permitting a bicultural program. The enabling act passed by the legislature only granted districts authority to mount a bilingual program, not a bicultural program, and there was increasing concern that biculturalism would lead to cultural divisiveness. At the same time, federal officials had come to believe that bilingual programs would be most effective if they were also bicultural, and while they did not issue regulations to that effect, the federal guidelines (which did not have the force of law) indicated that bicultural programs were preferred (see chap. 3). The parent advisory group also insisted upon the importance of raising the Spanish-consciousness of the pupils on the theory that with an increased sense of self-esteem student achievement would also rise. As matters now stand the state is threatening to cut off the state grant if the program remains bicultural and threatening legal action to bar the district from accepting the federal grant on the terms seemingly imposed by the federal government. Thus the possibility has been raised that the district lacks the delegated authority to accept federal grants that impose requirements that are inconsistent with state law and regulations.

The bicultural aspects of the program raised yet other problems. Spanish- and Mexican-American cultures involve very distinct sexual roles which the materials used in the school reflected. A local women's liberation group has protested to the school board about the use of such sexually biased materials and has threatened to seek through the state courts a prohibition of such materials on the ground that they violate the state's recently adopted law which prohibits the use in schools of materials that adversely reflect upon minorities and women. But since the law also requires that all school materials accurately reflect the role of minorities and women in the history of the state and nation, the school board has argued that the materials are consistent with the statute; nevertheless the board has conceded that the statute is not a model of clarity and that under one interpretation it could be read to bar the sort of materials used in the school. The board has offered to discuss the matter further to see if a compromise can be reached.

It might be noted here that the problems of this district would have been compounded if the district were in a state that relied upon state selection of textual materials (see chap. 4). In all likelihood, most of what the district might want to use in the way of materials would not be on the state list of approved textbooks, hence special permission, waiver, and the like, might have to be sought from the state board. Failing that, the district might have to use only approved texts in the hope that it could liberally introduce supplementary materials as long as they did not supplant the basic state-approved texts. In most states there are no clear rulings, however, as to what constitutes supplantation.

Besides these complications, parents of students who have been placed on the waiting list have filed a complaint with the Office for Civil Rights (OCR) in the Department of Health, Education, and Welfare (HEW), threatening to go to federal court on the ground that the district is violating the Civil Rights Act of 1964 by failing to provide special instruction in English to the students excluded from the program. The likelihood of the parents winning such a suit has just increased because of a recent Supreme Court decision upholding OCR's interpretation of the Civil Rights Act of l964 (see chap. 3). Under that interpretation all districts receiving federal funds must provide non-English-speaking students (those who are effectively excluded from the school program because they don't speak English) with special instruction in English. Not to offer such instruction means the loss of all federal funds. To comply fully with the ruling, however, the school district will have to raise taxes or shortchange some other part of the school program or increase class size throughout the district. At this point, however, the teachers' union is negotiating with the district and pressing hard for a lowering of class size. In any event, it appears the district is both going to have to cut its school program, somewhere, and increase the budget in the teeth of an ongoing taxpayer revolt.

OCR is not done with the district, however. It has begun an investigation of the whole project to determine if it violates federal rules against the segregation of pupils, since the requirements for admission to the schools have the effect of admitting only Mexican-American pupils and excluding other races (see chap. 2). It appears that a long and complicated set of negotiations between OCR and the school district is in the offing. Part of the difficulty the local board will have in negotiating with OCR is that OCR itself has not quite made up its collective mind as to what its policy is with regard to special schools serving the special educational needs of distinct ethnic groups.

In any event, the great publicity occasioning the controversies surrounding the bilingual school has alerted the parents of children with other special needs that their children are not getting specialized attention. Thus, the parents of children with learning disabilities have now gone to federal court arguing that their children are being functionally excluded from the schools, just as the non-English-speaking pupils who are not getting special instruction in English are being excluded (see chap. 2). Further, the failure of the schools to attend to the special needs of the learning disabled, say the parents, is a violation of their rights under the Equal Protection clause of the Fourteenth Amendment of the U.S. Constitution, since othe children in the system are getting programs suited to their needs. As matters now stand, the federal district court has refused to grant a motion to dismiss the suit for failure to state a claim upon which relief may be granted.

How precisely all these questions will be resolved is not clear at this point, but what does seem clear is that further changes will have to be made in the program of the school district. Some changes will have to be made in the bilingual program because is seems clear that more children will have to be served. Perhaps the program will have to be removed from the single building and dispersed throughout the school district. If this happens, major adjustments will have to be made in each building, especially if the district is not to be charged with intrabuilding segregation of pupils. Children with special needs will have to be placed in regular classes, and a system of releasing these students from regular classes will have to be devised. And it appears reasonably likely that the district is going to have to make some major budget reallocations, especially if it loses the learning disabilities suit. In any event, large sums of money will have to be set aside next year to pay for the legal services the district must now purchase.

Principles for the Allocation of Authority

That there has been a change in the last forty years in how the programs of the public shhools are controlled should not come as much of a surprise in light of the fact that there never has been any final agreement, since the time of Plato, on who should control the education of children. Strong arguments can be made for any number of governing arrangements, and choosing among these alternatives is no easy matter, for the principles that count in debates over governing structure conflict with one another and are subject to varying interpretations. Ten such principles seem to have played a role in the shaping of the old and new models for controlling education.

1. Paternalism. Although there exists a body of radical literature which argues that learning should be student directed, most people believe adults have a responsibility to guide the education of the young so as to protect the young from harm.[1] Minors today do not yet enjoy a right, vis-à-vis their parents, to control their own education. (The question of childs' rights vis-à-vis his or her parents was raised by Justice Douglas in partial dissent in *Wisconsin* v. *Yoder*.)[2] Thus, formal control of the education program remains in the hands of adults.

2. The Right of Parents. The Supreme Court has recognized a right of parents to control the upbringing of their children, but the precise scope of that right has never been definitely established (see chaps. 7 and 8). This right seems to rest on notions of individual liberty and privacy and on such other principles, to be noted later, as the principle of efficiency.[3] (Some people argue it may be most efficient to let parents control the education of their children as they have both the motivation to do a good job and the greatest knowledge of their children.) Carried to its extreme this principle points toward a totally decentralized system of education with each family providing or purchasing its own educatonal program. (State finacial support of the parents' purchase of educational services might be in the form of a chit or voucher worth a fixed sum of money which the parent turns into the private school of his or her choice and which the school, in turn, redeems for cash from the state [see chap. 9].) But one of the major compromises that has been built into the prevailing American models for governing education is that this principle has not been allowed to be carried that far. At least for the last one hundred years parent's rights have been significantly compromised. The efforts of recent years to give parents a greater voice in the running of public school systems can be viewed as an effort to give more meaning to this principle.

3. State and National Interests. One of the reasons parents have never had completely unfettered control over the education of their children is that it has been widely accepted that the public—both state and national publics—has an important interest in the education of the children. This interest has many facets to it: an interest in developing a loyal and patriotic citizenry; an interest in a literate citizenry which can meaningfully exercise the political and civil liberties which so importantly define our form of democracy; an interest in an economically productive and law abiding populace; and an interest in a populace that shares a common culture so as to reduce cultural divisiveness and political instability.[4] These interests point to the need for state regulation of private educational efforts; toward the need for neglect laws to protect children against the neglect and ignorance of their parents; and toward the need for compulsory education laws. These same interests also have led to the conclusion that we need a state supported and operated educational system: it has been thought that this is a more effective way of achieving the state's interest than the more cumbersome and legally complicated approach of regulating private educatonal efforts (see chap. 8). A further significant implication of this line of thought has been that the operation of the public educational system ought not be left entirely in the hands of local units of.government. Steps ought to be taken so that ignorant and lazy local populations cannot fail to provide minimally adequate educational programs or programs so culturally and politically slanted as to once again open the society to the dangers of cultural divisiveness. Thus, pure local control of education has never been formally recognized; what have tended to emerge are governing systems that represent a compromise among local and state and national regulation. The nature of that compromise, as we have seen, has recently shifted and differs from state to state.

4. Liberty and Democracy. The principle of liberty provides support for parental control of the child's education, but, as noted earlier, this principle has only been partially honored in the United States. Assuming public provision of educatonal services, the liberty principle has been the basis for arguing that decision making and administration should be left to the smallest unit of government competent to handle them.[5] Local government traditionally has been seen as a way of avoiding the emergence of an overweening centralized government. Local government encourages the development of initiative and self-reliance essential to all forms of self-government. Small units of government are likely to be made up of a more homogeneous population, which in turn enhances the likelihood that the preferences of all in the the local population will be realized. Local government is, thus, likely to be more responsive and accordingly more legitimate. But there also can develop in local government the village tyranny in which the majority overrides and neglects the interest of the minority; this possibility points to the need for state-level involvement in local government to protect minority interests. Finally, the principles of liberty and democracy point to the need for popular control of the educational system, as opposed to control by experts or professionals, at the national, state, and local levels of government.

5. Principle of Affected Interests. Stated broadly, this principle holds that everyone affected by a decision should have a right to participate in the decision-making process.[6] Taken to its extreme the principle points toward people in California participating in educational decisions reached in New York since, because of the mobility of the population, the educational failures and successes of New York have an impact in California. The principle points to a strong centralization of government, especially when the national and state governments participate heavily in the financing of local educational programs. The principle has been an important premise for justifying significant state involvement in education and provides a basis for the increase in federal involvement in educational decision making. The principle suggests that it is unlikely federal aid to education will ever be totally free of strings. The principle further suggests that policymaking should be shared by all three levels of government. Finally, the principle provides an important premise upon which teachers' unions justify their demands that such issues as the school curriculum be a subject of collective negotiations (see chap. 6).

6. No Delegation of Legislative Power. State constitutions devolve upon state legislatures legislative power for establishing basic educational policy for the state. The courts have interpreted such grants of legislative power as prohibiting the delegation of such power by the state legislatures to, for example, state or local educational agencies.[7] The purpose behind the delegation doctrine is to prevent the legislature from abdicating its responsibility for formulating basic policy. Under our governmental system the statewide community represented in the legislature has this responsibility, and it may not be given away. While as a practical matter the delegation doctrine has not been a serious obstacle to the delegation of authority to local school districts, it remains an important principle barring total decentralization of the governing system for schools.

7. Community Control. Having a sense of belonging to a group that wields governmental authority in a geographic area has always been an important value, and establishing local control or community control of education has been viewed as one way of achieving that value.[8] The notion of community control is also consonant with the attempt to maximize the realization of preferences since, if the community is in control of its own educational program, it need not struggle with the imposistion of requirements with which it disagrees. Defining the community that should be given authority is often no easy matter, however, as it could be done in terms of race, ethnicity, social class, religion, occupation, and the like. Further, defining communities in terms of race raises difficult constitutional problems. And community control may also encourage cultural and racial divisiveness.

8. Equality. One interpretation of the value of equality points to the need for greater national and state involvement in education to assure the educational program is equal from state to state, district to district.[9] But if the concept of equality includes the notion that different children ought to be treated differently, then the value points to local control of education to allow for the possibility that children may differ from district to district and that local control would permit each district to take the unique educational needs of its children into account.[10] This same understanding of the notion of equality, however, also points, once again, toward greater state, federal, and judicial involvement in the school program. This is so because often local districts neglect those very children who are a minority and different from the other children in the district. If these special children are to be given an equal educational opportunity, then higher authority may have to come to their defense.[11] Much of the present-day increase in the centralization of control of the school program can be attributed to greater weight being given this interpretation of the principle of equality.

9. Efficiency and Effectiveness. No one would doubt the value of having public schools that are effective in realizing their educational goals at minimum cost. But the principle has many conflicting implications for how authority ought to be allocated. First, the principle suggests the need for placing control in the hands of experts and professionals, yet it also suggests the wisdom of greater parental control since they know their children best.[12] The principle points to the wisdom of local control since this is where the greatest motivation for operating a good program exists, as well as the greatest knowledge of local conditions; but the principle also points to greater state and federal control since this is where greater knowledge of effective educational practices located throughout the country is collected.[13] The principle points to a few larger school districts to avoid duplication in central office staff and to achieve economies of scale, but it also suggests the need for many smaller school districts to avoid the decision-making problems and other costs associated with large and complex bureaucracies. As a general proposition, the principle suggests that the governing structure should be arranged to maximize student achievement while minimizing costs—but no one knows how to put such a principle into operation.

10. Keeping Education Out of Politics. There has been a persistent belief in some states that public education ought to be kept out of politics and politics ought to be kept out of public education.[14] Under one interpretation of this principle, more authority for running the system ought to be placed in the hands of experts—the professionals, such as the superintendent and teachers. It has meant establishing special governing units for controlling education separate from other local governments. The principle has also meant removing large city school districts from the control of the mayor; appointing school boards instead of electing them or, if they are to be elected, running the elections on a nonpartisan basis and at a time other than elections for other public offices. It has meant electing school board members at large, not by ward. At the state level, the principle in some states has meant insulating the governing of public education from the direct control of the governor and the legislative delegation of important policymaking responsibilities to a state board of education and chief state school officers who are supposed to be above and apart from normal state politics. As a practical matter, the principle of keeping education out of politics has often meant creating a governing structure that gives the white, Protestant, middle class a competitive advantage in gaining control of the educational system.

In brief, the ten principles create several different tensions: between parent and child; between the parent and the state; between the national government and state and local governments; between state government and local government; between the expert professional and general public; between the teachers' union and the governing board; and between the educatonal system itself and other political figures as the governor and mayor. Since the establishment of a public system of education in the United States, these tensions have never been fully resolved nor, as noted at the outset of the chapter, have they been resolved in the same way in all states. The principles, in short, lend themselves to the justification of different kinds of governmental arrangements. One example will illustrate this point. Some states use state-approved lists of textbooks as a central method for controlling the curriculum. This arrangement can be justified in terms of the principles of equality, efficiency, and affected interests. Those same principles, however, can be used to marshal an argument on behalf of total local control of education. Hence, given the malleabillity of the principles, it should come as no surprise to find that there are today different institutional arrangements for controlling the school program and, over time, modifications in those arrangements.

In the succeeding chapters the details of these changes will be explored. The authority and the exercise of that authority of the various participants as of the 1970s will be detailed. In addition, where possible, lines of future development will be pointed out and elaborated upon. With such an analysis it will be possible to discern new causes for concern with regard to how the public school program is being controlled and new bases for criticism in light of these ten principles adumbrated. We shall return to these problems in the concluding chapter, along with suggestions for what might now be done to once again change our system for controlling the school program to better fit with our emerging understanding of the application of the ten principles for allocating authority.

Appendix IA

The governing structure for controlling the content of the public school program can be thought of in terms of about a dozen tasks or roles. What follows is a brief discussion of each of these tasks.

1. Establishing Minimum Standards. The standards might be stated in terms of inputs (for example, this course must be taught; students must attend ten years of formal schooling) or in terms of outputs (students should achieve level x in reading by the eighth grade). Typically, state legislatures lay down such standards in the educational code of the state and delegate authority to the state board of education to establish their own additional minimum standards. Local school boards may establish their own additional minimum standards as long as they do not undercut those of the state. The antidiscrimination requirements which grow out of the Civil Rights Act of 1964 and Title IX might also be viewed as minimum standards. And the door has been opened for judicial determination of what constitutes a minimally adequate education (see chap. 2).

2. Establishing Educational Priorities. State legislatures traditionally have shaped the educational priorities of the public school system through legislation establishing the minimum standards for the school program. That is, minimum standards may also function as educational objectives and goals. The recent adoption of statewide testing programs is one way states have tried to force districts to pay greater attention to educational achievement in reading and arithmetic (see chap. 4). State and federal grants-in-aid may also serve to change educational priorities at the local level (see chap. 3). Recent litigation in the courts will have its effect by forcing districts to pay attention to the needs of children that heretofore have largely been neglected (see chap. 2).

3. Vetoing Educational Offerings. State legislatures have exercised their veto power by, for example, forbidding the teaching of communism in the public schools. In some states, authority has been given to the state department of education to veto new courses local districts may wish to offer. Where state authority exists to select educational materials, the state department may effectively veto a course by refusing to approve the materials necessary to teach the course. A form of veto is exercised by federal and state grant administration officials when they refuse to approve project proposals submitted by local districts. And the federal and state courts have vetoed religious services in the schools (see chap. 2). Occasionally, state courts have vetoed course offerings on the ground the local district lacked the delegated authority to mount the course (see chap. 5).

4. Establishing Graduation Requirements. State legislatures play an important part in establising these requirements but legislatures have also delegated authority to state agencies to set additional requirements. Local school boards in turn may be able to add to the minimum requirements set by the legislature and state department of education. Graduation requirements typically are stated in terms of course requirements, or credits, but recently some states have passed legislation which permits students who pass certain tests to meet graduation requirements.

5. Determining the Content of Courses. State legislatures only rarely specify in their statutes the details of the content of particular courses. Departments of education through their authority to establish minimum standards often have the power to specify course content but rarely do so, except, interestingly enough, when it comes to driver and physical education courses. Where state selection of textbooks exist, state agencies may have effective power to control the content of those courses for which they select books. New state legislation dealing with discrimination in curriculum materials may affect course content. Control by federal and state officials can only be exercised through the administration of the grant-in-aid programs. And the courts may get involved if legal arguments in support of a constitutionally required fairness doctrine are accepted. The courts may also deal with the kind of special instruction in English that must be provided to non-English-speaking students.

6. Determining the Method of Instruction. Legislatures involve themselves in this aspect of the curriculum when they specify the language that must serve as the medium of instruction or the method to be used in teaching non-English-speaking students English. State departments of education rarely involve themselves in this area except when it comes to specifying how, for example, the driver education courses are to be taught. States that rely upon state selection of materials have the power to control the method of instruction by approving materials, for example, that rely only upon the phonics approach to the teaching of reading. Basically, control over the method of instruction is left to the local boards of education and they in turn usually delegate this decision to the professionals employed by the system (see chap.6).

7. Selecting Educational Materials. In most states the task of selecting the materials to be used in courses is left to the local board which in turn delegates the choice to the professionals in the system, subject to ultimate board approval. As a practical matter the final choice may be left in the hands of the individual teacher and school building principal. Recent litigation protecting the academic freedom of teachers assures teachers of some leeway in introducing supplementary materials of their own choice (see chap. 6). Of course, in those states with state selection of materials, the choice of basic texts or basic courses is importantly constrained by the department of education, but even in those states some choice among approved materials is available to the local district. The selection of supplementary materials under these systems is not so tightly controlled by the department. Recent state laws prohibiting materials with a discriminatory content may ultimately lead to judicial involvement in this area (see chap. 4). And the Civil Rights Act of 1964 and Title IX lay down premises for federal involvemnt in the barring of racially and sexually discriminatory materials (see chap. 3). Teachers' unions have made an effort to make this role a subject of negotiations (see chap. 6).

8. Determining the Political and Cultural Bias of Courses. State legislation affects the choice of bias by excluding the teaching of communism in the schools; by requiring instruction in patriotism and loyality and in the benefits of the free enterprise system; by requiring the bilingual programs also to be bicultural (see chap. 4). The federal government, through its control of federal grants, may exercise its influence to encourage biculturalism (see chap. 3). Basic control, however, remains in the local board subject to whatever constraints are imposed by the courts through protection of the academic freedom rights of teachers (see chap.6).

9. Developing New Materials and Approaches. With regard to certain courses, state departments have been directed by state legislatures to develop materials for use in the schools. The federal government has had a long controversial role in this area (see chap. 3). Local districts have authority to engage in such developmental efforts but often are constrained by financial considerations.

10. Determining Staffing Patterns. Although the determination of staffing patterns in schools is not typically thought of as part of the problem of formulating the school curriculum, this task importantly affects what that curriculum will be. State tenure and certification requirements can significantly constrain local districts in establishing their staffing patterns, but many statutes in this area allow for some flexibility by providing for the waiver of these requirements under certain circumstances (see chap. 4). Within these constraints, local districts have the basic authority to determine staffing patterns, but with the advent of collective negotiations this area has increasingly become subject to the influence of teachers' unions.

11. Setting Up Pupil Classification Systems. To a surprising degree state legislatures have developed complex systems for classifying pupils, especially pupils who might be regarded as other than normal (see chap. 4). Federal and state grants-in-aid also influence the burgeoning pupil classification systems. Local districts have the basic authority to establish pupil classification schemes for normal pupils (see chaps. 4 and 7). The task of determining the classification into which a specific student will be placed has recently been placed under new laws in several states so that now special procedures must be followed in those states that classify pupils. These new laws often require some degree of parental involvement in the classification process (see chap. 7). Courts have become involved in reviewing classification systems and in the question of whether a particular student was properly classified (see chap. 2).

12. Exempting Students from Courses. State law often requires that students who object on religious grounds to health and sex education courses be granted an exemption from those courses (see chap. 7). The courts on occasion have required school districts to exempt objecting pupils from certain course requirements (see chap. 7). The Supreme Court has said students may not be compelled to take part in the pledge to the flag; and that released-time programs are permissible (see chap. 2).

13. Evaluating the School Program. In many states legislation has been passed requiring evaluation of the school program and students by the use of standardized tests (see chap. 4). Federally and state administered grant-in-aid programs also now carry mandatory evaluation requirements. The federal requirements can involve complex institutional arrangements in which local, state, and federal officials are involved.

2

The Federal Courts and the U.S. Constitution

The work of the Supreme Court and lower federal courts over the last twenty-five years has prompted one commentator to say that the courts have become a more important determinant of educational policy than the local school board.[1] Another observer has said that the courts have unconstitutionally usurped power and have moved toward becoming an "imperial judiciary."[2] These claims have been made in response to the significant change in judicial behavior which started in 1953 when Earl Warren became Chief Justice of the Supreme Court, and which has continued into the 1970s under Chief Justice Burger. As interpreters of the U.S. Constitution, the courts during this period have taken a more active role than ever before in making sure that the other agencies of government more directly responsible for the public school system operate within the confines of the Constitution. The courts' activism has been premised on the need to make sure that government, including the public schools, as it grows and extends its influence over the lives of the populace, does so in ways that are consistent with the values of liberty and equality. The expanded role of courts has coincided not only with an expansion of the role of government itself but also with an increasing recognition of injustices in society—injustices both perpetrated and tolerated by government. Thus there are powerful reasons to explain the recent unwillingness of the courts to defer to the judgment of other branches of government as they did between 1937 and 1953, when the courts effectively stepped aside as government grew under the New Deal.[3]

In this chapter, the courts' newer role is discussed first by assessing the Supreme Court's role in allocating decision-making authority between public and private decision makers. (The Supreme Court has also umpired the relationship between, on the one hand, the federal government, and, on the other hand, state and local government. This aspect of the Court's work will be taken up briefly in Chap. 3.) Next, the chapter turns to the Supreme Court's efforts to keep religion out of public schools. The subsequent sections deal with the Court's efforts to maintain the public schools as marketplaces for political and cultural ideas; the penultimate section reviews court cases touching on the adequacy of the school program and the problem of equal educational opportunity; and a concluding section provides a review of the chapter and deals with the question of whether there is such a thing as constitutionally required curriculum.

Allocating Authority between Public and Private Decision Makers

Plato, in his work *The Republic,* creates a utopian society in which all children are placed full time in state institutions, thereby denying parents any authority to control the upbringing of their children.[4] A step in that direction would be compulsory education laws which would not merely require that all children between certain ages attend school, but which would also require all children to attend only public or state operated schools. In *Pierce* v. *Society of Sisters* the Supreme Court refused to permit any such step toward the Platonic society by striking down a compulsory education law of the sort just described as an unconstitutional infringement of the liberty of parents to control the upbringing of their children. [5] Thus, parents today enjoy a constitutional right to choose between public and private instruction.

The *Pierce* decision, however, has left several fundamental questions unanswered: first, are compulsory education laws as we know them after *Pierce* constitutional, and, second, to what extent may states regulate the private educational efforts of parents and private schools? Although the Supreme Court has never explicitly answered the first question there are strong indications from the decision in *Wisconsin* v. *Yoder* that states may impose on parents the duty of educating their children formally.[6] In that case Amish parents sought for their fouteen- and fifteen-year-old children an exemption from the last two years of Wisconsin's compulsory education law so that the parents could have the students work on the family farm and thereby begin socializing them into the Amish religion and way of life. The Supreme Court accepted the argument of the parents, which was that not to grant the exemption would unduly infringe upon the right of the Amish freely to exercise their religion pursuant to the First Amendment and that the two-year exemption they sought would not frustrate the state's interests in assuring that the children were adequately educated. But in granting the exemption the Court was careful to suggest that the state's interest in compulsory education through the first *eight* years of schooling was sufficiently strong to override any interest the parents might have had in obtaining a more sweeping exemption than the one granted. And lower federal courts faced with challenges to compulsory education laws have upheld those laws, thus making it clear that parents may not claim total freedom from state control.[7]

The more difficult question remains, however: whether and to what extent may the state regulate private educational efforts? This has been the subject of litigation before the Supreme Court in only two cases. In *Farrington* v. *Tokushige* the Supreme Court struck down a state statute and regulations that had tried to limit the pupils who might attend foreign language schools to those who regularly attended some public school or an approved private school, or had completed the eighth grade, or were over fourteen years of age.[8] The state law also had given power to the department of education to regulate who could teach in the foreign language schools and to regulate the school program. The Court concluded that the statute and regulations went "far beyond mere regulation of privately supported schools" in that they could deny both owners and patrons "reasonable choice and discretion in respect of teachers, curriculum, and textbooks." The law and regulations "would deprive parents of fair opportunity to procure for their children instruction which they think important and we cannot say is harmful." In a similar case the Court also struck down a state law that prevented private schools from instructing students in the German language prior to the eighth grade.[9] With these rulings the Court barred states from trying to eliminate cultural diversity by strictly controlling the program of those private schools that served an alien population.

These rulings, however, do not preclude reasonable state regulation of private schooling.[10] The states may require privately educated students to be taught certain subjects such as English, arithmetic, and American history. And states may not prevent private education from including religious instruction. But whether states may, for example, require all private schools to attempt to produce patriotic and loyal citizens, or bar private schools from instructing children in communism or Marxism, is not so easily answered. The answers to these questions depend in part on (1) the scope of the parental right to control the education of the child and the scope of that right in turn depends on what the Court takes to be the basis of that right in the first place; and in part on (2) the scope of the free speech rights of private school teachers. It seems clear that the basis of the parental right to control the upbringing of the child is a set of personal liberties including freedom of speech, privacy, free exercise of religion, and, more generally, freedom of belief.[11] In terms of the allocation of roles, the Constitution and relevant cases strongly suggest that the formation of opinions, attitudes, values and beliefs should largely be in private hands and not governmentally controlled.[12] As for private school teachers, more traditional notions of freedom of speech seem amply powerful to obviate state control as to what goes on between teacher and pupil, absent a showing of possible harm to the student as a result of the instruction. (Public school teachers' rights are not nearly as strong. See chap. 6.) Hence, given the strong nature of the individual rights involved, it is unlikely that courts would sustain any regulations but those reasonably designed to assure the private education was minimally adequate. (Chapter 8 returns to question of the states' authority to regulate private educational efforts.)

While parents in the United States retain the right to educate their children privately, a right that may only be subject to reasonable regulation, the real difficulty facing parents today in exercising their rights is the cost of private education; thus, while parents enjoy a formal right to educate their children as they prefer, the worth of that right is not equal for all. By refusing to recognize a right for financial support to attend private religious schools and by refusing to permit most forms of state aid for religious schools, the Supreme Court has refused to lift an effective barrier in the way of most parents to the exercise of their formal right to control the education of their children. With the exception of permitting states to provide bus transportation and books to students attending private schools, the Supreme Court has religiously struck down all other attempts to aid sectarian elementary and secondary schools.[13] The courts have also denied parental claims that they had a right to state support to send their children to a sectarian school.[14]

Religion in the Public Schools

For a significant period of American history those parents who could not afford private religious education had the option of sending their children to public schools where religion remained part of the school program in the form of religious ceremonies involving readings from the Bible and the recitation of a prayer. But resting on the principle that what the public schools do may neither have the purpose nor primary effect of advancing or inhibiting religion, the Supreme Court has struck down these ceremonies even though objecting pupils could be excused from participation.[15] The Court also has barred the use of school facilities for the provision of religious instruction by local ministers, priests, and rabbis, even though voluntarily taken by the students.[16] Public property, money, and authority simply may not be used to promote religion.

The Supreme Court's sensitivity to the way religion may be promoted in the public schools is amply revealed in *Epperson* v. *Arkansas*, where the Court struck down a state statute that prohibited the teaching of the theory that mankind ascended or descended from a lower order of animal.[17] The Court found that the public campaign that had been mounted in support of the statute had been religiously motivated, hence the Court concluded the statute violated the principle set forth earlier. The Court seemed to be saying that the state's exclusion of Darwin's theory of evolution had the effect of placing the state's imprimatur upon the biblical account of the origin of mankind. In effect the state had established a religion. When a state passed a law that would have required all textbooks containing discussions of Darwinism to carry the disclaimer that the materials therein were not presented as scientific fact, that required the books to give commensurate attention to other theories of the origin of mankind including the account in Genesis, and when the same statute declared that the Bible was not to be deemed a textbook (and was thereby exempt from the required disclaimer), a federal circuit court struck it down.[18] The circuit court concluded that these provisions gave a preferential position to the biblical version of creation. Importantly, another circuit court concluded that schools that instructed children in the Darwinian theory did not also have to provide instruction in the book of Genesis.[19]

Decisions such as these seem to be pushing public school programs toward secularism, but the Supreme Court has also said that it would be a violation of the Constitution for the schools to establish a religion of secularism.[20] What the public schools may do is to provide students with an opportunity to objectively study religion and the Bible as part of a secular program of education.[21]

Where do these ambiguous and vague pronouncements of the courts leave the public schools? Perhaps the best way of exploring the implications of these rulings is by asking three questions: (1) What may the public schools not do? (2) What may they do? (3) What must they do? First, we know the public schools may not advance religion or a religion of secularism, but the Supreme Court has never defined these terms. But the prohibition apparently means at least the promotion of philosophical beliefs or a way of life by the public schools is permissable, as opposed to promotion of a religious belief.[22] We can determine a religious belief in part by finding out if the belief is directly based upon the Bible or other recognized religious documents.[23] (There are obvious problems of circularity of reasoning here.) As to the prohibition against promoting a religion of secularism it would seem that at the minimum the public schools may not overtly attack religious beliefs, for example, aggressively instruct pupils that explanations of the world that rely on what a Supreme Being did or did not do are not believeable. In any event, it is doubtful the prohibitions with regard to religion and a religion of secularism would be so broadly defined by the Court as to call into question every aspect of the school program. Beyond this, little can be said with certainty as to what is not allowed in the public schools.

Second, if the objective study of religion and the Bible is permitted, it is necessary to ask what constitutes objective study? The terms might mean only that the schools may not promote belief in a particular religious doctrine, or it might mean that in offering a course involving the study of religion and/or the Bible the schools must introduce students to the many atrocities and wars that have been undertaken in the name of religion.[24] Or the term might connote a requirement that, when religion is studied, more than one religion, more than one religious text, must be taken up so that students may make their own comparisons and judgments. Once again, what is permitted or required has not been made clear by the Court.

Third, practically speaking, are schools left with only one alternative, one form of educational program? A strong case can be made that the courts' rulings have had such an effect. First, it is doubtful that schools today could teach, even objectively, only the Genesis account of the Bible without at the same time instructing children in other theories of the origin of mankind. Chances are the Courts would view even objective instruction of Genesis as giving a preference to religion over nonreligion; this is one of the strong implications of the *Epperson* case. On the other hand, one lower court, as noted earlier, has already ruled that schools may teach Darwin's theory without having to refer to the book of Genesis. Further, the objective study of religion, however defined, seems to encourage a mental attitude of distance and reservation with regard to religion, the very opposite of commitment. The implicit message of such courses could be that no commitment is the preferred position and that religion should be approached from the outside, as a cultural phenomenon, and should be studied in the same way one would examine the culinary habits of a society. Thus, despite the Supreme Court's statement that public schools may not promote a religion of secularism, its rulings in many respects seem to leave the schools with no alternative but to offer at least a nonmilitant form of secularism.

The School as a Marketplace for Political Ideas

While the Supreme Court has made it quite clear that the public schools may not be used to perpetuate the religious culture of this society, the question still remains as to how far the public schools may go in perpetuating a particular political ideology. There are two basic schools of thought on what the public schools should be allowed to do in this area. John Stuart Mill opposed official imposition of political ideas on people but believed that publicly operated schools inevitably would be mere contrivances for molding people to be exactly like one another and that the mold would be that which pleased the predominant power in government.[25] As a consequence of this view, Mill was opposed to the establishment of publicly operated schools. In contrast, the American philosopher of education John L. Childs has argued that public schools should be used to make children over into patriotic and loyal citizens.[26] The question here is with which viewpoint does the Constitution tend to side. As we shall see, the Constitution tends to side more with Childs but public schools attempting to make children into loyal citizens must operate within certain limitations. As the Supreme Court has said on several occasions, the public schools must remain a "marketplace of ideas."

1. The Imposition of Beliefs. One way state legislatures have attempted to shape children into patriotic and loyal citizens is to require students to study the U.S. and state Constitutions, to learn the principles of citizenship and study American history.[27] Some states have gone so far as to require the public schools to instruct children in the benefits of the free enterprise system and in the evils and threat of communism.[28] But how far may the schools go in coercively imposing particular beliefs upon the students?

Our main guidance on this question comes from *West Virginia Board of Education* v. *Barnette*, in which the Supreme Court struck down a requirement that students participate in a flag salute ceremony in which they had to pledge allegiance to the country and confess a belief that this was a country in which liberty and justice were available to all.[29] Students who did not participate in such a ceremony faced expulsion from school, prosecution as delinquents; their parents could be criminally tried. The decision in *Barnette* was based upon an interpretation of the free speech rights of students or more specifically, the free belief rights of students. As a result of this case, any educational practice that involved compelling students to pledge loyalty to the country would be an impermissible invasion of the individual's intellect and spirit. But the opinion might also apply to any school attempt to compel students to profess a belief in certain value judgments with regard to the country, its people, its institutions. For example, a highly indoctrinary course might require students to answer "true" to the statement that the United States provides more equality of opportunity than any other country or that the free enterprise system is the only economic system compatible with liberty for all people. Such a practice would, most likely, be inconsistent with *Barnette* which was designed to bar the imposition of any "ideological discipline" and to protect "the right of self-determination in matters that touch individual opinion and personal attitude."[30]

It is doubtful, however, that the case reaches beyond this. Having students read, if not annunciate themselves, statements to the effect that the United States is the most peace-loving country in the world would be permissible. Similarly, students might still be compelled to read only favorable interpretations of American history or to memorize statistics about the quality of life in the United States which may be erroneous, incomplete, or subject to misinterpretation. These sorts of practices, which are common in the public schools, probably do not involve the sort of coerced confession of belief the Court has said cannot be allowed. These practices are merely a form of instruction. Besides, it is doubtful the Court would want to broaden too far the meaning of *Barnette* as this would plunge it too deeply into the process of formulating school curriculum.

There have been few other decisions dealing with the permissibility of the schools' imposition of doctrines and ideas on students. Several lower courts have been asked to decide whether high school students who object to compulsory ROTC courses on the basis of their religious beliefs may be granted an exemption, much in the same way the Amish were granted an exemption from the last two years of the compulsory education laws. The lower courts have split on on this issue.[31] And lower courts have upheld in the face of complaints by black students the official use by schools of such school names as "Rebels" and such school symbols as the Confederate battle flag, as well as the practice of playing "Dixie" at pep rallies.[32]

In short, the flag salute case apart, schools today may impose a significantly biased political education program. That is, schools may attempt to offer a program of study that is designed to produce loyal and even uncritical citizens. The public schools can be an instrument for the perpetuation of the prevailing political ideology in the country.

2. Maintaining Ideological Purity by Excluding Undesirable Materials. A question which has not yet been decided by the courts is whether schools may adopt rules with regard to the selection of courses and materials that purposefully exclude or have the effect of excluding political ideas with which the officials in charge of the system disagree. For example, it is common for states to pass statutes which prohibit the teaching of communism in the public schools.[33]

We have little guidance on this matter except a statement from Justice Stewart in a concurring opinion in the *Epperson* case, discussed earlier. Justice Stewart wrote that it is one thing for the state to decide not to offer a course such as biology in the public schools, but another matter for the state to make it a crime for a teacher to even mention the very existence of an entire system of respected human thought, such as Darwinism. Such a law, thought Justice Stewart, would infringe upon the constitutional guarantees of free communication.[34] By analogy, if a teacher were to mention communism in class and were then fired and criminally prosecuted, the chances seem good the conviction and firing would be reversed as an unconstitutional violation of the teacher's free speech rights. However, if the teacher were trying to indoctrinate the pupils in communism, then the courts would provide no protection. While teachers may have a limited right to introduce supplementary materials and comments into the class, they may not, at public expense, teach communism or provide a course of instruction wholly inconsistent with the prescribed curriculum. (See chap. 6.)

Another approach that might be adopted with regard to the discriminatory exclusion of materials and ideas with which the school district disagreed would be one that relied on the Equal Protection clause of the Fourteenth Amendment.

To discuss this question it is necessary briefly to review the standards of review (or tests) developed by the Supreme Court to assist it in applying the Equal Protection clause of the Fourteenth Amendment. (An understanding of these standards will be of use in analyzing other constitutional issues.) Four such standards of review have emerged from the Court. The oldest is the rational basis test, which provides that the Court will uphold state created classifications which bear some rational relationship to a legitimate state end.[35] This is the most lenient of the tests in that the complainant bears the burden of showing that no rational basis exists for unequal treatment meted out by the state to different classes of people, a task that in practice has proved to be almost impossible to achieve.[36] Under the second test, sometimes called the "new equal protection" standard, a legislatively created classification affecting a "fundamental interest" or involving a "suspect classification" triggers a stricter level of scrutiny.[37] (The Court has stated the test as follows: Where a fundamental interest is at issue or inferior treatment is afforded a suspect class, the state must show that a compelling interest is being served that cannot be satisfied by some less onerous alternative.) Now the burden of proof shifts to the state, which must demonstrate that its classification scheme is necessary to serve a compelling state interest. This test is so stringent from the state's viewpoint that while it is strict in theory, it has proved to be fatal in fact.[38] A third standard adopted by the Court falls between the old and new standards with regard to the strictness of review involved.[39] This test is like the rational basis test, but is used when an important but not fundamental interest is involved or when a classification is almost but not quite suspect. Under this standard the Court closely examines the relationship between the means used to effectuate a legislative end so as to determine if in fact that means substantially furthers the legislative purpose. This leads the Court to determine if, in fact, the claimed benefits of the legislative action are present, thereby providing a justification for the injury the complainant has sought to redress. Yet a fourth test may have been adopted by the Court.[40] This test is similar to the third test and the rational basis test, and, as under the third test, the Court closely examines the relationship of means to ends. But under this test the Court would not limit its inquiry to the question of whether the means in fact served the ends; it would go on to ask whether the end being served is sufficiently important to justify the unequal treatment about which the complaint has been filed.

The third and fourth tests avoid the result oriented nature of the first two tests and narrow the gap between the strict level of scrutiny of the second test and the minimal scrutiny of the rational basis test.[41] These last two tests encourage a genuine judicial inquiry into the conflicting interests in the case without the assistance provided by the manipulation of burden of proof as occurs under the first two tests. The last two tests are difficult to apply with consistency.

We may now turn to the problem of the exclusion from school of materials with a viewpoint offensive to the officials in power. The first question is, Which standard of review would apply? Since no semblance of a suspect classification is involved, the question becomes one of whether the interests of the complaining students are sufficiently important to be deemed fundamental, hence nevertheless triggering the use of the new equal protection test. The answer seems to be that the Supreme Court has already said that education per se is not a fundamental interest which warrants the use of the new equal protection test.[42] But are the interests sufficiently important to warrant use of the third or fourth tests outlined? Perhaps so. Assuming either the third or fourth test applied, the outcome of the suit would hinge upon how the courts conceived the purpose of the rules used by the school for deciding what will be taught and what will not be taught.[43] That is, before the courts could decide whether the selection rules were rationally related to the schools' purposes—were, in fact, realizing the benefits the school district set out to achieve—the court must decide on what it conceives the purpose of the school rules for selecting the materials to be. If the purpose is broadly conceived (for example, to select materials useful for producing educated citizens), it is probable that the school could show that its rules served this purpose, since almost any materials selected would serve such a purpose. The complainant could not demonstrate that the rules absolutely failed to realize the benefits to be achieved. But if the purpose were more narrowly conceived, (for example, to select materials which will produce politically educated and wise citizens), then the school might have trouble maintaining that its rules, which resulted in the exclusion of a discussion of many political viewpoints, actually served the purpose, and the challenge would have a better chance of being successful.

But chances are the courts would want to avoid getting deeply involved in this kind of a thicket and would insist upon using only the old or rational basis test for reviewing these challenges. Under this test the complainant would have to demonstrate that the rules used for deciding the content of the school program were not rationally related to any legitimate school purpose. Obviously the plaintiff could not win, bearing such a burden of proof, since the school could always argue its purpose was to produce well-educated citizens and its rules rationally served such a purpose. The complainant would have to convince the court that teaching students about the benefits of the free enterprise system was not rationally related to the purpose of producing well-educated citizens—a task not likely to meet with success. The complainant could only hope for success if he could convince the court that the school's conception of a well-educated citizen was not a legitimate school purpose, but again the chances of so convincing the court appear to be nil.

3. The Exclusion of Individuals. One important way the states have attempted to maintain the ideological correctness of the school program is to exclude certain people with whom the public officials disagree. And one way states have attempted to screen out undesirable teachers has been to require teachers to disclaim under oath past or present membership in the Communist party and the advocacy of the violent overthrow of the government. For a variety of reasons, this kind of disclaimer oath has been repeatedly struck down as unconstitutional.[44] What remains constitutional is that sort of oath that merely asks the teacher to affirm allegiance to the United States and to promise to uphold and defend the Constitution.[45] Thus, it appears that the mere fact of being a Marxist or communist is an insufficient basis for excluding a person from teaching in the public schools. It becomes a different question if such a teacher were to attempt to indoctrinate his or her pupils. (See chap. 6 and the discussion of academic freedom.)

Also excluded from teaching in the public schools in many states are aliens.[46] These laws have not, to 1976, been challenged under the Equal Protection clause of the Fourteenth Amendment, but once again the constitutionality of these laws turns on the questions of which standard of review applies and how the appropriate standard would be applied. Recent Supreme Court cases are suggestive of the fact that either test three or four would apply in a case challenging these laws; hence the question would be one of whether the state's purpose in excluding aliens was in fact being served by the exclusion. The state's case might be strongest with regard to excluding aliens from teaching history and social studies courses (on the grounds of lack of knowledge or expertise in American politics and ways of life), as opposed to excluding aliens from teaching science courses.

We have more guidance from the courts with regard to school district attempts to exclude from the schools particular teachers espousing viewpoints with which the administration of the district disagreed. The Second Circuit Court of Appeals decided two cases involving such an exclusion of teachers. In one case the teacher refused to participate in the flag salute ceremony and in the other the teacher wore a black armband to school in protest to the Vietnam War.[47] The opinions in both decisions were quite similar and will be discussed together here. The court began by noting that students had been given the right not to participate in the flag salute and to wear black armbands to school and that the behavior of the teachers in these cases had not disrupted the schools. The issue in each case became one of whether the school board could control the teacher's behavior as part of its general right to control the school curriculum. While agreeing that the school board had basic authority to instill in young minds a respect for the symbols of our government and to otherwise instruct them politically, the court said the question was whether the schools' requiring teachers to salute the flag and stop wearing the armband had caused unnecessary trampling on the rights of the teachers. What the court found was that enforcement of the schools' rules was not necessary as the students still, in the one case, continued to recite the pledge under the guidance of another teacher in the room and the course of study in the classroom of the teaching wearing the armband was still being pursued. Neither teacher had engaged in unrelenting indoctrination of the pupils. Besides, the pupils involved in both cases were old enough to understand the conflict involved and did not need to be shielded. Thus, to an extent, the schools must remain open forums for the expression of political ideas—even those with which the school board and officials disagree.

This point is underscored by the decision in *Tinker* v. *Des Moines Independent School District* in which school officials excluded two children from school for wearing black armbands in protest against the Vietnam War.[48] The basis of the school's action appeared to be mere disagreement with the political viewpoint of the students. The Supreme Court, in reinstating the students, said that students may not be suspended or expelled from school for exercising their First Amendment right of free speech unless they had materially and substantially disrupted the school or unless the school officials had some reasonable basis to forecast that the exercise of those rights by the students would materially and substantially disrupt the schools. In this case, the students who had worn the black armbands to school and who had been suspended for doing so had to be reinstated with the right to wear the armband. In other cases, students have been protected against suspension for distributing student newspapers which contained views with which the school officials disagreed. However, it should be noted that the material and substantial disruption standard is subject to many interpretations and in practice has not always provided students with protection against disciplinary action. Nevertheless, the recognition of student rights is an important element in maintaining the school as a marketplace of ideas. Today student organizations may not be denied official school recognition merely because of official disagreement with the organizations' views. Thus the public schools can be thought of as a sort of forum at which students may express their ideas and communicate with each other and the faculty, so long as they do not materially and substantially disrupt the school. As the Supreme Court said, students are not merely closed-circuit recipients of only that information that school officials choose to communicate.

The School as a Cultural Marketplace

Just as many educators have argued that the public schools should be used to perpetuate the political ideas of the country, they have argued for using the public schools for perpetuating one set of cultural values. Given the multinational and multiracial background of the country, it has been feared that unless children were educated in one set of values the country would be faced with severe problems of cultural divisiveness. It was this sort of thinking that led in the past to the attempt on the part of states to eliminate, or at least severely curtail, private foreign language schools.[49] But how far may the schools go in promoting cultural ideals? This section explores several aspects of this question.

1. English as the Basic Medium of Instruction. One important way in which states have attempted to avoid the problem of cultural divisiveness has been to require that English be the basic medium of instruction through most of the school years.[50] (In some states, in the early grades, bilingual instruction may be offered in which the basic language of instruction may be other than English.[51] Eventually it is assumed, however, that students will learn English and be taught primarily in English.) To date this all-English policy has not been attacked head-on in a case claiming that students have a right to be taught only in their mother tongue. (This claim should be distinguished from those suits, to be discussed later, that have claimed a right on the part of non-English-speaking students to be given special instruction in English so they can effectively partake of the school program.)

An argument on behalf of a challenge to English as the medium of instruction might go as follows: Using English as the language of instruction is a form of racial-ethnic discrimination because this means that white, English-speaking students obtain instruction in their mother tongues while the non-white, non-English-speaking students obtain no instruction in their mother tongues. Since race, a suspect classification, is involved, the new equal protection test applies, and the school must demonstrate that its language policy is necessary to achieve a compelling state interest. The school, the argument would continue, cannot meet that burden of proof as its language policy is not necessary for the achievement of its purpose, namely, to assure that all children speak English. The school could simply provide special instruction in English to these non-English-speaking students but maintain for them, through all the school years as the basic medium of instruction, their mother tongues. The school district could reply that while such an approach would be possible, it believes that making English the basic medium of instruction, especially after the first few grades in elementary school, is the only way to really make sure that all students speak English well, and it is essential, if our society is to maintain its cohesiveness, that all people share a common language. Hence, the school would argue that its language policy was necessary to achieve a compelling state interest. It would be very surprising if the courts did not accept the school's reply, thereby permitting what some people call cultural imperialsim.

2. The Exclusion of Other Languages. Could states attempt to promote the learning of English by passing statutes which prohibit the public schools from offering any instruction in any other language? Our only direct guidance on the question is a Supreme Court decision striking down a similar statute that applied to private schools.[52] But states presumably have more authority to regulate public schools so it is unlikely that such a law would be unconstitutional with regard to public schools unless the quotation from Justice Stewart's opinion in the *Epperson* case noted earlier could be stretched to cover this kind of law, or unless the law had a discriminatory effect with regard to non-English-speaking students. Certainly school rules which banned, for example, Spanish-speaking students, from talking Spanish among themselves, as schools in the southwestern part of the country have attempted to do in the past, would be viewed as an impermissible form of discrimination.[53]

3. The Schools and Sexual Roles. Cultural education goes beyond language requirements to include instruction with regard to the social roles appropriate for the sexes. In this regard, the courts may yet be asked to overturn on constitutional grounds such course requirements as home economics for girls and shop for boys. Since sex has not yet been declared by the Supreme Court to be a suspect classification and since education is not a fundamental interest according to the Supreme Court, yet since education is still an important interest and there is an element of unfairness in classifying people in terms of immutable characteristics, such requirements may be tackled under tests three and four instead of the old equal protection test.[54] Using the third or fourth test, the courts would explore the nature of the stigma imposed by such a classification scheme, its purpose, whether the means actually achieve the purpose, and whether the purpose is sufficiently important to outweigh the restriction of liberty and stigma imposed. It would be surprising if today such requirements would withstand this degree of judicial scrutiny.

As for the exclusion of, for example, female students from shop courses or athletic programs or male students from home economics courses, a new question enters the analysis: To what extent may schools attempt to bar students from choosing courses that might encourage them to adopt social roles or behaviors different from the traditional roles and behaviors for the two sexes? The answer given in cases in which women have challenged such exclusionary rules is that schools may not try to close out options in this way.[55]

Another question is whether schools could require, for example, all students to take home economics or shop or both. The element of sex discrimination would not be present in such requirements. Indeed, there would be no element of discriminatory treatment in such a case as the requirement applies equally to all. Thus, it appears the schools could engage in one form of cultural imperialism, encouraging new thinking about social roles despite a possible desire of parents to maintain traditional sexual roles for men and women.

4. Sexually Biased Materials. The chances are that today the problem of sexually biased materials would be challenged under federal statutes prohibiting sex discrimination in programs receiving federal funds. (See chap. 3.) But mention should be made of the possibility of challenging such materials under the Constitution. That is, the question raised here is whether schools may perpetuate traditional sexual roles by imposing on students textual materials reflecting these older traditions with regard to appropriate roles for males and females. Since sex has not been termed to be a suspect classification, chances are such a case would be decided under either the third or fourth tests. Assuming the courts could decide if a given set of materials were discriminatory in content—no easy task, as will be brought out more clearly in the next chapter—the prospects are reasonably good that such materials would be struck down as serving no legitimate state purpose.

5. The Imposition of Rules of Behavior. Schools have attempted to maintain the hegemony of particular cultural ideals by establishing hair and dress codes. Such codes have met a mixed reception in the federal courts. Some courts have upheld these codes even in the face of claims by such groups as Pawnee Indian students that their braided hairstyle was traditional in their tribe and even rested on religious beliefs. But other federal courts have struck short hair style requirements down as an invasion of privacy and the personal liberty of students.[56] The Supreme Court has consistently refused to review these decisions despite the split among the circuits, thus the extent to which schools may constitutionally impose a particular cultural idea upon students by excluding students who deviate from the prescribed standards depends on the circuit in which the school is located. What the status of these cases is in 1976, in light of the recent Supreme Court decision upholding hair length regulations imposed on policemen, is not certain.[57] In that case the Court both played down the importance of the liberty at stake while playing up the rationality of the policy of requiring uniformity in appearance for police. Students are different from police, however, and the reasons for controlling the hair style of students may very well be less compelling than the reasons for controlling the hair style of the police.

Aside from hair and dress regulations, schools also have attempted to educate their students as to proper sexual standards of behavior by excluding pregnant and married students from the regular school program. The schools argue that not to exclude such students leaves the impression that approval is given to early pregnancy, pregnancy out of wedlock, and teenage marriages. Allowing these students to remain in school runs the risk that they will become models other students will emulate. There have been few federal court decisions dealing with such policies, but the tendency has been for courts to uphold the rights of students not to be so excluded.[58] (See chap. 5 for a discussion of state court cases.) The courts have stressed the importance of a formal education for the students and have pointed out that the schools have other less coercive means of educating students with regard to pregnancy and early marriage. Excluding pregnant females from schools can also be viewed as a form of sex discrimination since fathers of these children are not excluded (see chap. 4).

Schools also have attempted to exclude married teachers in their fifth month of pregnancy on the ostensible ground they are no longer physically fit to teach and to exclude unmarried pregnant teachers on the ground they are a bad example for students.[59] Teachers in both cases have been successful in their suits to bar exclusion. The Supreme Court, as to the married teachers, said there was no medical substantiation for the claim that all pregnant teachers in the fifth month were physically unfit to teach. As for the unwed pregnant teachers, a lower court said the claimed adverse effect of these adult models on student behavior was purely speculative.

As for school boards excluding or restricting access to books deemed unacceptable, the courts have sustained the actions of the boards in the face of claims that these restrictive policies violated the free speech rights of teachers, parents, and students.[60] Absent charges of racial, religious, or sexual discrimination, it would be surprising if the courts would step in to control school board discretion in this area. To get involved would, in the eyes of most judges, convert the courts into local school boards. Thus, boards constitutionally remain free to select books according to their own cultural lights. The kind of cultural-religious disputes that have arisen from time to time over textbook selection must remain a matter for the political decision-making process.

6. Race and the Curriculum. Racism has been an important part of American culture and its bearing on the school curriculum raises several interrelated issues. First is the question of whether the school constitutionally could impose upon students racially discriminatory materials—for example, materials that encouraged the belief that blacks were inferior to whites and were to enjoy only certain socioeconomic political roles in the society. In light of the Supreme Court's strong stand against the purposeful segregation of pupils it would be surprising if the courts did not prohibit, on the basis of the Constitution, materials that were deemed racially discriminatory.[61] But the real question would be whether a particular item were purposefully discriminatory in content.

Is the story *Little Black Sambo* an example of racially discriminatory materials because the hero is repeatedly identified as black or because of the perjorative connotations which the name "Sambo" has taken on? Is Shakespeare's *Othello* discriminatory? Second, when materials totally omit any black characters or omit references to black people, are those materials racially discriminatory? If they are to be so declared, presumably it is because such materials cause some form of harm, but can it be established by present-day methods of social science that failure to make reference to black people injures pupils? A very difficult problem of proof is involved here. Third, how materials are used may be as important as the content of the materials. A teacher may have introduced a blatantly discriminatory article for purposes of discussing racial prejudice. There thus may be a strong justification for the use of such materials, even if racially discriminatory in content. In any event, assuming *Othello* were deemed to be racially discriminatory, could its use be justified simply because it is a great piece of literature? Could a course in English literature, which took up the classics but did not involve reading any material that had blacks as heroes, be barred despite the obvious justifications that would be offered in support of such a course? Because of these problems it is not likely the courts will quickly or willingly involve themselves in such cases.

A second problem involves the exclusion from schools of materials—especially magazines and newspapers—with a black viewpoint. There is no doubt that school rules for selecting magazines and newspapers for use in the classroom or library which purposefully excluded such materials would be reviewed under the new equal protection test.[62] Purposeful racial discrimination is prohibited by the Constitution and only if the Supreme Court were willing to relitigate that issue would there be any doubt on this point. Rules for the selection of materials, which merely as a practical matter had the effect of excluding black-oriented materials, pose a more difficult question. Such rules might be deemed to be racially discriminatory only if it could be shown that even unintentional exclusion of such materials harmed the complaining pupils. That is, while it is obviously harmful to black students when a school engages in purposeful racial discrimination, it may not be so obvious as to what the injury is if the rules have only the incidental effect of excluding black materials. Presumably proof of harm in this instance would involve establishing that black children are injured by not having available materials that provide them with role models and that serve to develop a positive image for black people. Whether social science today can establish such propositions remains uncertain. If such proof could be established, however, the new equal protection test would apply as it would in the case of purposeful exclusion, because such school policies would involve treating students differently on the basis of race, a suspect classification.

Under the new equal protection test the school would have the burden of demonstrating that its rules were necessary to achieve a compelling state interest. To meet this burden school officials might argue that the excluded materials threatened materially and substantially to disrupt the school by heightening racial tension or inciting students to violent action. It is doubtful, however, that such a claim could be sustained with regard to all black-oriented materials. A close comparison of excluded with included materials in the school probably would uncover, in most instances, no differences in content.[63] The school rules would have to change and the Equal Protection clause would have served the function of maintaining the school as a marketplace of ideas.

The problems discussed to this point have all involved an element of coercion, either the imposition of courses or the exclusion of ideas and people from the schools. We turn now to the issues raised when schools offer as electives full-time special programs in ethnic studies, such as black or Spanish studies programs.[64] Problems arise with these programs because the students who enroll in them all tend to be of one race and/or ethnic background even if the programs are officially open to anyone. Given the complexion of the student body in these programs, a school board might be accused of operating a segregated program. Such a charge could rest on several bases: First, it might rest on the belief that despite the official claim that enrollment is open to all, a closer examination of the school's policies would reveal that the program was purposefully segregated. Second, the charge might be based on the argument that the policy of the board had the foreseeable result of producing a segregated program, hence it is unconstitutional. Third, it might be argued that the fact that the program is concerned only with one race creates a prima facie case of purposeful racial segregation which the school board must rebut or face closing down of its program.

In response to these arguments the school might present three rebuttals. First, neither race nor ethnicity was in fact used to exclude students from the school. Second, while in practice the programs have turned out to enroll only students of one racial and/or ethnic background, the programs are justified by the educational benefits achieved (for example, greater self-esteem resulting in increased learning achievement). Third, the policy for admissions was one of freedom of choice, and such methods for assigning students to schools have not been declared by the Supreme Court to be unconstitutional per se.[65] Freedom of choice plans have only been deemed to be unconstitutional when they have been adopted by school districts that have been ordered to desegregate their schools; that is, when the freeom of choice plans did in fact fail to eliminate the pattern of single-race schools in the district. As of this writing, the constitutional issues raised by these ethnic studies programs have not been resolved.

The Minimally Adequate Education

Using various means of litigation, educational organizations, parents, and lawyers interested in the education of children have been trying to get the courts to review the adequacy of the public school program. Suits have focused on such different things as the exclusion of children from school, the methods of instruction, the amount of money spent, and the racial mix of the student body. The success of these suits has been quite varied.

1. Exclusion of Children. Two suits raised claims on behalf of two groups of students (mentally retarded children and children with behavior problems) who were excluded from school on the grounds that they were noneducable—that no school program would or could meet their needs. In one of the cases the parties reached an agreement, which the court approved, that required the identification of all excluded students, a thorough medical and psychological evaluation of those children, and placement of them in a free public program of education and training appropriate to the child's capabilities, as well as protection of the child through required periodic reevaluation of the child's educational needs.[66] In the second case, the federal court also ordered the establishment of elaborate procedures to identify the educational needs of the excluded children and ordered that all excluded children be provided with a program suited to their needs.[67] But it is important to note that neither opinion made clear what an appropriate or suitable program must be. Yet the cases represent a tentative first step in judicial involvement in assuring all children of an adequate education and in rejecting the proposition that there are certain groups of children who are noneducable.

2. The Methods of Instruction. Another kind of challenge to the adequacy of the school program arose in California where parents of Chinese-speaking students claimed their children were effectively or functionally excluded from the school program because the program was conducted solely in English; no special efforts were being made to instruct their children in English.[68] Second, the parents argued, the exclusion of their children was a form of racial exclusion: the all-English policy of the school had the effect of excluding a specific, identifiable national and racial-ethnic group from obtaining any benefits from the school program. Third, because the school in effect classified pupils on the basis of race, the new equal protection test should apply. Fourth, the school district, thus, had the burden of establishing that its policy was necessary to achieve a compelling state interest, but, the parents continued, no such justification exists. For example, that school finances were tight, the plaintiffs argued, did not constitute a justification for singling out one group of students for effective exclusion from the school program. As a remedy the plaintiffs demanded that the school undertake to provide special instruction in English to their children to afford them access to the educational opportunities offered to English-speaking students. The parents did not say whether that special instruction should be in the form of English-as-a-Second-Language (ESL) or bilingual education; apparently the parents doubted that the courts would be willing to impose a specific method of instruction upon the schools, despite the fact that there was mounting evidence that bilingual education is the more effective method.

The case ultimately reached the Supreme Court where the right of the non-English-speaking children to special instruction was upheld, not on the basis of the constitutional argument outlined in the previous paragraph, but on the basis of an interpretation of the Civil Rights Act of 1964 which required school districts receiving federal funds to effectively include non-English-speaking children in the school program.[69] Thus, school districts receiving federal funds and enrolling non-English-speaking pupils must provide them with special instruction in English or face losing their federal assistance. Whether the constitutional argument outlined is acceptable to the Supreme Court remains unsettled. Also left open are such questions as whether ESL or bilingual instruction will meet statutory and regulatory requirements, and what kind of effort to provide special instruction must districts make which enroll, for example, one Polish-speaking child.

Perhaps the soundness of the constitutional arguments outlined may yet be decided by the Supreme Court. Parents of children with learning disabilities have brought suit in Philadelphia, charging their children are functionally excluded from the school program.[70] The complaint states that children with specific learning disabilities who are not receiving instruction specially suited to their handicaps are discriminated against in several respects. First, the school district is providing normal children with an education appropriate to their needs but denying an equal educational opportunity to the learning disabled. Many of the learning disabled, it is alleged, cannot derive *any* educational benefits from the normal curriculum. Second, it is claimed the school district is providing the mentally retarded with an education suited to their needs but is denying the learning handicapped an education adapted to overcoming their handicaps. Third, it is alleged that the district unlawfully discriminates between those few learning disabled students who are getting special instruction and those who are not. A federal district has recently ruled that the complaint states a colorable claim under the third equal protection test: that is, the school's handling of learning disabled students may not in fact be providing all children with an education appropriate to their needs.

The preceding two cases relied on claims that the students were absolutely excluded from deriving any benefits from the program to which they were exposed while other students were obtaining an education from which they could benefit. But the suit has not yet been brought which alleges that, while not absolutely excluded, the injured students were not obtaining a program as well suited to their needs as other programs were to other students. The reason such a suit has not been brought is that it is highly unlikely judicial intervention could be obtained. Courts are not likely to insist that educational programs perfectly realize their purposes.

However, courts have been willing to tackle the suitability of educational programs for particular groups of children if racial discrimination is involved. Black students and students from lower socioeconomic classes have gone to court to argue they were being provided with an education unsuited to their needs because they had the effect of classifying them not on the basis of ability but on the basis of their race and socioeconomic background. In one such case the IQ tests allegedly had the effect of creating a racial imbalance in the classes for the mentally retarded because, it was argued, the tests were biased against the culture and experience of black children.[71] Because race was an element in the case the court adopted a standard of review that placed the burden of proof on the district to justify its tests. The court concluded the school did not demonstrate that the IQ tests were rationally related to the purpose of classifying pupils by their abilities, at least with regard to black children. In another case, the court concluded the tests used discriminated on the basis of the student's social class and race and that the tracking system in the school district was deficient. That is, once students were placed in the slower tracks (as a result of the discriminatory tests) there they remained (because they were given no compensatory instruction), receiving only a watered down and inadequate education.[72] It should also be noted that special education classification systems may be vulnerable in the courts if the plaintiffs can establish that such schemes stigmatize the pupils and do not in fact serve the purpose of educating the children.[73]

But absent possible stigmatization in special education classification schemes or elements of racial discrimination, or a claim of absolute functional exclusion, it is doubtful that the courts would be willing to strike down the educational program provided a child simply because the parents think the program is not fully suited to the child. The courts are likely to conclude that these cases are nonjusticiable and ought to be left to the educational experts in the schools. While it is fairly easy to determine if children are absolutely functionally excluded from school, or discriminated against on the basis of race, or stigmatized without *any* offsetting educational benefit, it is much more difficult to determine if this or another school program might be marginally better for a child. If the courts, nevertheless, did try to deal with the suitability of school programs for particular children they would have to refer to the following kinds of criteria to make their task easier:[74] (1) a bona fide effort is being made to identify the background factors which bar effective student utilization of school services and facilities; (2) the instruction offered is adequate in light of existing knowledge and could reasonably be expected to help the student overcome the incapacitating factors in his background; (3) the school is continuously upgrading the diagnosis of the student, constantly making efforts to assure that the program is suited to a student's particular needs; (4) the particular program is adequately staffed and funded. Although somewhat vague, these criteria are not so vague as to be nonjusticiable. And they do not force the court into the untenable position of specifically decreeing that one or another method of instruction be adopted; nor do they impose upon schools the impossible demand that all children reach a certain level of achievement. The criteria loosely constrain the selection of programs and services without usurping the power of the local school district.

3. Funding School Programs. Whether programs suitable to the needs of children will be mounted in a school district importantly depends on the amount of money available to that district. Accordingly, some reformers concerned with the adequacy of the school program have focused their attention upon existing systems of school finance. Under most such systems great interdistrict disparities in the amount of money spent per pupil are permitted, with the result that there are significant differences in the programs offered from district to district.

Assuming these differences in the program were educationally significant, some people argued that these systems of finance were unconstitutional.[75] The first point in the argument was that since existing systems for financing education relied so heavily upon the local property tax, and since property wealth per pupil drastically varied from district to district, this meant the amount of money spent per pupil became a function of the varying wealth of the district. Second, the quality of education thus varied from district to district with a higher quality education being provided in wealthy districts which could afford to spend more for education. The children who were hurt by this system of financing education were (a) all children in relatively poor districts; (b) the children from poor families in relatively property-poor districts; and (c) minority children who tended to be located in relatively poor districts. The third point in the argument was that this discriminatory system had to be reviewed pursuant to the new equal protection test because the system discriminated on the basis of a suspect classification (the wealth of the district where children resided) and because a fundamental interest, education, was affected. Fourth, the plaintiffs argued the system could not withstand the strict scrutiny of the new equal protection test because the existing system did not serve any compelling state interest, including the interest of local control. The interest of local control was not served because property-poor districts had no real control over the amount of money they could spend on their children.

The Supreme Court rejected all these arguments in a case challenging the educational finance system of Texas.[76] The Court said the use of the new equal protection test was not required in this case because under the Court's precedent (a) there was no suspect classification as it had previously been defined and (b) education was not a fundamental interest. The second point is important because the Court went on to say that children might have a fundamental interest in a minimally adequate education, but in this case no one argued that the property-poor districts with their lower levels of spending were offering less than a minimally adequate education. It was perhaps not an education equal in quality to the more adequately supported programs in wealthy districts, but it was not inadequate. In saying this, the Court overlooked the observation that where a good such as education is valued because of its usefulness in a competitive activity (for example, seeking income and status), relative inequality in the provision of the good may entail the same evil as absolute deprivation of the good. Inequality implies absolute deprivation. In any event, the court went on to review the case in terms of the rational basis test and concluded that the system, despite its inequalities, was rationally related to the purpose of maintaining local control. Additionally, the Court in several places in the opinion expressed its unwillingness to get involved in a case that (as this case did) involved so many complexities of the taxing and spending powers of states and unresolved disputes with regard to the relationship of money to the quality of education provided.

Thus, as matters now stand, it appears the Supreme Court may only get involved in educational finance cases if the case involves proof that the programs affected are not minimally adequate. But the Court has not defined what it means by this term, so it is hard to predict when it might intervene.

4. Racial Segregation. In *Brown* v. *Board of Education*, the Supreme Court struck down as inherently unequal schools that had been purposefully segregated under statutes and local regulations that required that black children attend school only with black children and white children with white.[77] The Court gave its approval to a finding of the Kansas district court, which stated:

Segregation of white and colored children in public schools has a detrimental effect upon the colored children. The impact is greater when it has the sanction of law; for the policy of separating the races is usually interpreted as denoting the inferiority of the Negro group. A sense of inferiority affects the motivation of the child to learn. Segregation with the sanction of law, therefore, has a tendency to [retard] the educational and mental development of Negro children and to deprive them of some of the benefits they would receive in a racial[ly] integrated school system.[78]

The finding, the Court said, was "amply supported by modern authority," which was set forth in the infamous footnote eleven of the opinion.

The *Brown* decision leads one to conclude that the legally enforced separation of the races in public schools is constitutionally wrong because it ultimately results in an inferior education for black students. Hence, one can argue that judicial concern with purposefully segregated schools stems from, at least, in part, a desire to be sure that all children regardless of race obtain equal educational opportunity, a program of equal quality. Today the issue of whether purposefully segregated schools do in fact systematically damage the learning achievement of black children is foreclosed from relitigation by the decision in *Brown*.

What remains unsettled by the Supreme Court is whether segregation in schools that results solely from segregated residential patterns, that is, from the actions of real estate agents, housing authorities, banks, and the like, is unconstitutional.[79] (Most racially segregated schools result from school districts' manipulation of attendance zones, strategic construction of new buildings, and creation of optional attendance zones.) If genuinely segregated (that is, where segregation does not involve any action by the school district) education is to be declared unconstitutional, it will have to be because it violates the Equal Protection clause, and for that to be established it probably will have to be shown that even genuine de facto segregation provides black children with an inferior education. Several lower courts have come to this conclusion.[80] Remedying genuine de facto segregation thus can be viewed as a form of judicial involvement in the curriculum of the schools.

It should be noted, however, that there is disagreement among the social scientists as to whether nonpurposeful segregation harms the education of black children.[81] Indeed, one basis for the argument of community control of schools is that black schools controlled by a black community can provde a high quality education. And at least one black legal scholar concerned with integration is not convinced that segregation regardless of cause stigmatizes black youth and should be eliminated regardless of cost.[82] In light of this controversy it is highly unlikely that the Supreme Court will soon extend the *Brown* case to encompass genuine de facto segregation.

Where an end to discrimination has been ordered the courts have on occasion been forced into a more direct consideration of curriculum-related issues. In several desegregation cases the lower courts have ordered the provision of compensatory education to black students.[83] In several other cases pupil assignment to schools and classes on the basis of standardized achievement or IQ test scores has been struck down when the intended or actual effect has been the perpetuation of the now prohibited dual school system.[84] In another case the schools were forced to offer compensatory education to a large group of students who had been illegally excluded from the schools.[85] Additionally, the integration of schools may force school districts to change their curriculum in a vareity of ways: books and materials may have to be changed to reflect the interests and backgrounds of more diverse student bodies; black history and literature courses may have to be developed; racially offensive books will have to be removed from use; and vocational education may have to be paid more attention.[86]

Perhaps the most difficult problems are posed when the desegregation order involves white and Spanish-speaking students. Several courts have ordered or approved massive program changes in this kind of situation.[87] The changes have included provision of bilingual instruction to both the Mexican-American and white student populations; changes in the curriculum materials to reflect the cultural diversity of the student body; the hiring of bilingual teachers; changes in the home economics course to reflect the different life styles of the pupils; new teaching techniques such as team teaching, individualized instruction, and small group instruction; a staff training program; and the establishment of multiethnic school community councils to make a yearly evaluation of the new education programs and to assist in the formulation of educational goals and objectives.

Conclusions

This breadth of involvement of the federal courts in shaping the educational program to which children may be exposed is impressive. The Supreme Court and lower federal courts, because of their authority to interpret the U.S. Constitution, allocate power between the public and private sectors. They involve themselves in the religious, political, and cultural content of the school program as well as concern themselves with the minimal adequacy of the school program. The work of the courts has touched and might touch upon the setting of minimal standards, determining the content of courses, determining methods of instruction, selecting educational materials, determining the religious, political, and cultural bias of the school program, setting up pupil classification systems, labeling and identifying individual pupils, and exempting students from courses. In short, the federal courts have been involved or might involve themselves in most of the ways in which the educational program of the schools are controlled. (See app. 1A.)

But breadth of involvement should not be mistaken for depth of involvement. In many respects the courts have restrained themselves, placed sharp limits on how far they are willing to go in executing these various roles. For example, while the courts have taken some steps to assure the schools remain marketplaces for political ideas, it is still possible for schools to mount political education courses with strong biases. Also, judicial involvement in assuring that the educational program is minimally adequate is still at an early stage of development.

To a certain extent, we can discern a kind of constitutionally shaped school program emerging. The program must be secular, not religious, but it may not be militantly secular or overtly antireligious. English may remain the dominant language of instruction. But the program may not fail to meet the needs of non-English-speaking pupils and perhaps also the needs of other students with special problems. The program may be politically biased in that the school may encourage belief in a particular political viewpoint. However, students may not be coerced into a confession of the school-approved doctrines and the school may not discriminatorily screen out people or perhaps even curriculum materials with which it disagrees. The school must remain a marketplace of competing ideas even if the official viewpoint retains a competitive advantage. In the realm of culture, schools in many places may continue to use school dress and hair codes to educate students to approved standards of taste but course requirements no longer may be rigged to force students into stereotypic sexual roles. On balance, schools need be less of a marketplace with regard to cultural ideas than with regard to political ideas. The major exception to this rule is the perpetuation of racism—public schools may not officially attempt to prolong the existence of that aspect of American culture. In short, the schools may not perpetuate the religious, racist, and sexist aspects of our society but may within bounds perpetuate its political ideology.

3 The Federal Government

In 1965 the total federal investment in elementary and secondary schools was running at the rate of about $1 billion a year.[1] The major pieces of legislation then in existence that had (and today still have) a bearing on the school curriculum were the National Defense Education Act (NDEA), various vocational education acts, and the statute establishing the National Science Foundation.[2] (NDEA's Title III provides grants on a matching basis to states that, in turn, hand money over to localities for support of instruction in science, mathematics, modern foreign languages, and other subjects critical to the national defense. The money can be used for equipment and minor remodeling to improve instruction. Title V of that same act provides financial assistance for guidance, counseling, and testing at the secondary school level. Vocational education is assisted under the Vocational Educational Amendments of 1968, which provide assistance for construction of area vocational schools for demonstration and experimental programs; for programs for the socioeconomically disadvantaged; for residential vocational education projects; for consumer and homemaking training; for work-study programs; for curriculum development and bilingual vocational education. Among many other activities the National Science Foundation supports curriculum development in the sciences at the secondary school level.) These programs were funded at modest levels in 1964—about $100 million for funding all three pieces of legislation—and they did little to disturb the relationship that had prevailed since the founding of the republic between, on the one hand, the federal government and, on the other hand, state and local government.[3] That is, the legislation offered no challenge to the authority of the states and localities to control the public school program. The federal government simply shipped the money out with few restrictions on its use and the states acted as middlemen, passing the money on to the localities. The United States Office of Education (USOE) eagerly tried to avoid complaints of interference with local districts. Little in the way of changed behavior was demanded by Washington of the states and localities.

In 1964-65 all this changed with the passage of the Elementary and Secondary Education Act of 1965 (ESEA) and, most importantly, Title I of ESEA.[4] As will be discussed in greater detail later, Title I authorized USOE to demand from local school boards significant changes in their educational programs. No longer would the federal government be merely a check-writing machine; rather it would attempt to realize its own con-

43

ception of a proper educational program despite the disclaimer in the legislation that "[n]o provision . . . shall be construed to authorize any department, agency, officer, or employee of the United States to exercise any direction, supervision, or control over the curriculum, program of instruction, administration, or personnel of any educational institution, school, or school system."[5]

The passage of ESEA also meant a dramatic increase in the level of federal support for elementary secondary education. Compared to the $1 billion spent in 1965, spending now moved to $2 billion in 1966, and roughly $3 billion at the end of the 1960s.[6] In fiscal year 1975, Title I alone provided $1.8 billion in federal aid and served six million children in 13,900 school districts.[7] Local education thus derives about 7 percent of its financial support from the federal government. This is not a large average percentage, but for some school districts it is the difference between being able to offer something more than a bare-bones program.[8]

Thus, the loss of federal aid can loom as a significant threat to school districts, and it is from this fact that the federal government obtains a significant point of leverage over the local board. Title VI of the Civil Rights Act of 1964 and Title IX of the Educational Amendments of 1972 prohibit racial and sexual discrimination in programs receiving federal funds.[9] Schools that do not comply with federal regulations barring racial and sexual discrimination face the loss of their federal funds. Consequently, the power of the federal government to cut off federal funds provides a significant tool by which to control these two forms of discrimination in the school program.

A third area of federal involvement that will be discussed is that of federal support of curriculum development efforts. While the influence of the federal government in this area is more indirect, nevertheless in recent times it has become quite controversial.

The Constitutional Basis of Federal Involvement in Education

In theory the federal government is a government of enumerated powers, meaning it has no authority to act in a given area unless that authority has been granted to it by the Constitution. Federal authority can be contrasted with that of the states which are presumed to have authority to act in a given area unless provisions of the Constitution oust them of that authority. And since education is nowhere mentioned in the Constitution, a question arises as to the constitutional basis for the federal legislation mentioned earlier.

The question was answered by the Supreme Court in *United States* v.

Butler and other related cases.[10] In those decisions the Court settled a long standing debate as to whether Article I, Section 8 of the Constitution could be interpreted to allow for federal spending for purposes other than those explicitly enumerated in the Constitution. Article I, Section 8 begins as follows: "The Congress shall have power to lay and collect taxes, duties, imposts and excises, to pay the debts and provide for the common defense and general welfare of the United States; . . . " The Court held the scope of Section 8 authority was not delimited by the areas enumerated in that section and that Congress could tax and spend for the general welfare broadly conceived, including education.

But authority financially to support state and local educational efforts is a different matter from authority to control educational policy. Whether Congress has authority to control educational policy depends importantly on the scope of its authority to attach conditions to grants-in-aid it authorizes. On this question the Supreme Court has expanded congressional power by allowing Congress to establish conditions which, if not complied with, result in the denial of federal funds.[11] The result is Congress today has the authority, for example, to deny federal aid to school programs that discriminate on the basis of race or sex.

The nondiscrimination and other conditions attached to federal grants to public schools are often vaguely stated and must be given more specific meaning by the federal agencies charged with enforcing those laws; thus we need to know the scope of the authority of federal agencies to interpret the statutes. The question is important because it is widely recognized that "Whoever has interpretive authority over written or spoken words is the lawgiver for all intents and purposes, not the person who wrote or spoke them."[12] The Supreme Court has said in this connection that the interpretations of federal agencies such as the Department of Health, Education, and Welfare will be upheld so long as they are reasonably related to the purposes of the legislation.[13] As a practical matter this test has led to a grant of considerable discretionary power to federal agencies.

Title I, ESEA

The first title of the Elementary and Secondary Education Act of 1965 is singled out for discussion not only because it is by far the most heavily funded piece of federal legislation directed to elementary and secondary education but also because Title I represents the most ambitious attempt on the part of the federal government to control the educational program offered in the public schools. An examination of the design, intent, and actual impact of the Title I should throw much light upon the extent of federal influence over curriculum.

The purpose of Title I is stated in a preamble:

In recognition of the special educational needs of children of low-income families and the impact that concentrations of low-income families have on the ability of local educational agencies to support adequate educational programs, the Congress hereby declares it to be the policy of the United States to provide financial assistance (as set forth in the following parts of this title) to local educational agencies serving areas with concentrations of children from low-income families to expand and improve their educational programs by various means (including preschool programs) which contribute particularly to meeting the special educational needs of educationally deprived children.[14]

To carry out this purpose the statute establishes a formula for the distribution of federal funds between states and localities, a formula that bases the level of funding for which a locality is eligible on the number of children from low-income homes residing in the area. This money is then turned over by USOE to the states which in turn hand money over to the local districts once the districts have submitted a detailed proposal to the state (which the state must approve in accordance with basic criteria set forth in the legislation itself and promulgated in the form of regulations and guidelines by USOE) as to how the money will be spent to meet the special educational needs of educationally deprived, even if not poor, children in the district. Once the local district has obtained its money and executed the project in accordance with its proposal and the law, at least annually it must evaluate the project and report the results to the state. In turn the states must evaluate their Title I programs and submit a report to USOE, which must also carry out its own evaluation and report to Congress. Thus, money flows down while project proposals and evaluation reports flow up.

The real potential for control of the local school program arises out of the possibility of forceful administration of several statutory requirements which districts must meet in order for their project proposals to be approved and for them to continue to receive funds. But since the enactment of Title I, the implementation of these statutory requirements has been marked by considerable political infighting between USOE and the local districts.[15] The result of these struggles has been that at the outset of the implementation process it was difficult for USOE to impose upon local districts as strict a set of regulations and guidelines as it seemed to prefer. This USOE-local struggle was compounded by an internal USOE debate between those reformers in USOE who viewed Title I as a vehicle for reforming education at the local level to make sure that the federal aid would serve the special needs of educationally deprived children and those traditionalists in USOE, members of Congress, and local districts, who viewed Title I as basically a way of providing general aid to local districts for use largely as those local districts saw fit. As the former head of the Title I office of USOE has written, Title I has been "a grueling test" of USOE's capability to provide educational leadership.[16]

The first statutory requirement to be discussed provided that local districts use their money in school attendance areas having high concentrations of children from low-income families.[17] This basic requirement meant, without going into the various exceptions and qualifications spelled out in the statute and regulations, that school districts had to rank their schools in terms of indexes of poverty and then use their Title I funds in those schools that had percentages of children from low-income families as high as the percentage for the whole district or average numbers of poor children as large as the average for the school district.[18] Elementary and secondary schools could have been placed in separate rankings and funds need not have been used in secondary schools even if they ranked higher than elementary schools in terms of the indexes of poverty. This allowed districts to concentrate their Title I efforts at the elementary level, where many educators, USOE, and state departments thought the greatest compensatory educational effort ought to be made. The selection of target schools on the basis of indexes of poverty was based on the theory that it was educationally more important to concentrate compensatory education in schools largely composed of low-income children, since research showed that the mere fact of large concentrations of low-socioeconomic children in schools lowered the educational achievement of those students. These targeting requirements, when coupled with other requirements, forced school districts to mount Title I compensatory education programs in only a limited number of schools. As a further consequence of the targeting requirement and other regulations, a limited number of schools were provided with a more expensive program than other schools. A form of reverse discrimination occurred, with poor schools reaping the benefits.

Second, within the target schools the money had to be used to meet the special educational needs of educationally deprived children, whether or not they were poor. To carry this out, USOE required school districts to assess as part of each project the special educational needs of educationally deprived children. A recent statutory amendment now also exhorts districts to develop individualized written educational plans for each child, which are agreed upon by the local district, the parent, and, when appropriate, the child.[19] The proposed regulations from USOE also would require that an order of priority be established for addressing the needs which have been identified.[20] These requirements are part of the general reform effort to encourage local districts to stop directing their concern solely toward the middle-class child with no learning difficulties and start directing their concern toward the unique educational needs of the educa-tionally deprived, on the assumption that the regular school program can-not serve those needs.

Third, all Title I projects had to meet an additional set of related re-quirements such as:[21] the project had to be directed to the children who had the greatest educational need; it had to be directed to a limited num-ber of educationally deprived children; and it had to be of sufficient size, scope, and quality as to give reasonable promise of substantial progress toward meeting the needs of the educationally deprived. The guidelines currently in force say that one measure of this concentrated effort is the amount of money spent per child.[22] Districts are expected to supplement by one-half the amount of money that they spend per child from local and state funds. And the project has to be broad enough in its attack on educa-tional problems to get at any of several possible causes of low achieve-ment (for example, health problems as well as reading problems). Other requirements call for the coordination of Title I efforts with other similar compensatory efforts funded from other sources.[23]

Fourth, Title I funds had to be used only in schools already receiving services which taken as a whole were comparable to services being pro-vided in schools not receiving Title I funds.[24] This statutory requirement was interpreted by USOE to mean that, for example, in target schools the pupil-teacher ratio and the amount of money spent per pupil (other than longevity pay) had to be roughly equivalent to those ratios in nontarget schools. The point of the comparability requirement was to make sure that Title I funds tipped the scales in favor of the educationally deprived and were not merely used to bring target schools up to a level of services already available in nontarget schools.

Fifth, Title I funds had to supplement, not supplant, local and state funds.[25] For example, if a compensatory education program funded by state and/or local funds was already being provided in an eligible school, Title I funds could not be substituted for those state and local funds, but had to be used to increase the level of funding in that school.

Sixth, local districts, states, and USOE were all expected to evaluate the effectiveness of Title I programs with appropriate objective measure-ments of educational achievement.[26] The results of these evaluations were supposed to feed back into the redesign of the projects to improve their effectiveness in meeting the special educational needs of education-ally deprived children.[27]

Taken all together and fully enforced these statutory requirements, as spelled out in greater detail in the regulations and guidelines, had the po-tential of forcing a virtual revolution in educational programming at the local level. First, a local school board would have to stop providing un-equal educational services to schools attended by children from low socioeconomic backgrounds. (The unequal provision of money and services within school districts is not uncommon.[28]) Second, the school district would then have to go one step further and provide the target schools with a level of services that was more amply funded than nontarget schools. Next, the district would have to single out within the target schools yet a smaller group of educationally deprived students who would receive the primary benefits of the Title I program. In order to make sure that Title I funds were not so diffused throughout the whole school, thereby benefitting ineligible children, the Title I project would have to be significantly separated from the regular program. Further, if the projects were to be truly effective they presumably would have to be based on a concept of education drastically different from the regular school program which had been proven inadequate in meeting the needs of the educationally disadvantaged: schools would have to adopt wholly new educational theories and methodologies. These new programs would have to be directed toward improving that form of educational achievement that could be measured by objective methods. And the schools would have to adopt methods of educational planning and development that relied upon the use of evaluation data. Such an approach to educational decision making was and is not common in most school districts and itself represents a significant reform above and apart from the required curricular changes. In short, Title I potentially represented an effort to transform public education in the United States by means of the device of the grant-in-aid.

But the full potential of Title I has not been realized. Almost from the very start of the implementation process, reports began to surface of abuses in the use of the Title I money, and today the catalog of these abuses is extensive.[29] Title I funds have been used for noneligible children so that the educationally advantaged in some places have reaped more rewards than the disadvantaged.[30] Title I money has been spread too thin, so that today the extra amount of money spent per pupil averages $175 per year.[31] The money has been used for purchasing large amounts of educational hardware which languishes unused in closets and cabinets.[32] Pools have been constructed with Title I funds and offices furnished.[33] The money has been used to supplant local funds by picking up the salaries of school personnel who previously had been supported by local funds.[34] The comparability requirements have been systematically ignored and Title I funds have been used to equalize programs in schools that had up to that point been shortchanged by the local board.[35] The money has been used to reinforce segregation by directing its use to all-black schools to encourage black students to stay in these schools and not transfer to white schools where compensatory services were not available.[36] The assessment of needs has been carried out in a superficial way and the evaluation of programs has been shoddy.[37] Perhaps as a consequence of these abuses all indications are that Title I has not improved the educational achievement of the target population.[38]

This picture of abuse should not, however, be overdrawn. Some cities did make genuine efforts to carry off the educational revolution implied by Title I.[39] There are reports of individual projects scattered throughout the country which do seem to have made a difference in the level of educational achievement.[40] But why compliance seems to have been achieved in some districts, partial compliance in others, and total abuse in yet others is unclear. Perhaps the abuses are good indicators of the obstacles faced by those administrators who do try to implement Title I programs.

Those obstacles include the following.[41] First, some administrators and politicians at all three levels of government viewed the program as one of providing general aid to school districts, not one primarily directed to the needs of educationally deprived children. Second, inadequate staff at the federal and state levels of government made enforcement of all the requirements difficult. Third, those charged with enforcement responsibilities did not have the stomach for confrontations with local districts over the misuse of Title I funds. Fourth, a desire on the part of USOE officials to get the program off to a fast start resulted in a willingness to forego strict enforcement of all the statutory requirements. Fifth, too strict enforcement of all the statutory requirements was thought by some in USOE to be dangerous as it might encourage Congress to amend the Title to move away from a categorical aid program to a general aid program. Sixth, officials in USOE felt politically weak and believed their best chances for obtaining compliance with the regulations was through persuasion rather than through threats and confrontation. Seventh, to actually cut off funds from noncomplying districts would have hurt the students, the very group of people the legislation was designed to help; thus this ultimate and only truly effective weapon for obtaining compliance was rarely used. Eighth, at the local level the syndrome sometimes called organizational rigidity helps to explain the unwillingness or inability of local districts to reform themselves along the lines demanded by the statute and regulations. Ninth, strong political pressures at the local level pushed local decision makers into widely dispersing Title I funds so as to spread the benefits of the funds to as many people as possible. At the same time there was no strong and active political opposition at the local level that sought complete compliance with the statute and basic regulations. Given this balance of political forces, local boards tended to go with those who pressed for spreading the money around. To have concentrated funds on a select group of students could only have been accomplished by local boards by paying a heavy political price. Tenth, full compliance often would have conflicted with districts' own concepts of a sound program and would have caused many administrative problems and internal strains within the school organization. Eleventh, local decision makers did not, in any event, have at hand adequate theories on the educational process to design truly effective educational programs; no one knew what it would take to improve the learning achievement of the educationally disadvantaged.

In sum, the incentives brought to bear on local decision makers to comply with the statute and regulations simply were not as powerful as the incentives not to comply. This said, what is missing is a deeper understanding of why even partial compliance was achieved in most districts, given the balance of incentives, and why reasonably full compliance may have been realized in yet another select number of districts.

Putting together the fact that we do not have a well documented picture of the pattern of compliance with Title I nor good explanations for that pattern means we lack today a complete understanding of the role the federal government has played in controlling the educational program at the local level. What we do know is that a significant group of people in Congress and in USOE have attempted to control and have been partially successful in controlling the school program at the local level. We also know that this break with tradition with regard to the role of the federal government was accomplished in order to achieve educational opportunity for educationally deprived students—in order to break the correlation between low social class background and low achievement. The achievement of this social policy was deemed sufficiently important to warrant a reform in our federal system for governing education.

Title VI, Civil Rights Act of 1964

The Civil Rights Act of 1964 provides:

No person in the United States shall, on the ground of race, color, or national origin, be excluded from participation in, be denied the benefits of, or be subjected to discrimination under any program or activity receiving federal financial assistance.[42]

This provision is enforced against school districts by the Department of Health, Education, and Welfare (HEW) and more particularly the Office for Civil Rights (OCR). These agencies promulgate regulations and guidelines which spell out in greater detail the specific duties of school districts receiving federal funds. A failure to comply with the Act as interpreted and enforced by HEW and OCR can result in the loss of all federal funds for those programs in which discrimination has been proved to exist. To date the most important use to which Title VI has been put is tackling pupil segregation in the south.[43] The implications of desegregation for curriculum were discussed in chapter 2.

In 1970, Title VI took on even more significance for local districts. The story begins with HEW's interpretation of Title VI. HEW's Title VI regulations provided that recipients of federal aid may not:

(ii) Provide any service, financial aid, or other benefit to an individual which is different, or is provided in different manner, from that provided to others under the program;

(iv) Restrict an individual in any way in the enjoyment of any advantage or privilege enjoyed by others receiving any service, financial aid, or other benefit under the program . . .[44]

The prohibition against discrimination on account of race or national origin included "discrimination . . . in the availability or use of any academic . . . or other facilities of the grantee or other recipient."[45] Even in the absence of affirmative acts purposefully designed to discriminate, a school district might be in violation of Title VI if it adopted policies that had an impermissible effect. A recipient of federal aid

may not . . . utilize criteria or methods of administration which have the effect of subjecting individuals to discrimination . . . or have the effect of defeating or substantially impairing accomplishment of the objectives of the program as respect to individuals of a particular race, color, or national origin.[46]

And, in a memorandum dated July 10, 1970, HEW added the following significant clarification:

Where inability to speak and understand the English language excludes national origin-minority group children from effective participation in the educational program offered by a school district, the district must take affirmative steps to rectify the language deficiency in order to open its instructional program to these students.[47]

At the time this memorandum was issued, San Francisco Unified School District was the recipient of $11 million in federal aid and enrolled 16,574 Chinese students, of whom 2,856 did not speak or understand English. Of the 2,856 students, 1,790 received no special instruction in English. Six hundred thirty-three did receive help on a part-time basis and 433 received help on a full-time basis. Only 260 of the 1,066 who received help were taught by a teacher who spoke Chinese.[48]

Special assistance was not provided the 1,790 students because the school distict said it lacked the funds. The district also said that the unaided pupils were provided "the same facilities, textbooks, teachers, and curriculum as is provided to other children in the district."[49] But the district did agree that the result of being exposed to an all-English program without special assistance was that the non-English-speaking child was "frustrated by [his or her] inability to understand the regular class work," performed below average in school, and was "almost inevitably doomed to be a dropout and become another unemployable in the ghetto."[50]

To rectify the situation a suit was brought in federal court by several non-English-speaking Chinese pupils who were receiving no special help at all. The petitioners sought an injunction requiring the school district to provide them with special instruction in English. Petitioners argued failure to provide them with special instruction was a violation of the Equal Protection clause of the Fourteenth Amendment and Title VI as interpreted by HEW and OCR. The court of appeals denied the claim but petitioners appealed to the Supreme Court where their claim was upheld on the basis of Title VI.[51]

Justice Douglas, who wrote for a unanimous Court, implied that while it was not entirely clear that the school district's policies violated Title VI standing alone, it certainly was clear that those school policies did violate Title VI as authoritatively interpreted by HEW. Further, Justice Douglas said the federal government did have the power to fix the terms on which it disbursed its money and that, whatever the limits of such power were, they had not been reached in this case.

In a concurring opinion Justice Stewart wrote:

The critical question is, therefore, whether the regulations and guidelines promulgated by HEW go beyond the authority of § 601. Last term, in *Mourning* v. *Family Publications Service, Co.* we held that the validity of a regulation promulgated under a general authorization provision such as § 602 of Title VI "will be sustained so long as it is 'reasonably related to the purposes of the enabling legislation. ' " I think the guidelines here fairly meet that test. Moreover, in assessing the purposes of remedial legislation we have found that departmental regulations and "consistent administrative construction" are "entitled to great weight." The Department has reasonably and consistently interpreted § 601 to require affirmative remedial efforts to give special attention to linguistically deprived children.[52]

Thus, the Supreme Court placed its imprimatur upon a significant expansion of the power of HEW and OCR to shape the program of local school districts. Shortly after the *Lau* decision, Congress affirmed this expansion of federal authority by adopting a piece of legislation that enacts into law the holding of the *Lau* decision.

The significance of this expansion of federal authority should not be underestimated. In 1970, HEW estimated there were 5.4 million children between the ages six and eighteen whose mother tongue was other than English.[53] The most prevalent of these language minorities are the groups that have suffered racial and cultural discrimination at the hands of the white majority, namely, people of Spanish origin, American Indians, the Chinese, and the Japanese.[54] Of the 5.4 million children HEW estimates that about 1.8 to 2.5 million need special assistance in learning English.[55] Further, it appears only a very small percentage of those who need instruction have been obtaining it in the public schools. In 1973 approximately 109,000 pupils obtained help from federally funded programs.[56] Only 6.5 percent of the schools in the southwest in 1970 had any kind of bilingual education program despite the fact that schools in that area enrolled 1.4 million Spanish surnamed pupils.[57] Rough estimates indicated that 47 percent of these students did not speak English as well as Anglo pupils.[58] And it has been estimated that of the 250,000 Puerto Rican pupils in New York City public schools, 118,000 are non-English speaking, while only 4,418 receive special assistance to learn English.[59] In sum, OCR identified, in the fall of 1972, 353 school districts with at least over one thousand national origin minority students and less than 10 percent of these students were receiving bilingual education.[60]

The extent of the non-English-speaking student problem defines the scope of potential federal involvement in local school districts. Between July 1970, and March 1974, OCR reviewed 72 school districts and notified 37 of noncompliance with the July 10, 1970, memorandum.[61] For the future OCR has planned several major initiatives to enforce the July 10 Memorandum. These plans have been influenced by five findings:

1. Compliance reviews have clearly showed that a range of discriminatory educational practices wider than that identified in the Memorandum were limiting the educational access and opportunity of minority students.

2. Many of these discriminatory practices were having an adverse impact on blacks as well as on national-origin minority children.

3. The investigation and analytic techniques which had been developed needed substantial automated data processing support if they were to be applied to medium-sized or large school districts.

4. Cost effectiveness and institutional burden considerations dictated that reviews of large urban school districts should be comprehensive and unitary, both in terms of issues and client groups.

5. Congress has passed Title IX of the Education Amendments of 1972, adding sex discrimination as an important new compliance criterion to the area of equal educational opportunity.[62]

In view of these findings, OCR plans the initiation of a two-pronged enforcement effort. It first plans to continue to seek compliance with the July 10 memorandum among school districts enrolling significant numbers of non-English-speaking children. In the spring of 1974, OCR planned to move against 133 districts in ten states and in the fall of 1974, against an additional 172 districts in fourteen states.

Second, OCR plans to adopt a more sweeping approach to the enforcement of Title VI by engaging in massive investigations of five major cities: New York, Chicago, Houston, Los Angeles, and Philadelphia. The treatment of traditionally recognized minority groups, including blacks, was to be investigated, as well as the treatment of Italians, Greeks, French, and handicapped children. And since it was concluded that the problems faced by these children result not only from language discrimination but also from other varieties of discrimination, a vast array of possibly discriminatory policies will be investigated, specifically, those involving expenditures, facilities, all pupil services, equipment, tracking, special classes, curriculum, instructional methodologies, assessment techniques, the compatibility or noncompatibility of educational environments with the nature of the child, referral functions, guidance and counseling programs, drug programs, extracurricular activities, and disciplinary procedures.[63] (It should be noted that despite the impressively sweeping plans HEW and OCR laid out for themselves for enforcing Title VI, their enforcement policies have come under considerable criticism. The critics charged in a letter to the secretary of HEW in December 1975 that of 350 districts cited for discriminating against non-English-speaking pupils, OCR followed up with only fifteen on-site investigations.[64])

Returning to the more specific problem of protecting non-English-speaking pupils, an important issue has yet to be resolved by the courts, namely, whether OCR and HEW would have the authority not merely to require a district to provide some kind of special instruction to help non-English-speaking children through English-as-a-Second-Language (ESL) or bilingual instruction, but also to specify which method is to be used. But on this point OCR has said it will not require that one or another method be used. Presumably OCR's position on this point rests importantly on a belief that to specify precisely what method of instruction must be used would occasion strong protests from local districts over federal control of the curriculum.

But the method of instruction that should be used is of some importance as evidence is beginning to accumulate which shows that ESL is not particularly effective in teaching students English, that bilingual instruction is preferable.[65] Research suggests that forcing a child to learn English before he or she has learned to read and write in his or her mother tongue can lead to cognitive confusion and emotional disturbances which can result in stuttering and stammering. A child who is forced to learn English before mastering the mother tongue may end up knowing neither language well, becoming a person without a language.[66] The U.S. Commission on Civil Rights has criticized ESL approaches on the grounds that in such programs students are expected to read English before they have mastered speaking it, since these children must follow the regular English curriculum with their native English-speaking peers.[67] The Commission also noted that ESL students do experience retardation in the learning of subject matter while they slowly learn English, a retardation they may never overcome.[68] The Commission concluded that ESL is only useful in communities where children obtain enough exposure to English outside the school to learn to speak it fluently in a relatively short period of time.[69]

Bilingual education avoids these problems. Since the children already speak their mother tongue, learning to read in their mother tongue follows the correct sequence in learning. Further, their mother tongue serves as the medium of instruction until they have mastered English, so the children experience no retardation in the learning of subject matter. And the slower introduction to English avoids problems of cognitive confusion, frustration, and damage to the child's self-esteem. The Commission for Civil Rights thus concludes that in most communities the preferred approach to teaching children English is the bilingual approach.[70]

In light of these conclusions OCR may be forced and/or tempted to begin requiring school districts to adopt bilingual instruction in order to comply with Title VI. But whether OCR would have the legal authority to impose such a requirement raises an interesting legal problem. First, we need to ask whether Title VI would support OCR regulations and guidelines which required bilingual instruction. As noted earlier, the Supreme Court has given federal agencies considerable leeway in interpreting the statues they are to administer, hence it is possible OCR would be deemed to have the statutory authority to issue such a requirement.

The second question is whether such a policy would withstand a challenge that it did not rest on "substantial evidence."[71] Rules of federal agencies must be based on substantial evidence and, as might be expected, this standard for the legitimacy of administrative action is subject to no single interpretation.[72] In general, however, as the courts have interpreted this requirement they will not overturn an agency's finding (1) even if the agency might reasonably have made a contrary finding based on the same body of evidence, and (2) even if the court itself might have made a contrary finding and believes the agency should have made a contrary finding.[73] The agency's decision will be upheld so long as there is enough "relevant evidence as a reasonable mind might accept as adequate to support a conclusion."[74] From this it can be seen that the substantial-evidence rule works heavily in favor of the federal agency. Even when experts might conflict over the soundness of a particular finding, the courts will not intervene because of the belief that the agency has greater expertise in deciding which experts are more likely to be correct. Indeed the Supreme Court has said that mere "expert opinion," so long as it is not contradicted by empirical evidence, will in and of itself be deemed to be "substantial evidence" when first-hand experimental evidence on a question is unavailable.[75]

Given this legal background there is little doubt that OCR could legally impose upon schools a requirement that only bilingual methods of instruction be used. As noted, there is a body of expert opinion which would support such a requirement and the existence of that body of opinion would seem to be sufficient basis on which OCR could act. Thus, the potential exists of a significant step being taken toward direct federal control of the local school curriculum.

Title IX

It has not been uncommon for schools to reflect the cultural biases of the larger society through the establishment of course and program requirements that work to maintain accepted socioeconomic roles for men and women.[76] Thus, schools have excluded female students from vocational educational schools and courses. Female students have been required to take home economics and male students shop. If vocational programs were offered women, they often were restricted in both the number of occupations in which training would be offered, and what occupational training there was would reflect prevailing notions of what sort of work women could do in our society; for example, secretarial training would be offered women but not automobile repair. Course descriptions reflected this bias with female pronouns being used for descriptions of courses only women were expected to take. Outside of the vocational area, female students have been discriminated against by having higher admission standards applied to them when they try to gain access to the supposedly high powered academic high schools. This form of discrimination has been justified on the ground that without higher standards female students would overrun the academic high schools. Perhaps these requirements reflected a cultural bias against women going on to college and entering the job market.

All these forms of sexual discrimination and others have been brought into question by the promulgation of Title IX of the Education Amendments of 1972. The central provision provides:

No person in the United States shall, on the basis of sex, be excluded from participation in, be denied the benefits of, or be subjected to discrimination under any education program or activity receiving federal financial assistance . . .[77]

This provision closely parallels Title VI in that failure to comply with the statute, regulations, and guidelines developed by HEW and OCR can mean the loss of all federal funds. But there are three ways in which Title IX differs from Title VI. First, the congressional opposition to sex discrimination seems less adamant than toward race discrimination. While Title VI absolutely prohibits race discrimination, Title IX contains certain exceptions that explicitly permit some degree of discrimination and separation of the sexes. (As regards admissions policy, the basic nondiscrimination provision applies only to vocational, professional and graduate schools, and public undergraduate schools. Public undergraduate schools that have had a continual and traditional policy of admitting only students of one sex are exempted. Educational institutions controlled by religious organizations are exempt if the application of the basic provision would conflict with the religious tenets of the organization. Schools training individuals for military service are totally exempt. And educational institutions are specifically permitted to provide separate living facilities for different sexes.[78])

Second, the statute explicitly states that the no-discrimination requirement should not be interpreted to require preferential treatment of any sex on account of a sexual imbalance which may exist in the program.[79] This antiquota provision reduces the tools that may be used to bring about compliance with the basic antidiscrimination provision quoted. Third, Congress limited the enforcement powers of HEW and OCR in another way by providing that if funds are to be cut off, the cutoff must be limited in its effect to the particular program, or part thereof, in which noncompliance has been found.[80] Thus, if discrimination is found in the vocational high school it appears federal funds for special education may not be cut off. Such a limiting provision is not to be found in Title VI.[81]

These provisions, in reflecting a less hard-nosed attitude toward sex discrimination than toward race discrimination, raise questions with regard to the scope of the basic antidiscrimination provision quoted. While there is no doubt that overt sex discrimination based on no other justification than prejudice or tradition is barred by the statute, there is doubt as to what the statute has to say to the following kinds of issues. Does the law extend to policies that are facially neutral, that appear on the surface to be nondiscriminatory, but in their effect impose substantial burdens on one or the other sex. The problem raised here is analogous to the problem in *Lau* in which the facially neutral-language policy had a significant impact on non-English-speaking students. An example in this area would be the establishing of a competitive standard for gaining a berth on an athletic team that has the effect of substantially excluding all women from participation. Another problem has to do with whether the offering of separate but equal services and facilities, such as separate locker and toilet facilities, is permissible under the statute. More broadly, are there forms of differentiated treatment of the sexes which while suspect may nevertheless be permissible if justified by a sufficiently strong educational policy?

These questions in turn raise problems for the authority of HEW and OCR to interpret and enforce Title IX. May these agencies extend Title IX to prohibit facially neutral policies which have a discriminatory impact even if the statute itself does not explicitly reach such issues? May HEW and OCR permit separate but equal services and facilities if they deem it wise to do so or would they be precluded from issuing regulations permitting such practices? More generally, what standard should be followed in determining the legality of the regulations issued by HEW and OCR? On this last point the answer clearly is the same standard used by the Supreme Court in upholding the regulations and guidelines issued by HEW and OCR referred to in the *Lau* decision.[82] That is, the regulations promulgated under Title IX should be upheld as long as they are reasonably related to the purposes of Title IX. But since the Congress seems less intent on ending sex discrimination than race discrimination, the power of OCR and HEW in enforcing Title IX may be somewhat less than their power to enforce Title VI.

With this background we may turn to a description and legal assessment of the regulations HEW has in fact promulgated. As for the provision of courses, the regulations state a recipient of federal aid may not carry out any of its educational programs separately on the basis of sex, including health, physical education, industrial, business, vocational, technical, home economics, music, and adult education courses.[83] Sex education courses, however, are explicitly exempted from this requirement.[84] Whether HEW is justified in not extending the nondiscrimination requirements to sex education courses is in some doubt, as the notion of privacy which seems to provide a limitation on HEW's authority does not seem to extend to this situation. The notion of privacy behind the residence exemption is one of protecting physical privacy and would not seem to encompass privacy with regard to the discussion of reproductive systems and sexual behavior. Thus it may be possible for an individual to bring suit to force integration of sex education classes despite the exemption allowed by HEW.

As for admitting students to courses or special schools, the regulations are clear in that they bar the establishment of sexual quotas, giving preference on the basis of sex, or relying on tests or other admission criteria which discriminate on the basis of sex.[85] The regulations go on to bar the use of a criterion for admission "which has a disproportionately adverse effect on persons on the basis of sex unless the use of such test or criterion is shown to predict validly success in the education program . . . and alternative tests or criteria which do not have such a disproportionately adverse effect are shown to be unavailable."[86] Thus, HEW has prohibited admission criteria that might be facially netural but have a discriminatory impact, unless there is a strong educational justification for the use of these criteria or tests. This extension of Title IX by HEW seems justified in light of the *Lau* decision and the standard used there in upholding HEW's and OCR's regulations and policies.

Schools have not only relied on overtly discriminatory rules and regulations to push males and females into different lines of development but also have relied on approaches less explicitly discriminatory. One of the most powerful school socializing techniques has been counseling. Title IX and the regulations now prevent discrimination in this area also.[87] More specifically, reliance on biased psychological, personality, and vocational interest tests is now prohibited, as is the use of separate male-female tests and counseling materials. The regulations also attempt to get at forms of sex discrimination in the counseling situation less easily proved and stopped, such as counselors encouraging female students to take up careers traditionally dominated by women and discouraging females from entering fields traditionally dominated by males, or discouraging female students from taking certain courses and programs. The regulations provide:

Where a recipient [of federal aid] finds that a particular class contains a substantially disproportionate number of individuals of one sex, the recipient shall take such action as is necessary to assure itself that such disproportion is not the result of discrimination on the basis of sex in counseling or appraisal materials or by counselors.[88]

When we turn to extracurricular activities, the regulations generally prohibit all discrimination.[89] Neither aid, benefit, nor service can be denied or given in a different manner or under a different set of requirements on the basis of sex. School organizations such as social and service clubs supported by the school must be available on a nondiscriminatory basis.[90] Opportunities for recreation must be equal.[91] And students may not be segregated on the basis of sex for gym or physical education classes.[92] Thus it appears that separate but equal physical education programs are barred. However, separate but equal locker, shower, and toilet facilities are permitted.[93] Again, this protection of physical privacy seems consistent with the intent of Congress in light of the residential exemption.

When we turn to the regulations as they bear on competitive athletics, the regulations become somewhat ambiguous and legally complex. A general prohibition against discrimination attaches to any interscholastic, intercollegiate, club, or intramural athletics.[94] But separate teams for each sex may be offered in contact sports.[95] Similarly, when selection for teams is based upon competitive skill, separate teams may be offered.[96] But if a school offers only one team for one sex in a noncontact support, "and athletic opportunities for members of that sex have previously been limited," the members of the excluded sex must be allowed to try out for the team.[97] Beyond this, schools must provide equal athletic opportunity for both sexes.[98] The regulations list a set of factors in considering whether such equal opportunity is being provided, including unequal aggregate expenditures for the members of each sex. However, unequal aggregate expenditures by itself does not constitute noncompliance.

(The factors to be considered along with unequal aggregate expenditures are: (1) whether the selection of sports and levels of competition effectively accommodate the interests and abilities of members of both sexes; (2) the provision of equipment and supplies; (3) scheduling of games and practice time; (4) travel and per diem allowance; (5) opportunity to receive coaching and academic tutoring; (6) assignment and compensation of coaches and tutors; (7) provision of locker rooms, practice and competitive facilities; (8) provision of medical and training facilities and services; (9) provision of housing and dining facilities and services; (10) publicity.[99])

The mere recitation of the provisions of the regulations show how ambiguous they are. What seems possible under these regulations is the following: unequal amounts of money may be spent on male and female athletes, and male athletes may be provided with a chance to compete competitively in contact and noncontact sports without the same opportunities being provided females. The only check on this discrimination is that final and vague requirement that equal athletic opportunity be provided both sexes.[100] Thus it is not at all clear as to the legal status of even the following extreme problems: (1) A school offers only one noncontact sport in which no girls compete because they have not passed the tryouts. Are the girls simply out of luck or does the requirement of equal athletic opportunity require the school to provide a separate team for the girls? (2) A school offers contact athletic opportunities to males in wrestling, football, and basketball but no such opportunities for girls. Does the requirement of equal athletic opportunity provide relief or can the school avoid offering such opportunities to girls because only a few are interested?

Beyond these problems of interpreting the regulations are the questions surrounding their legality. It may very well be that HEW has permitted a degree of inequality which the statute precludes. Yet Congress, as noted, seems willing not to root out all sex discrimination and this looseness in the regulations may be consistent with the statute. There is yet another very peculiar problem with HEW's authority. Title IX can be read to prohibit separate but equal provision of noncontact and contact sport opportunities. But what happens if only one basketball or skiing team is available and no girls can make the team because they cannot meet the competitive requirements? Here we would have a situation of Title IX allowing the total exclusion of women from these sports. Facially neutral criteria for getting on the team have had, in this case, a discriminatory impact on the girls. But this result may be unconstitutional under equal protection tests three and four (see chap. 2) but permitted under Title IX. To an extent, HEW's regulations try to cope with this problem and, thereby, save the constitutionality of Title IX itself. That is, the regulations go beyond Title IX by permitting schools to offer separate teams, even in noncontact sports, when selection for the teams is based on a competitive position and retain the opportunity to compete, albeit on all-female teams. Yet, by providing this kind of protection for women, HEW may have violated its authority under Title IX. Indeed, by seeming to allow separate teams, even in the elementary grades when the physical differences between boys and girls have not yet developed, HEW may have gone beyond Title IX with its apparent push toward the elimination of differences in treatment on the basis of sex.[102] We have here an extraordinary legal problem ripe with irony.

Putting athletics aside, the regulations also touch upon hair and dress codes by forbidding discrimination in the application of any rules of appearance.[103] Thus it seems girls must be allowed to wear pants and boys must be permitted to wear their hair as long as they wish. Apparently schools may not even justify their hair length rules with regard to males on the ground that long hair is "disruptive" of the school program. And the regulations prohibit different behavioral rules or sanctions for the two sexes.[104]

That prohibition should be read in connection with another general prohibition against applying any rule concerning a student's actual or potential parental, family, or marital status which treats students differently on the basis of sex.[105] This section of the regulations goes on to provide that schools may not exclude any student from any class or extracurricular activity on the basis of the student's pregnancy, childbirth, false pregnancy, termination of pregnancy, or recovery therefrom.[106] But a student who desires to remain in the regular program may be required to provide a certificate from a doctor showing the student is physically and emotionally able to continue participation. But this required certification must be asked of all students for other physical or emotional conditions which require attention of a doctor if required of pregnant students.[107] If a school operates a separate program for pregnant students who voluntarily enter that program, the program must be comparable to the regular program.[108] In general schools must treat pregnancy, childbirth, false pregnancy, termination of pregnancy, and recovery like any other temporary disability with respect to medical services, and pregnancy must be treated as a justification for a leave of absence for so long a period of time as is medically necessary as determined by the student's doctor, "at the conclusion of which the student shall be reinstated to the status which she held when the leave began."[109]

In sum, Title IX as implemented by HEW, despite the deficiencies noted, goes a long way toward forcing the public schools to purge themselves of the sexual biases that have marked the culture in the schools of an older America. The public schools, to an important extent, may not be the instruments for perpetuating this aspect of our culture, by forcing students into or out of certain courses and programs, by the counseling provided, or by the rules of dress and behavior.

Sex and Race Bias in Educational Materials

In releasing the proposed regulations for enforcement of Title IX, then Secretary of HEW, Casper Weinberger, said the department recognized that sex-stereotyped curricula were a serious matter, but that no regulations on this question would be issued as that would raise grave First Amendment issues.[110] Title IX regulations today provide that nothing in the regulations shall be interpreted "as requiring or prohibiting or abridging in any way the use of particular textbooks or curricular materials."[111]

But HEW's position on sexual discrimination (and racial discrimination) in educational materials may misrepresent the law. First, both Title IX and Title VI may themselves bar materials that discriminate on the basis of sex and race even in the absence of regulations promulgated by HEW. The scope of these two statutes is not determined solely by what HEW says about them. In any event, HEW has not said that these provisions do not prohibit sexually and racially biased materials, only that the regulations issued to date do not deal with the subject. While HEW and OCR may not enforce these provisions against school district use of biased materials, individual suits based on these statutes remain possible. If in the future HEW changes its mind and decides to regulate the use of educational materials, Title IX and Title VI provide the legal basis for such a move.

Assuming then, either enforcement by individual suits or by HEW in the future, let us consider the constitutional issues Secretary Weinberger was worried about when he issued his statement. Would the free speech and press clauses prevent enforcement of Titles VI and IX against discriminatory materials? First, it is doubtful that teachers have a First Amendment right to choose whatever materials they want for use in the classroom; the selection of basic materials is usually controlled by school boards (see chap. 6). Thus, the question is whether school boards have a First Amendment right to be free of rules limiting their use of discriminatory materials. Here the question becomes murky because it has never been decided if a public corporate entity, such as a school board, is a "person" for purposes of the First Amendment. Assuming the school board did enjoy a First Amendment right of free speech, it is doubtful that it would have a constitutional right to impose sexually and racially discriminatory materials upon a captive audience.[112] Thus, it would seem that Congress, with its power to attach conditions to the use of federal money and with its power to enforce the Fourteenth Amendment, certainly would be within its rights to bar local school boards from carrying out policies that probably are unconstitutional. (Section 5 of the Fourteenth Amendment explicitly grants Congress the power to enforce, by appropriate legislation, the provisions of the article.) Indeed, Congress even has the power to broaden the rights protected by the Fourteenth Amendment. As for publishers, they undoubtedly have a constitutional right to produce and attempt to sell sexually and racially discriminatory materials, but such a right probably does not encompass a right to have those materials purchased by governmental agencies such as local school boards. And it seems highly doubtful that parental rights with regard to the upbringing of children include freedom from federal laws barring the use of discriminatory materials in the public schools. Thus, precisely whose free speech rights Secretary Weinberger was concerned about becomes unclear, and we are forced to conclude that his refusal to issue regulations dealing with instructional materials was based on other considerations.

Undoubtedly an important consideration was fear of being charged with a federal attempt to control the public school curriculum. Perhaps equally as important is the practical problem of drafting administratively enforceable regulations and guidelines which define sexual and racial discrimination in curriculum materials and which are consistent with Titles IX and VI. These problems can be explored by suggesting some general regulations for dealing with both racial and sexual discrimination:

The materials for a course will be deemed to be sexually discriminatory and thereby prohibited for use if they have some or all of the following characteristics:

1. They are male centered and fail to adequately represent the role of women in history and society.
2. The materials adversely reflect upon women and glorify males.
3. The materials depict women in a stereotyped way and place them in stereotyped social and family roles.
4. The materials depict women as dependent on males; define women in terms of who they marry; the children they bear; the father to whom they were born; while depicting men in terms of their activities and accomplishments.
5. The materials tend to depict women in passive, observer, and highly domestic roles, while depicting men in adventuresome, risk-taking, outgoing roles.
6. The materials include pejorative references to women and sexual slurs.
7. The materials suggest that women ought to have certain "feminine" traits, for example, be loving, caring, nurturing, sweet, and that men

ought to have certain "masculine" traits, for example, courage, physical strength, sportsmanship, inventiveness.

8. The materials use references in which such terms as *men* and *mankind* stand for people in general; use occupational terminology that ends in *man*, for example, workman, or cameraman; or adds feminine suffixes to words, for example, poetess, as though to indicate a poet and poetess were different and unequal. [113]

A similar but different set of regulations might be suggested with regard to race and school materials.

The materials for a course will be deemed to be racially discriminatory and thereby prohibited for use if they have some or all of the following characteristics:

1. The materials are white centered and fail adequately to represent the role of minorities in history and society.
2. The materials adversely reflect upon minorities and glorify "whiteness."
3. The materials depict minorities in stereotyped ways and place them in stereotyped social and economic roles.
4. The materials depict minorities as dependent on whites and treat minorities in a patronizing and demeaning manner.
5. The materials tend to show minorities in economically and socially inferior roles while depicting whites in roles deemed to be admirable and important.
6. The materials are strongly associated with a past history of racial prejudice and, thus, tend to perpetuate that prejudice.
7. The materials contain racial slurs and racially pejorative references.
8. The materials suggest that the proper virtues for minorities are those of submissiveness, passiveness, and dependence.[114]

We must now question whether these regulations would be consistent with Titles IX and VI. Presumably the courts would give HEW considerable leeway in interpreting the scope of those provision, but would HEW have the authority to bar the use of a book if, for example, it failed to comply with sex discrimination regulation number 7? How many of the eight requirements would have to be violated before HEW had the statutory authority to act? Next, how would a requirement that materials not be male centered or white centered be interpreted? If the reader used in the first-grade class had as its main character a white male, would it per se be barred from use? In other words, must all first grade readers under these requirements have at least four coequal central characters, for example, white male, white female, minority male, minority female? And which minority group must be represented? Must more than one minority be represented as a lead character? And how does one define a lead character? The problems of interpreting these regulations could be infintely expanded upon. Obviously, deciding actual concrete cases could become quite complex and very controversial. Yet the regulations laid out do capture some of the central problems with regard to materials presently in use in schools, hence it would seem these problems can't be avoided if sexual and racial materials are to be excluded from the public schools by federal statute and regulation.

Curriculum Development and Dissemination

The National Science Foundation (NSF) was established by federal statute in 1950 in order "to develop and encourage the pursuit of a national policy for the promotion of basic research and education in the sciences."[115] In 1957 a combination of factors, namely, the launching of Sputnik I and the poor performance of armed service personnel on achievement tests during World War II, led to a closer examination of science education in the United States. It was found that while scientific knowledge had grown immensely, teachers were out of date with that material, the science curriculum in the public schools was neither extensive nor of high quality, and published materials were inadequate. Hence a need was felt for training teachers and developing more adequate curriculum materials, and in 1957 NSF set up its first organizational unit to consider proposals for science curriculum development.[116]

Since that time NSF has funded fifty-three curriculum development projects in such areas as physics, biology, anthropology, mathematics, political science, social studies, and geography for high school, junior high school, and elementary school. Some of these projects are among the most well known in the curriculum area: PSSC physics (Physical Science Study Committee); Harvard Project Physics Course; and *Man: A Course of Study* (MACOS). About $196 million was spent in support of these projects during fiscal years 1956 to 1975, much of it simply for development of the materials, but a considerable sum for the dissemination and implementation of the courses once developed.[117]

NSF itself does not develop curriculum materials; it merely funds proposals sent to it by groups interested in developing the materials. When NSF receives a new set of course materials, it reviews it with the assistance of outside reviewers and then decides upon funding. If a project is funded, then the developers are merely obligated to fulfill the promises made in their proposal and to turn in periodic progress reports. NSF loosely monitors the project, perhaps with the assistance of outside evaluators and perhaps with an occasional site visit by NSF officials. NSF is careful not to direct the development of the project or influence the content of the materials being developed. Once the project is completed, the developer typically seeks a publisher who would be willing to reproduce and sell the materials under a contract with the developer; royalty fees ranging between 3 percent and 20 percent have been negotiated between developer and publisher. The developer also turns royalties over to NSF which in turn is supposed to remit them to the U.S. Treasury. At the same time NSF has funded extensive implementation projects to help with the dissemination of the newly developed materials.[118]

We must now pose the question of whether this sort of government support of curriculum materials tends toward the imposition upon schools of a nationally created uniform curriculum.[119] Does this federal effort result in an undermining of the tradition of state and local control of curriculum? Since it is clear NSF does not itself develop the materials and has no legal authority to require any state or local school district to adopt the materials it has supported, the general question must be resolved into several narrower questions: (1) Has NSF, through its policies for selecting proposals, effectively turned curriculum development over to an interlocked, unified cadre of people with an agreed upon set of values which they want to see promoted in the public schools? (2) Do federally supported curriculum materials have a competitive advantage in the curriculum materials market because publishers can offer these materials at prices lower than would have been the case without federal support of the developmental effort? (3) Has NSF given its own materials a competitive advantage through its support of dissemination and implementation projects? (4) Do NSF materials have a competitive advantage because of an implied federal endorsement of the materials?

To begin to answer these questions, let us examine the extent to which NSF-supported curriculum materials have been adopted by local school districts. Here the data are very sketchy. NSF has concluded that its efforts have brought about a major change in the content of science teaching at the precollege level and has stimulated developmental efforts in other federal agencies, the industry, and school systems.[120] A small quantity of available data supports this conclusion. A chemical study program, NSF says, has reached a minimum of 25 percent of all high school students.[121] A 1971 NSF survey found that 34 percent of the schools sampled used these same materials. That same study found that 31 percent of the sample used materials from a project called *Introductory Physical Science*.[122] NSF estimates that in 1972-73 950,000 pupils used the materials.[123] Elementary Science Study materials were used by 3.5 million students; another project, entitled *Science—A Process Approach*, involved 3 million students, and two other projects reached approximately 1 million students each.[124] Obviously, not all NSF-funded projects have had such an impact.[125] For example, the controversial project called *Man: A Course of Study* reaches between 200,000 and 328,000 pupils.

MACOS is a social science curriculum designed to move toward answers to the following questions: What is human about human beings? How did they get that way? How can they be made more so? The course begins with a study of such lower forms of life as the salmon, which develops from an egg without any parental contribution; the herring gull, the young of which depend upon their parents for food and other assistance; the baboon, the young of which are dependent upon their mothers and other troop members in many ways for a long period of time. Then the course turns to the Netsilik Eskimos who live in a very harsh environment. The near marginal food sources force the Netsiliks to be constantly on the move for food and sometimes dictates their leaving behind to die an aged person unable to continue the traveling, or to abandon a female infant who would not be as productive in producing food as a male and who was just one too many mouths to feed. Also the need for the Netsilik male for a wife to carry on the tasks necessary for life have led to wife-lending and wife-stealing.

Not only are students expected to learn about these behaviors but also to debate their morality and to engage in playing the role of a Netsilik. Teachers are instructed to treat all questions as open-ended, to help students think through the problems for themselves and to come to their own conclusions.[126]

Current estimates of the use of MACOS are that 1700 school districts have picked the materials up in 47 states; thus about 1 to 2 percent of all students are served by the project. Yet other projects serve even fewer students, such as one entitled *Man-Made World* which reached 20,000 pupils in 1972-73.[127]

While some data, though scanty, exist on the extent of adoption of NSF-funded projects, there appears to be no information as to whether these projects are more widely adopted than similar materials produced without governmental assistance. Nor is there information available to shed light on why school districts adopted NSF-funded products rather than commercially developed products: Was it because the price was lower; the quality higher; some combination of the two factors; because NSF had effectively proselytized its own products while the other products had not been as effectively advertised; or because the materials seemed to carry the sanction of the federal government? We do know that publishers who have the opportunity to publish NSF-developed materials have to pay royalties on the materials so that they, in theory, cannot undersell others. But the data also show that the royalties they have had to pay are sometimes as low as 3 percent, as in the case of two projects. A widely adopted biology program involves royalties of 20 percent, but the chemical program noted involves no royalties, only a payment of $35,000 by the publishers to pay for the right to publish the materials. About half the projects were contracted out at the rate of 8 to 12 percent during the period of exclusive rights.[128]

Additionally, we know NSF has engaged in extensive efforts to introduce the materials it has funded, as well as some materials wholly commercially produced. For example, in fiscal year 1973, NSF spent about $14 million promoting the use of new curriculum materials among secondary school teachers alone; in that same year additional millions were spent on other kinds of promotional activities.[129] It is not in fact uncommon to find that NSF has spent more money on the promotion of the use of one of its projects than it spent to develop the project in the first place. Thus the chemical materials mentioned cost $2.6 million to develop and $4.6 million to implement.[130] While NSF will support dissemination of non-NSF-developed products, 80 percent of the implementation monies were spent in support of NSF funded projects in 1975.[131] These implementation projects include mere distribution of information about the projects as well as in-service training of teachers in the use of the materials, the development of teams of people who can help school districts change over to the new curriculum, and the introduction of college-level people to the materials on the theory that they in turn would spread the good word to the elementary and secondary schools.

The data thus do not belie the hypothesis that NSF support for development and dissemination of a particular package of curriculum materials gives those materials a competitive advantage in the marketplace. In other words, we cannot rule out as foolish the claim by some that federal involvement has had a strong, albeit indirect, influence on the school curriculum in the area of science education. Hence, the anxiety that has been raised over such NSF-supported projects as MACOS becomes more understandable, as here is a project that touches upon some of the most important value questions facing humans.

NSF has also been charged with working through its selection of projects only with a select group of people, sharing a common value base sometimes called "cultural relativism" or "humanistic secularism" or "environmental determinism."[132] Some fear that this particular viewpoint, because of the competitive advantage of NSF-funded products, is gaining a foothold in the schools at the expense of diversity in the school curriculum. The data supporting such charges at this point are sketchy at best. All that is clear is that most of the grantees are college-/or university-based and that the Educational Development Center of Cambridge, Massachusetts, the producer of MACOS, has received more grants than any other grantee, seven in all.[133] But whether these grantees tend to share the same value viewpoint, and what the content of that viewpoint might be, has not been established. Neither has it been established that the materials produced by the grantees all tend to espouse the same viewpoint on the nature of science, humans, or society.

In sum, it does seem plausible to conclude that NSF and its grantees have had an influence upon the curriculum of the public schools, but the precise extent, reasons for, and nature of that influence remain obscure.

Conclusions

This chapter focused upon only three aspects of federal involvement in shaping the local school program. Beyond what has been discussed here, the federal government is attempting to shape local education programs by offering grants-in-aid to support education for handicapped children and children of limited English-speaking ability.[134] Recently the federal government has started to offer grants for "career education" projects which some charge is but another name for vocational education and which others deny, saying career education aims at vocational adaptability so that a student will be ready to move to a range of jobs rather than having been trained to do only one kind of work.[135] Money has also been available for guidance, counseling, testing, and educationally innovative programs and projects. Indeed, the list of types of grants and other efforts the federal government has supported in order to shape the public school program is very extensive.

But as broad as has been the effort to shape the local program, one should not immediately conclude we now have full federal control of the local program. As the materials in the chapter indicate, even some of the more significant efforts to influence the local program have been blunted or thwarted. And in some respects the federal government has tried to restrain itself to avoid exercising too great control over the content of the school program. Nevertheless, the potential for increased federal control of the curriculum is enormous, whether it be through the attachment of conditions to grants, enforcement of the nondiscrimination requirements of Titles VI and IX, or development of curriculum materials. Ways have been found for a strong federal involvement in an area hardly contemplated to be a subject of concern by those who drafted the Constitution.

Perhaps it is as much the threat of federal control as it is the reality that there have been recent efforts to change the existing grant-in-aid system from one relying on specific categorical grants, such as Title I, ESEA, to a system that relies on block grants. In 1974 Congress consolidated several smaller grant-in-aid programs into two kinds of block grants thereby giving states greater leeway in administering these monies.[136]

And on March 1, 1976, President Ford sent to Congress a proposal to consolidate twenty-four more grant programs, including Title I, ESEA, into a $3.3 billion block grant to states. The proposal would eliminate most federal guidelines on the use of the money and would let the states formulate their own plans as long as they spent most of the money for poor and handicapped children. President Ford said he hoped the plan would cut administrative costs and red tape and provide "a minimum of federal regulation and a maximum of local control."[137]

4 The Changing State Role

Despite the significantly increased formal and informal role that the federal agencies—judicial, legislative, and executive—play in controlling the curriculum of the public schools, the most important participants in the curriculum policy-making process remain the states and local school districts. The U.S. Constitution leaves to the states the basic authority to control public education within their borders albeit within the confines of the Constitution, federal law, and the various state constitutions. Amendment X of the Constitution states: "The powers not delegated to the United States by the Constitution, nor prohibited by it to the states, are reserved to the states respectively, or to the people." State constitutions typically require little more than that there be some kind of free public schooling in the state and that there be established a state board of education and a chief state school officer.[1] Some state constitutional provisions also include brief references to the subjects that must be taught.[2] The exact design of the system of free public schooling to be provided is left to the legislatures to choose, be it a completely centralized and state-operated system of education, a kind of mixed centralized-decentralized system, or a totally decentralized system of education which could even include the use of educational vouchers. It is also within the legislature's power in most states to determine the precise authority and duties of the state board of education and the chief state school officer; some state constitutions are, however, more specific than others in this respect, as in the case of California, where the state board is given the authority by the state constitution to control the selection of textbooks for use in the public schools.[3]

The state legislature, with its basic authority to control the public school system, may prescribe the basic course of study down to the last detail, select the books and materials to be used (except in a state such as California), and even determine the methods of instruction to be used.[4] But no legislature has chosen to so totally control the curriculum of the schools. What we do find is a variegated pattern ranging from the not fully centralized to the not fully decentralized. These differences will be described in greater detail by beginning with a description of the decentralized states and then adding to that model bit by bit the features that characterize the moderately decentralized and then the centralized systems.

A. Decentralized States

While it is always risky to categorize, the following states may be considered to be decentralized states: Alaska, Colorado, Connecticut, Delaware, Idaho, Illinois, Iowa, Kansas, Maryland, Massachusetts, Michigan, Minnesota, Montana, Missouri, Nebraska, New Hampshire, Ohio, Pennsylvania, Rhode Island, Vermont, Washington, Wisconsin, and Wyoming. In a decentralized state, the allocation of authority between state agencies and localities strongly favors local discretion in the shaping of the school program. The number of legislatively mandated courses and other curriculum requirements are significant but not overwhelming. Thus, for example, local districts might be required by state law to offer in the elementary schools instruction in arithmetic, reading, spelling, writing, the English language, geography, United States history, civics, physical training, and state history.[5] Additionally, instruction might be required in health, the effects of alcohol, fire safety, kindness to animals, and conservation of natural resources.[6] It is not uncommon for states to require instruction in the U.S. and state constitutions, patriotism, loyalty to country, and the ideals of good citizenship.[7] These requirements might be coupled with compulsory flag salute ceremonies.[8] An old Massachusetts statute requires the schools to instill in the students

principles of piety and justice, sacred regard for truth, love of country, humanity, universal benevolence, sobriety, industry, frugality, chastity, moderation and temperance, and those other virtues the basis upon which a republican constitution is founded.[9]

In most states these curriculum requirements are merely listed in the statute without any specification as to the amount of time to be devoted to each subject or course. Some states do go a step farther and require in their statutes that a given subject be taught four times a week, or that three full-year courses in U.S. history be offered, or that a certain number of units be provided in a given subject.[10] The statutes do not go beyond such requirements in that they do not specify the course content or method of instruction. These decisions are left to the local district. Districts also have the discretion—although this is sometimes subject to legal challenge in the courts—to offer additional courses beyond those listed in the statutes;[11] for example, a district might want to offer physical education, although not specifically authorized to do so. But court challenges have been raised when a district lacked the explicit delegated authority to offer a course. Decisions on such issues have come out both ways (see chap. 5).

In addition to specifying course requirements, older state statutes reflect nascent pupil classification schemes. Typically, the classifications are in terms of elementary and high school pupils;[12] or in terms of normal children who can benefit from the regular school program and those who cannot benefit from the program and therefore are excluded;[13] or in terms of those children in public schools and those children in private schools.[14] The classification scheme is thus quite rudimentary, and local districts retain considerable discretion in deciding upon the grade structure, ability grouping schemes, standards for promoting, and the grade and group placement of individual children.

Beyond the statutory code is the administrative apparatus for enforcing and carrying out the requirements laid down by the legislature. This apparatus includes the state board of education, the chief state school officer, the state department of education, and the local school districts, as well as the governor, who often is given the responsibility of appointing the state board. A central characteristic of decentralized states is that these state agencies have no real statutory power to control the educational program at the local level. The statutory grants of authority typically give to the state board and chief state school officer authority only to prepare course outlines to assist local districts, or general power to promote the improvement of education, or power to review subjects and courses of study or to approve or accredit schools.[15] Pennsylvania's code requires local districts to conform to the course of study set out by the state superintendent of instruction "so far as local conditions in the respective districts permit."[16] But in some of these decentralized states the state board has the authority to set minimum standards and while such a statutory grant of authority could lead to significant state control of the local program, the fact is this authority is rarely interpreted to warrant detailed state control of the program offered in the local districts.[17]

It is also of interest to note a modest relationship between weak state authority over the curriculum and the fact that in these states the chief state officer and state board tend to be appointed. Of the states listed, only Idaho, Indiana, Montana, Washington, and Wisconsin have elected chief state school officers. Seven of these states have elected state boards.[18] This relationship between weak state authority and appointed officials suggests a reluctance on the part of state legislatures to give significant authority to appointed officials not directly accountable to the public.

B. Moderately Decentralized States

Included in this category are the states of Maine, New Jersey, New York, North Dakota, Oregon, and South Dakota. These states are placed here because the state officials—state board and chief state school officer—enjoy a modicum of authority with regard to the curriculum above and beyond that enjoyed by the state boards and chief state school officers in fully decentralized states. For example, in Oregon and Wyoming there is what might be called a weak statewide textbook adoption law. The Oregon law provides for the development of a list of state-approved textbooks but local districts of under twenty thousand average daily membership may adopt books in place of or in addition to those adopted by the state with the approval of the state board; and districts over twenty thousand in average daily membership may ignore the state list altogether if they choose books which conform to the criteria for selecting books established by the state board.[19] In South Dakota the state board has the power to review the books used in the schools and to force them to be withdrawn from use.[20]

The codes of New Jersey and Maine give the chief state school officer authority to approve or disapprove courses to be offered by the local district.[21] The New York commissioner of education claims in the regulations he has promulgated a similar authority but no explicit statutory provision grants such authority.[22] Additionally, the chief state school officers in New Jersey, New York, North Dakota, and Wyoming have been given quasi-judicial authority to resolve disputes between parties at the local district.[23] To this end these chief state school officers may hold hearings, hear witnesses, take evidence, and then render a decision. This power gives the chief state school officer a chance to overrule curricular decisions by local officials. In Delaware, quasi-judicial authority is enjoyed by the state board of education.[24]

A recitation of the statutory provisions which set the moderately decentralized states off from the decentralized states does not fully capture the differences between these types of states. To better capture the difference we should consider in greater depth one state, New York. Not only has the commissioner in New York been given quasi-judicial powers but the Board of Regents, elected by the state legislature, is to exercise "legislative functions" over the public school system of the state.[25] The regents also may confer such honorary degrees as they may deem proper and establish examinations to determine the attainment of persons to whom the regents may award a suitable diploma; the regents must also establish examinations in the high schools of the state "in studies furnishing a suitable standard of graduation" and certificates are to be conferred on students who pass the examinations.[26] In another provision the state department of education (which is controlled by the regents) is given the authority to "alter the subjects of instruction" prescribed in the statute.[27]

Pursuant to these provisions the regents have ordered that starting in June 1979 no high school student may receive a high school diploma unless the student demonstrates ninth-grade reading and mathematics skills on a test. The purpose of this new requirement is to force a change in the school curriculum, said the commissioner of education, a change that should reach the elementary grades.[28]

The regents and commissioner have also established other graduation requirements; issued detailed regulations dealing with driver's education and physical education; and spelled out in greater detail than in the statutes the kinds of efforts local districts must make to educate the handicapped and non-English-speaking students.[29]

Additionally, for years now the regents have had available a set of regents' examinations which students may take in order to test their competence in certain core and elective subjects. Students who pass the examinations obtain a regents' seal on their diploma which may have some benefit when applying for admission to college.[30] Since school districts have in the past been interested in seeing to it that their students do well on the regents' examinations, they have tended to design their courses in order to teach to the tests. In this way the state has had an important influence on the high school program. And, the commissioner of education has an opportunity to shape the local school program in several other ways. It is his job to approve plans for school building construction, and to the extent that the nature of the building affects the curriculum, the commissioner can affect what goes on in the building by the requirements and restraints he puts on building plans.[31]

Finally, we should take note of a strong relationship between the increased power of state officials in these states and the fact of their being elected. In North Dakota, Oregon, South Dakota, and Wyoming, the chief state school officer is an elected official. In New York, the regents are elected by the legislature. In Maine and New Jersey, however, the governor, an elected official, appoints both the board and the chief state school officer.[32]

C. Centralized States

The states included in this category are Alabama, Arizona, Arkansas, California, Florida, Georgia, Indiana, Kentucky, Louisiana, Mississippi, Nevada, New Mexico, North Carolina, Oklahoma, South Carolina, Tennessee, Texas, Utah, Virginia, and West Virginia. Hawaii is a unique state in that it has no local school districts; the state as a whole constitutes one school district. Centralized states tend to share two features of great significance for local control of education: statewide prescription of the course of study by the state board of education and/or state adoption of lists of approved texts from which local districts must choose those books they intend to use in the classroom. There are states included in this category, like Florida, that have statewide textbook adoption, but the state board does not exercise vigorously what authority it has to prescribe the basic course of study. Thus, the key feature which leads to the inclusion of Florida in this category is its use of statewide textbook adoption. Alabama was included despite the fact some larger districts have the local option of not following the approved list because of state board control of the basic course of study. Similarly, Virginia was included despite the fact local districts can avoid the approved list if they follow state board regulations in choosing texts. West Virginia only requires local boards to use approved basal texts.

Before turning to a discussion of these two main features, however, it is important to pause a moment to discuss a third feature found in some centralized states, such as Arizona and California. What makes California a centralized state is not so much that it has a textbook selection law (the California law applies only to the elementary grades and districts must be allowed to choose from lists per grade/subject of at least five books and perhaps as many as fifteen books) nor the fact that the state board has been given authority to regulate specific courses and programs, nor the fact that the board also has the authority to approve or disapprove courses offered by local districts in grades seven through twelve which are above and beyond those required by statute.[33] California obtains its unique degree of centralization from the fact of having a statutory code that is both detailed in the extent to which it prescribes a course of study and "restrictive" in nature.[34] A restrictive code is one that is to be interpreted narrowly, meaning that unless a local district explicitly has been given the authority to undertake a course or program, it must be presumed the district lacks the authority. In less centralized states the educational codes tend to be permissive in that the codes are interpreted liberally so as to give local districts the benefit of the doubt in cases where it is not clear whether or not they have the authority to carry out the new course or program. Whether a state's educational code is permissive or restrictive has obvious important implications for the degree of local autonomy.

Turning now to state authority to prescribe the curriculum, the statutes granting this authority are models of brevity. The typical statute tells the board little more than that it has the power and duty to prescribe and enforce the course of study in the schools or to prescribe the subjects to be taught.[35] Except for the listing of a few legislatively mandated courses in other parts of the code, little other guidance is given to the state board. Not only is it not clear from these laws as to what additional courses should be prescribed, but it is unclear as to whether the board has the power to spell out every detail of those courses or only authority to mandate their general thrust. For example, we might ask of these statutes whether the state board has the authority to go so far as to draft daily lesson plans for each course. While this question has not been authoritatively answered, it does seem clear that the state board—often with the required advice of the chief state school officer or an advisory commission—does have the power to decide which values are to be emphasized; which to be ignored; which to be attacked; what general method or approaches to be adopted in teaching such courses as history or reading; and what concepts and theories are to be taught.

With this kind of power it becomes important as to which political model of decision making the state board and its advisors follow in reaching their decisions. Under a consensus model every element of a course of study (or textbook) would be acceptable to all the members of the state board or advisory committee. This agreement may be the result of a thorough hammering out of all the issues or a result of avoidance of any decision on controversial points. Under a bargaining model the parties trade with each other so that one party agrees to allow one item in the guide if the other will agree to let another item enter the guide. The result is a product no one fully agrees with and which may contain inconsistencies with the further result that local districts are left with more leeway than the product of the consensus model may. Under the third model it is majority rule and winner take all. Here one group simply imposes its preferred view of the curriculum upon the other and strong state control of local districts is the outcome.

While most states operate according to a consensus or bargaining model, occasionally a majority on a state board will reject these modes and resort to winner take all. This seems to have occurred in Arizona between 1968 and 1974, when a conservative coalition got control of the state board and a conservative was elected as chief state school officer. This resulted in an attempt to impose on all schools in the state detailed curriculum guides. The controversy became so bitter in October 1972 that eight members of the advisory commission on social studies resigned in protest. The tangled issues involved right-wing ideology versus moderate and liberal ideology; state versus local control; use of the schools to indoctrinate versus the need for a politically neutral curriculum; basic education versus a behavioral approach, and other issues. The attempt by the conservatives to carry out their reform of social studies was ultimately beaten back by a strong public reaction. The matter came to a quiet end when the state superintendent said publicly he viewed the social studies guidelines as only suggested requirements. The commission on social studies completed its work by issuing a short document, instead of long detailed plans, which suggests the commission reverted to a consensus model of decision making addressing only those issues on which agreement could be obtained.[36]

Finally, as for who has actual power at the state level, as opposed to formal authority, to control the curriculum, research shows that state boards neither initiate nor formulate curriculum policy.[37] Rather boards tend to give their approval to what the chief state school officer says should be done. But this is not always the case, as shown by the resistance Max Rafferty met when he tried to have the California state board issue regulations imposing on schools a requirement to carry out his conception of a moral education program.[38]

Turning now to statewide textbook adoptions, how the states have structured this process varies in terms of: (1) the grades to which the state system for approving texts applies; (2) the kinds of materials subject to the system; (3) who has been given the ultimate authority to establish the approved lists; (4) the criteria that must be followed in establishing the lists; (5) the procedures that must be followed in drafting the approved lists; and (6) who at the local level has been given the authority to select from the approved lists.

As for the first point, while it is common for states to require approval of texts to be used in all grades, California, for example, only requires state approval of textbooks for use in grades one through eight.[39] Second, the states define differently the kinds of materials that are subject to state approval. Some states limit the process simply to textbooks, but others such as Florida and California have amended their statutes so as to extend state approval to cover "instructional materials" which includes textbooks, workbooks, and audiovisual materials.[40] Of course the broader the scope of the statute in this respect the less discretion at the local level to control the selection of materials.

Third, it is common for the state board to be given the final authority to establish the approved list of textbooks after obtaining the advice of an advisory commission appointed by the board itself with the advice of the chief state school officer or, as in the case of North Carolina, with the advice of an advisory commission appointed by the governor.[41] The statutes also vary in their requirements as to the kind of person to be appointed to the advisory commission. Typically they require that professional educators be involved who hold teaching or supervisory posts in the public school system of the state; also, geographical spread in appointments may be required and occasionally a lay person must be appointed to the advisory commission.[42]

Staying with the question of who has final authority to approve the list of texts, Kentucky, Oklahoma, Utah, and Tennessee give this power to a separate state textbook commission appointed in some instances by the governor and in others by the state board and in the case of Utah by both.[43] The membership of these commissions must be made up largely of professional educators in all these states—Utah, however, includes five lay persons along with the professionals.

Texas's law is worth noting for the intricate relationships it sets up.[44] The board, upon the recommendation of the state commissioner, appoints fifteen experienced educators to an advisory committee. This committee is charged with developing a list of approved texts for recommendation to the commissioner. The commissioner may remove any book from that list but cannot add to it nor can he reduce to a single adoption any list for a given grade/subject. In turn the commissioner recommends the list as modified to the board which may remove books but not add books to the list; it also may not reduce to a single adoption any list for a given grade/subject.

Fourth, what criteria must boards and commissions follow in developing lists of approved texts? Typically the statutes require the adoption of multiple listings.[45] The statutes do not make clear if the multiple listing requirement means not merely a listing of more than one book but also that the books must differ in theory, content, approach, method, and so forth. For example, the statutes do not explicitly preclude the adoption of reading systems that all rely on one method of instruction, such as the phonics approach. Sometimes this requirement is spelled out by requiring the adoption of a specific number of books such as requiring the listing of between three to five books per grade/subject.[46] California places the limits between five and fifteen.[47] Such requirements are a way of compromising between full state control and local discretion in the control of the curriculum. As for other criteria, few more substantive requirements are imposed. Most states only prohibit texts with a partisan or religious viewpoint.[48] Some states go beyond this however. California and Florida, for example, bar the use of texts that reflect adversely on women and minority groups; approved texts must accurately reflect the contributions of women and minorities to the history of the country and state.[49] Also, California and Florida now require the adoption of texts that have been learner-verified. But the general absence of standards in most states means that those formulating lists of approved texts enjoy considerable degree of discretion.

As for the fifth feature of textbook approval laws, state statutes typically are short on prescriptions as to the procedures that must be followed by those establishing approved lists. These statutes often merely prohibit those with interests in textbook publishing companies from serving on advisory or adoption committees and may require that the final adoption meeting of the state board be an open meeting which the public may attend.[50] But these kinds of requirements afford little protection against corruption and abuse of discretion. Florida has found it necessary to revise its textbook selection law after the legislature uncovered a considerable body of evidence pointing to both abuse of discretion and the prevalence of bribes, kickbacks, and conflict of interest. Today Florida's textbook selection law requires open meetings at all stages of the process, participation by lay people, greater involvement of local districts, the display of books before their adoption, and various other rules designed to prevent a recurrence of the corruption that occurred. The rules touch on such matters as public notice for public meetings; equal time provisions for all publishers; the makeup of advisory committees at all levels of the selection process; the maintenance as public records of all council motions, votes, and summaries of debates; and the public display of materials being considered for adoption.[51]

Once the approved lists have been promulgated the question becomes, Who has authority at the local district level to select from the approved lists? In most states this task is left either explicitly or implicitly to the local board.[52] But in Alabama, Arkansas, Oklahoma, and Tennessee local boards must establish special textbook selection committees.[53] In Arkansas, Oklahoma, and Tennessee these local committees are to be made up largely of teachers—Oklahoma requires there be one lay member per committee. Alabama law leaves the composition of the local committee up to the local board.[54] The practical result of these requirements is to place the selection of text materials in these states wholly in the hands of professional educators. This is especially true for Oklahoma and Tennessee, where the drafting of the original list from which local teachers are to select is given over to a separate textbook commission appointed by the governor and made up entirely of professional educators.

As for selecting supplementary materials, local districts are left with more discretion. This is so because state lists for approved books are largely limited to basal texts, although in some states supplementary materials are also listed for certain courses.[55] The discretion of the local district may also vary with the type of course in question. Books are usually listed by the state for required courses and less often for courses not prescribed by statute or state regulation.[56] When books are listed for a course, local districts are not permitted to supplant the approved texts with books of their own choosing; but defining what constitutes supplanting as opposed to supplementation is not easy and the statutes tend to provide no help on the point. California's statute does provide a definition of "supplementary materials."[57] All these complicating factors, coupled with the fact of multiple adoptions per grade/subject, underscore that even where state adoption of approved lists of textbooks exists, local districts have not lost all control of the selection of materials.

Final note should be made of the striking correlation between strong state power over the curriculum and the election of the state officials who wield that power. Only four of the centralized states do not either elect the state board or the chief state school officer: Arkansas, Tennessee, Virginia, and West Virginia. In all the other states either the state board or chief state school officer is an elected official and most frequently the election is run on a partisan basis. The picture of which states elect their boards and which elect their chief state school officer is as follows: Alabama—board; Arizona—chief state school officer (CSSO); Arkansas—both appointed; California—CSSO; Florida—board made up of governor and other statewide elected officials and CSSO elected; Georgia—CSSO; Hawaii—board; Kentucky—CSSO; Louisiana—board and CSSO; Mississippi—CSSO; Nevada—board; New Mexico—board; North Carolina—CSSO; Oklahoma—CSSO; South Carolina—CSSO; Tennessee—both board and CSSO appointed by governor; Texas—board; Virginia—both board and CSSO appointed by governor; West Virginia—both appointed. Indeed, only in California where the chief state school officer is elected and in Nevada where the board is elected are the elections run on a nonpartisan basis.[58]

Recent Developments

In all three kinds of states changes that are similar have occurred in the law. One change that marks many educational codes is the addition of new mandated courses such as driver education, physical education, science, music, art, and consumer education.[59] Courses in business administration and vocational and industrial arts education have also become required parts of some high school curricula.[60] Courses in the effects of drugs have been added to some lists of mandated courses and in several states local districts have been given explicit statutory authority to offer sex education.[61]

When the so-called cold war was at its peak several states passed statutes requiring students be taught about the evil and threat of communism.[62] More recently Arizona and Texas have passed laws requiring students to receive instruction in the benefits of the free enterprise system.[63] Most states bar instruction in communism but California merely prohibits indoctrination in communism.[64] States have also begun to take into account the racial and ethnic diversity of the school population by requiring instruction in black history or more generally, the contribution of minorities to the history of the country.[65] The older concern with the conservation of natural resources has given way in some states to required instruction dealing more broadly with the environment.[66]

Several states have become concerned with racial and sexual discrimination in the schools.[67] California adopted, in 1975, far-reaching new provisions that bar all forms of sex discrimination in the school program whether it be in assigning students to courses, guidance, vocational education, or athletics.[68] New restrictions have been placed on the kinds of materials that may be selected for use in the schools. California and Florida have adopted legislation that prohibits the adoption of instructional materials that adversely reflect upon women or minorities.[69] Since both California and Florida establish state-approved lists of textbooks, the state level agencies charged with developing these lists have an important responsibility in enforcing these nondiscrimination requirements. There is evidence, however, that to date enforcement at the state level has not been vigorous.[70]

In Pennsylvania and New York it has been the state agencies and not the legislatures that have promulgated policies on sexism in school materials. The Board of Regents in New York has told local districts care must be taken not to use materials that depict men and women in stereotyped sex roles and has asked them to revise their courses so that they reflect a balanced account of women's contributions to civilization.[71] As a follow-up, the New York Department of Education issued an eighty-seven page booklet providing highly detailed guidelines for reviewing and changing materials to avoid sexism.[72] In Pennsylvania the Secretary of Education announced that schools would be evaluated in terms of the elimination of sex-segregated and sex-stereotyped classes, programs, activities, and courses, the inclusion of feminist materials in libraries, and the use of materials that portray women favorably in nontraditional roles. There seems to have been little compliance with the secretary's directive to date.[73]

And there have been changes in state laws dealing with what has been called state textbook adoption. In California and Florida the textbook adoption laws have been amended to increase lay involvement, to lessen somewhat the centralized nature of the system by increasing the involvement of local districts in formulating the approved list and by requiring that the final approved list allow for choice among alternative books within a given category.[74] The nondiscrimination requirements noted were added to the laws as was a requirement that materials selected be "learner verified."[75] The learning verification requirement roughly means that publishers must provide evidence that the books they propose for adoption will contribute to the learning achievement of students. The nature of the evidence to be supplied by the publisher is not strictly controlled by the statutes. Indeed, it is hard to imagine what would constitute a sound study that both showed a given book contributes to the learning achievement of students and at the same time controls for such other variables as a teacher's competence and a student's motivation and ability. There are those who believe the learner verification requirement will not lead to an improvement in student achievement but will only create confusion, create administrative strains on the school system, drive up the cost of educational materials, and perhaps even drive smaller publishing companies out of business.[76]

Educational Accountability

The concern with learning achievement reflected in the learner verification requirements has manifested itself in other ways. There is evidence to indicate the states are moving toward a radically different approach to the control of the curriculum; namely, states are attempting to regulate not what goes into the school program but what comes out, that is, achievement in certain basic subjects. Thus states like New York, California, and North Carolina have begun to incorporate requirements in their statutory codes that local districts offer programs and courses from which "students may benefit" or which will improve student achievement in reading or which "actually benefit" the child.[77] Some states, like New York, have moved toward redefining graduation requirements in terms of achievement standards. Similarly, Arizona requires students, before graduating from junior high school, to achieve a certain level of competency in reading.[78] In a related development California has passed legislation permitting students to "test-out" of high school.[79] Oregon permits students to be exempted from compulsory education requirements if they can show they have acquired equivalent knowledge to that acquired in grades one though twelve in public school.[80]

Beyond these developments is the fact that over half the states have now adopted legislation designed to pursue educational accountability.[81] In most of these states the legislation has taken the form of requiring the state department of education to undertake each year an assessment of educational achievement in the state by administering standardized tests in certain subject areas to certain grade levels.[82] Typically, the legislation requires that these tests be given in reading and other language skills as well as in arithmetic and mathematics, but such other areas as the social and natural sciences may also be tested along with student attitudes toward school, achievement, and themselves.[83] As might be expected at the start of these testing programs state departments have concentrated on developing a battery of tests in reading and computational skills. The kinds of tests used are norm-referenced in some states, for example, California, and criterion-referenced in others, for example, Florida.[84]

The legislative purpose behind these testing programs in all states has been one of collecting information on the school program so as to make decision making more rational, thereby making schooling more efficient and effective.[85] In Michigan, the legislature stated that the information was needed to assist in allocating state funds and professional services to equalize educational opportunities.[86] And Florida, by forcing widespread public reporting of the test results, has attempted to use the testing program to bolster and encourage its policy of promoting parental involvement in educational decision making.[87] Perhaps the most important driving force behind the legislation has been the widespread concern over whether taxpayers were getting their money's worth for their tax dollars.

Execution of these laws has not been free from controversy. From the beginning, in Michigan, the state assessment program has been the subject of protests from those who saw the testing program as an invasion of privacy because of the questions asked of students about family backgrounds. Others have called the testing program racist because of an alleged cultural bias in the tests. Conservatives attacked specific questions on the test as communist propaganda and anti-American. There were fights over whether some of the data should be made public and on the significance of the results once they were made known. The very notion of standardized testing was attacked as antihumanist. Teachers expressed fears that the tests would be used for purposes of deciding who will get fired and who will get pay raises. And others expressed fears that the testing program might result in schools focusing most of their attention on students who failed to achieve minimum levels of education while other students languish in the classrooms.[88]

Beyond these kinds of issues, statewide testing programs raised a set of complex questions with regard to their implications for state control of the curriculum in the public schools.[89] In states in which criterion referenced tests have been adopted, the initial problem was to settle upon the goals and objectives that were to be tested. Clearly, if state agencies alone were involved in deciding this question it would have amounted to state determination of the basic goals and objectives toward which all school districts should be directing their efforts. Realizing this, state officials, in establishing the list of goals and objectives to be tested, have attempted to involve the local districts of the state, but this involvement necessarily is limited for most districts lack the time and staff to carry out this complex developmental effort. As matters have worked out in a state like Florida, some of the larger school districts have participated, but in a real sense final decisions and choices have been made by state bureaucrats.

The question of who controls becomes even more difficult when it comes to choosing the test items to be used to test each of the objectives. This has proved to be such a technically complex matter that in Florida primary responsibility has been left to state officials assisted by university-based educators and private companies in the business of producing standardized tests.

An opportunity for state control arises again when the decision has to be made on how many test items a student must successfully complete in order to be deemed to have mastered the objective being tested. Must three of the four test items used to test a single objective be successfully completed, or two, or all four? The choice on this matter typically has been left to state officials who thus have the basic power to define the notion of minimum achievement.

Similarly, state control exists in the authority to determine how many of the, for example, 120 objectives must be successfully completed for a student to be deemed a minimally competent reader.

States can also choose between different ways of reporting data and that choice can affect the behavior of local school officials. Composite reading scores for each building in a district and for each district as a whole can be reported, thereby providing a basis of comparison between buildings and districts: this kind of report creates enormous pressures for educational reform when the comparisons are not to the advantage of a given building or district. Or data can be reported by region, avoiding comparisons between administrative units. Or, while the data can be reported by building and district, no composite or average score need be reported for each administrative unit, but instead, as is done in Florida, average scores for each single reading objective can be reported for each building, leaving the reader of the report the problem of figuring out what the significance of 120 average scores on 120 objectives for a building or a district ultimately means.

Finally, the long-term impact of the state-controlled testing program will depend in part on how the test results are interpreted. The Florida Department of Education warns that differences in achievement between buildings and districts may be accounted for by factors other than the efficacy of the school program, such as the socioeconomic background of the pupils, the instructional priorities of the district or school, or the sequence in which a school or district has taken up the objectives tested in that some of the objectives tested for had not yet been taught in the school. But it is important to note that as part of the testing program in Florida and other states only the skimpiest background data on the students were collected, and no school program data; hence there is no way to make meaningful building or district comparisons while holding these factors constant.

Nevertheless, despite these problems and difficulties in the use of the data, and the dangers involved in the misuse of the data, there is evidence from Florida and Michigan that the tests are having an impact on the local school curriculum. Teachers have begun teaching to the tests and curriculum materials are being revised to take the tests into account. School districts fear the adverse publicity that can come with publication of test scores lower than other districts. We thus see the start of a new set of state-local relationships in these statewide assessment programs with the state setting the objectives and testing to see how well the objectives have been achieved, and the localities beginning to shift their educational efforts in order to improve the performance of their children on the tests. In time these statewide testing systems could become a powerful tool for shaping the local school program.

Children with Special Needs

The concern with achievement has caused state legislatures also to become concerned with children with special educational needs who might not be able to benefit from the regular school program. A North Carolina statutory provision is an excellent example of this concern in that it expressly announces that the state recognizes the diverse educational needs of many children and commits the state to the achievement of equal educational opportunity for all these children. As noted previously, the statute goes on to commit the state to the provision of programs that actually benefit the child.[90]

A related development has been the virtual explosion in the number of statutorily defined pupil classifications. In addition to the classifications listed in the discussion of decentralized states, state legislatures have added such classifications as: students in vocational or career education programs; the mentally gifted; the educationally disadvantaged; underachieving students; migrant children; non-English-speaking children; American Indian children; handicapped children, including physically handicapped, emotionally handicapped; educably mentally retarded; trainable mentally retarded; specific learning disabled; autistic children; the multiply handicapped; children with behavior problems such as the delinquent or near deliquent. For each of these classifications special programs may or must be offered which take into account the student's special needs or capabilities.

Special Education

A highly diverse group of about seven million children who recently have received much state legislative attention are the physically and mentally handicapped, 40 percent of whom have been receiving special services.[91] Of the 60 percent not receiving services about one million are excluded from public schools under state laws that permit students to be exempted from schools on the grounds that they suffer from physical, mental, or emotional disabilities and are unable to profit from further schooling.[92] Frequently those who do obtain special services get nothing more than baby-sitting services.[93]

Because of these and other problems states have begun to introduce new legislation to cope with the mentally, physically, and emotionally handicapped. Since 1966 money spent on the handicapped has more than tripled and in one year alone, 1972, 800 bills were introduced in legislatures dealing with handicapped children, and 250 have been enacted into law.[94] All states now have some sort of legislation dealing with handicapped children.[95] This legislation is, however, quite diverse. Some legislative provisions merely call for state or local planning with regard to the education of the handicapped; other provisions go a step further and require the state and/or local district to provide programs for the handicapped; states like California and New York provide a sort of voucher to reimburse parents for sending their children to private schools; and some states, such as Massachusetts and California, have passed complex codes dealing extensively with many aspects of the problems involved in educating the handicapped.

An examination of the features of the California legislation for the mentally retarded will be useful in illustrating the direction legislation in this area is moving.[96] The California statute declares that every mentally retarded or physically or multiply handicapped child has a right to a free public education and school districts have an obligation to provide services for these children. Before a child is labeled as mentally retarded, however, the statute requires an elaborate examination involving a teacher, psychologist, and nurse. The testimony and advice of a wide variety of people are required as well as the consent of the parent. Parents must be given a chance to bring in their own experts to testify. The tests must be both verbal and nonverbal and must be given in the home language of the child. The complete psychological examination must include estimates of adaptive behavior and take into account the child's developmental history and cultural background as well as school achievement. Thus the pupil is evaluated as a total person, not only in terms of within-school achievement. Parents must give consent to the assignment of their child to a special education class and may appeal the withdrawal of their child from such a class if the child has been so placed and later removed. No child may be placed in a special education class who scores higher than two standard deviations below the norm. Students ultimately classified as mentally retarded are placed in special classes or training classes or in occupational training programs. The special classes may not have an enrollment of more than eighteen unless a waiver of this limitation is obtained from the state so as to assure accommodation of students who would otherwise go without an educational program. These special classes may not have a disproportionately high enrollment of children from any socioeconomic, minority, or ethnic group. Classes that are disproportionate in this respect must be justified to the state by the local district.

Massachusetts, a state noted for its strong belief in local control of education, also has adopted a special education law, perhaps even more sweeping in its implications for educational practice at the local level than the California law.[97] The act is designed to define the needs of children requiring special education in a "broad and flexible manner" by providing a full range of programs for children requiring special education, programs that hold out the promise of benefiting the children. The act applies to a wider range of children than the California law. Thus it appears from the broad language of the act that if a child is in danger of not being promoted or actually fails, the child may be referred for services. Four other kinds of children may also be referred: (1) Students suspended for more than five days in a quarter; (2) those absent more than fifteen days in a quarter without medical excuse; (3) those who demonstrate distinct learning or behavior changes after illness; (4) those considered delinquent. In brief, the act is designed to provide "special" education (not just for those who are mentally retarded, but for any child in need of special services).

Furthermore, Massachusetts wants to avoid the use of labels that may stigmatize pupils. The parent must consent before a child may be evaluated and may participate in the evaluation process and in drawing up an educational plan for the child. If a plan cannot be agreed upon, the examiner must hold a prompt hearing, to be followed, if needed, by an appeal to a state agency or court. The plan must be monitored. If possible a child is to be "mainstreamed," that is, placed in a regular class and given supplementary services and treatment without isolating or segregating the child from the regular program. If the evaluation results in a decision that the child cannot be mainstreamed, the parents must be told what the child must achieve before he may reenter the regular classroom.

The California and Massachusetts laws impose upon local districts requirements that schools have heretofore not had to meet. Entirely new kinds of students must be given service, students who before had been exempted or suspended from school. Entirely new educational programs have to be mounted, of a kind never before undertaken by many schools. New individualized evaluation procedures have to be established and parents must be brought into school decision making in ways never done before. New working relationships need to be established among regular classroom teachers, special education teachers, school psychologists, administrators, and parents. Old methods of testing and pupil evaluation have to be abandoned, especially under the California law which aims at avoiding misclassification of pupils because of possible cultural bias in the evaluation procedures. Attitudes have to be changed with regard to the children who need special assistance and jealousies over the extra money being spent on those children have to be mitigated. New teachers and psychologists have to be hired and perhaps new facilities provided. Care must be taken to be sure these new personnel and facilities are not usurped for use for normal children or otherwise not directed to the children they were designed to help.

Meeting these demands, the evidence seems to show, has been difficult. In fact, to date the reports on compliance with state laws in California and Massachusetts indicate many failures and, as a result, the impact of these laws at the local level has not been fully felt.[98] Full compliance with the laws would put considerable strain on the local districts, forcing them to divert energies and resources into these new programs. New programs the schools might otherwise have undertaken would have to be reduced in scale or abandoned, and even ongoing programs might have to be changed to accommodate and adjust to the newly mandated programs. The overall impact of these laws will be considerable even though extra state aid is frequently available to assist local districts in serving the handicapped child.

Bilingual Education

Just as the federal government has begun to provide federal grants to support programs for children who have limited or no English-speaking ability and to require, pursuant to Title VI, all districts to provide special instruction in English to those children, so have the states begun to develop policy in this area. (Congress has passed two pieces of legislation establishing a grant-in-aid program for bilingual education. The first was adopted in 1968, the second in 1974, amending the 1968 act, 20 U.S.C. 880[b] [Supp. 1975]. Between 1969 and 1973 $117.9 million was spent under Title VII.) The pattern of state policy remains, however, quite diverse. Some states, such as Delaware and Nebraska, have on the books legislation that mandates that English alone be the medium of instruction. About a dozen states have no legislation on the question. Another sixteen states permit instruction in a language other than English, sometimes with the limitation that such non-English instruction may be provided only in the first three years of schooling. As many as eight states require local districts to offer bilingual instruction.[99]

Before turning to an examination of the acts mandating bilingual education it is important to note that those states that permit bilingual instruction do not always explicitly permit bicultural instruction. For example, while New York's legislation makes it clear that bilingual instruction is to be bicultural, Arizona's act is silent on the question, thus leaving local districts in Arizona in doubt as to whether they could, if they wished, offer a bicultural-bilingual program.[100] Thus Arizona has left in doubt the question of the extent to which bilingual programs may be designed to preserve minority cultures or must be used to blend minority pupils into a mainstream of English-speaking Americans.

The states that have adopted mandatory bilingual education programs include Alaska, Illinois, Massachusetts, Michigan, New Jersey, Pennsylvania, and Texas.[101] The features of the legislation adopted in these states are quite similar. What are described here are the provisions of the Massachusetts law.[102] School districts that enroll twenty or more children of limited English-speaking abilities must establish three-year, transitional, bilingual-bicultural programs under the Massachusetts law. To determine if the law applies to them, school districts must conduct annual surveys of the number of language minority children in the district.

Parents, under the provisions of the law, may withdraw their child from the program at the time of the original notification of enrollment or at the close of any semester thereafter. Additionally, parents must give their consent to the continuation of their child in the program for a period longer than three years, and parents must approve the transfer of their child out of the program prior to the third year of enrollment. Parents may not compel the school to keep their child in the bilingual program beyond the third year if the district decides to remove the child from the program.

The statute also speaks to the nature of the bilingual program that is to be offered. Whenever feasible, the classes must be located in the regular public schools rather than in separate facilities. The program must include instruction in all courses or subjects which a child is required by law or by the local district to receive. There must be full-time instruction in the reading and writing of the mother tongue of the child and in oral comprehension, speaking, reading, and writing of English. The program must include study in the history and culture of the country that is native to the parents of the child. Whenever possible a child should be placed in classes with children of approximately the same age and level of educational attainment, but if the group is heterogeneous, instruction must be individualized. Only qualified teachers may instruct in the programs.

In courses in which verbal skills in English are not essential to understanding, such as art, music, and physical education, non-English-speaking students are to participate with English-speaking students. And the non-English-speaking students must be assured of a practical and meaningful opportunity to participate fully in the extracurricular activities of the school. The Massachusetts law also establishes a Department of Bilingual Education in the State Department of Education to enforce the law, collect information, provide technical assistance, evaluate the programs, and provide for the maximum practicable involvement of parents in the planning, development, and evaluation of these bilingual programs.

This description of the Massachusetts law should make clear that once again the new state laws impose far-reaching requirements on the local districts—requirements that not only cost a considerable amount of money but entail significant programmatic changes that may affect the entire school program. Adjusting the existing school program to take into account the special needs of a minority of pupils is no easy task, and one can see why, until forced to do it, local districts have to date neglected their responsibilities toward these children.

Experimentation and Innovation

At the same time as states have been moving toward increased state control of the curriculum, legislatures have recognized a need for greater flexibility at the local level. Thus legislation has been adopted that is designed to open the door to greater experimentation and variety. Some states permit the chief state school officer to waive statutory requirements upon request from local districts. Legislation has been adopted that allows specially qualified *noncertificated* people to come into the schools to teach courses, for example, lawyers, craftsmen, artists.[103] States have also begun to grant credit toward graduation experiences other than public school work, such as employment outside of school, courses in local junior and four-year colleges, training in the Army.[104] California permits local districts to set up programs that are not subject to the usual statutory requirements for children who cannot benefit from the regular school program.[105] (There are obvious dangers in such a statute as it permits the schools to exclude from regular classes any child the school finds to be troublesome in any respect. Without standards for administering this provision, abuse is possible.)

Drastically different forms of schools are permitted by legislation in several states. For example, in Massachusetts the state board of education is authorized to establish three experimental school projects for the development of educational innovations.[106] Under this authority the state board has established the Massachusetts Experimental School System which now includes three schools offering K-12 instruction. The schools are a cross between magnet schools designed to attract a multiracial population from several municipalities and a community controlled school because of the mechanism for parent participation in governance. For another example, the California legislature has adopted a bill entitled the Demonstration Scholarship Act which permits the creation of four experimental projects involving vouchers.[107] Under the law, a demonstration board is created which can be either an existing local school board or a new board appointed by a participating local district. Public and private schools may participate, but the private schools may not be religious schools. While important controls over all participating schools are placed in the hands of the demonstration board, an important degree power to make decisions remains in the hands of the participating schools, including general control of the educational program. Pursuant to this legislation, a demonstration voucher project funded with federal funds is now going forward in Alum Rock Union School District in Northern California.[108]

As of July 1976, local districts in California have been authorized to establish one or more alternative schools within the district in which not more than approximately 10 percent of the student population of the district may enroll. Students may not be selected for these schools on the basis of previous classroom performance or on the basis of sex, race, or ethnicity. The schools are to be innovative and should be designed to maximize the opportunity for students to develop the positive values of self-reliance, self-motivation, initiative, kindness, spontaneity, resourcefulness, courage, creativity, responsibility, and joy.[109]

Legislatures have also tried to encourage new kinds of courses and programs by passing legislation authorizing districts to mount new courses and programs and then providing state funds for those programs and courses. One of the more significant developments in this area has been the recent interest in career education. By the end of 1974, twenty-five state legislatures had authorized career education and appropriated funds for these programs. Arizona alone has appropriated over $10 million in four years.[110]

Administering Grants-in-Aid

The passage of Title I, ESEA, and related state grant-in-aid programs created an enormous opportunity for the state departments of education to influence education at the local level. It will be recalled that under Title I the amount of money to which a local district was entitled was determined by federal formula, but in order to receive the money the local district had to submit a project proposal to the state for approval (see chap. 3). The state then had to determine if the proposal met with federal regulations, but it could also impose its own more stringent standards if it wished.

A handful of states took advantage of this opportunity, most notably Ohio, Connecticut, and California.[111] There, under the leadership of Wilson Riles, who subsequently was elected state superintendent, the California Education Department strongly enforced federal regulations and imposed its own more stringent regulations in the areas of concentration of Title I funds, targeting funds on those schools with the highest concentration of low-income families, and targeting projects to elementary schools. Riles was able to carry out this policy because of several factors. The state legislature and state board of education supported these policies and refused to listen to appeals to overturn the priorities established by Riles; the state governor, who traditionally did not get deeply involved in the running of the department of education, was Ronald Reagan, and he was more concerned with higher education than with elementary-secondary education.[112]

Other states also made some use of the opportunity afforded by Title I. The department of education in Michigan stressed the distribution of federal aid to those districts and students with the greatest need.[113] New York's department of education sent the word out that it preferred Title I projects that involved instruction in reading in the elementary grades. The result was that in New York, by 1970, 40 percent of all projects submitted to the state for approval had a reading component.[114]

But these examples are the exceptions. The general pattern was one of state departments doing nothing more than checking to see that Title I money was fiscally accounted for and going through the motions of making sure that federal regulations were being complied with.[115] Indeed, some states such as Massachusetts, with a long tradition of local control of education, a tradition that has been termed a religion of localism, hardly enforced federal regulations let alone promulgate and enforce stiffer state regulations. In Massachusetts the small Title I staff was lucky to be able simply to read the applications which they then routinely approved. No district ever lost its funding and the minor adjustments that were asked of districts were largely handled over the phone. Little in the way of monitoring or evaluation was undertaken. The Massachusetts state bureaus involved in administering Title I and other federal grant programs, Title II, ESEA, vocational education, NDEA, Title III, confined themselves to writing checks and letting the local district determine what to do with the money.[116]

Conclusions

In the nineteen states that have been classified as centralized, there has been a long history of significant state influence over the educational programs offered in the public schools. But in these states as well as the less centralized states there have been in recent times significant changes that have tended toward greater centralization in all three types of states. This new influence of the states can be seen in the new statewide testing systems, the special education laws, the bilingual education laws, the state created grant-in-aid programs, and, to a lesser degree, in the new federal grant-in-aid programs. To date this expanded role for state government in education has not resulted so much in a total takeover of the local program, but in creation of a required dialogue between state and local officials. Increasingly local officials cannot act unilaterally but must consult state regulations and guidelines and talk to state officials to find out what is permissible and what regulations might be bent or waived. Local control of education as that term was once understood now means something quite different in decentralized states as well as the moderately decentralized and centralized states.

5 The State Courts

The entrance of the federal courts into the process of shaping educational policy is a relatively new phenomenon, but the state courts for many years have been involved in the resolution of a variety of disputes arising out of the operation of the schools. For most of this period, however, the state courts have acted with considerable restraint, avoiding as much as possible intrusion upon the prerogatives of either the state legislature or the local school boards. They have tried to avoid striking down state legislation as unconstitutional, interpreting statutes in new or unexpected ways, or attempting to control or direct the exercise of discretion by educational administrators. But in several respects this pattern of state judicial restraint is changing. This chapter will review those changes in three areas: constitutional litigation; interpretation of statutes; and review of the exercise of discretion.

Right to an Education

It is common for state constitutions to contain provisions requiring the legislature to provide for a system of common schools, or a uniform system of free public schools.[1] Sometimes these state constitutions go one step further, imposing not merely a duty to establish a school system, but a system which the "needs of the people may require" or a system in which all children "may be educated."[2] By imposing upon the legislatures of the states certain duties with regard to education, these provisions also seemingly create a right on the part of children to demand certain educational services from the state. Put somewhat differently, these provisions seem to create a right to an education which if broadly interpreted could become the basis for massive judicial involvement in shaping the public schools of the state.

It would seem that at a minimum these provisions would severely limit the discretion of state legislatures and local districts to decide who will or will not be educated at public expense, and consequently limit their discretion to decide what sort of educational program must be mounted. (If children cannot be excluded from the schools, they must be served by the schools, which means mounting programs to accommodate their special needs. When courts put an end to the exclusion of children from the pub-

97

lic schools, they perforce impose upon the schools a change in the school curriculum.) Early litigation interpreted these provisions to prevent the total exclusion from public school of black and Indian children (but did not prevent their assignment to separate and segregated facilities);[3] these early cases did not, however, stop the exclusion from the schools of the mentally and physically handicapped.[4] The exclusion of these children was authorized under state compulsory education laws which permitted school officials to exempt from the compulsory attendance law requirements those children who may not be able to benefit from the regular school program.[5] The obvious purpose behind these laws was to save the state and localities the money, time, and effort that would have been necessary to develop educational programs suited to the needs of these children. In upholding such exclusions these older cases relied on such arguments as that a state constitutional requirement of the provision of a common school education for all children did not require provision of educational services for children who were not common.

The practical impact of these decisions has recently been undercut in several ways. First, there are indications that the courts may be turning away from their previous literal interpretations of the state constitutional provisions and are coming to accept the argument that the state constitutions create a right to a public education for all children. Second, amendments in educational codes such as the special education laws discussed in chapter 4 have moved toward assuring handicapped children of a publicly supported education. In New York if the public schools do not have available educational services suitable for physically handicapped children, the parents may seek financial support from various appropriate units of government in order to send their children to private school.[6] Third, as noted in chapter 2, several lower federal courts have issued orders based on the U.S. Constitution which uphold the right of the mentally retarded and others to obtain access to a publicly supported education.

Not only are state courts beginning to bar the absolute exclusion of certain kinds of children from the public schools, some courts are beginning to show concern about the adequacy of the educational program provided. Thus, the Michigan Supreme Court ordered school districts to supply textbooks without charge to all children, since books were an essential part of a system of free public schools, guaranteed by the Michigan State Constitution which provided that the legislature "shall maintain and support a system of free public elementary and secondary schools as defined by law."[7] Similarly, an Idaho court struck down textbook fees and a general fee for extracurricular activities levied on all students regardless of their participation; but the court said in dicta that a true user charge associated with extracurricular activities would be constitutional.[8] Thus both these courts read their respective state constitutional guarantees as requiring a free education for all, not simply as providing protection for the poor who might not be able to afford the fees. In Arizona, however, the State Supreme Court refused to strike down a textbook fee despite the claim that the state constitution assured *all* students a free public education.[9] However, the court decided that the plaintiff's complaint was valid under the Equal Protection clause of the Fourteenth Amendment of the U.S. Constitution:

[W]e hold that indigent high school students who cannot afford textbooks must be provided as adequate an educational opportunity [to receive a "basic education"] as students who can afford to buy their own textbooks.[10]

The Court presented this holding as an application of the rational basis equal protection test (see chap. 2). Given the state's commitment to give every student the opportunity to obtain a basic minimum education, said the Court, there was no rational reason related to a legitimate objective for making access to this opportunity significantly more difficult, if not impossible, for indigent students. Because textbooks are an integral part of the educational process for which cheaper substitutes are usually unavailable, indigent students must have a substantial opportunity to use appropriate textbooks and may not be penalized for failing to purchase any text. It was not necessary for the state to furnish free textbooks to everyone, or for that matter to furnish them to *anyone* enrolled in a course on a full-time basis. Arrangements could be made for short-term borrowing by indigent students or a similar system so long as it did not put a significant burden on indigent students who were trying to obtain a basic education. Textbook fees have been upheld in some states, for example, *Hamer* v. *Board of Education*.[11]

These textbook fee cases represent a relatively modest intrusion by the courts into the operation of the public school system, but they do reflect a growing willingness on the part of state courts to consider challenged inequalities and inadequacies in the provision of public education. The most famous of these cases is the California decision in *Serrano* v. *Priest*.[12] The California system of educational finance at the time of the decision (and even after the legislature modified the system shortly after the decision) relied heavily upon the use of a local property tax for raising local expenditures for education. Because of wide discrepancies in the amount of taxable property per pupil available in the various districts in the state, there were wide differences in the amount of property tax monies available per pupil from district to district. State aid did not make up these differences; hence, the amount of money spent per pupil in the districts was alleged to be a function of local district property wealth. The plaintiffs charged that to the extent inequalities in local expenditures were the result of these differences in the available taxable property, these inequalities were unconstitutional under both the Equal Protection clause of the Fourteenth Amendment of the U.S. Constitution and then Article I, Section 21, now Article I, Section 7, of the State Constitution. (Article I, Section, 7, of the California constitution provides in part that a person may not be denied equal protection of the laws. Thus, the provision is similar in wording to the Fourteenth Amendment of the U.S. Constitution.) The defendants demurred and the lower court dismissed the complaint.

On appeal from the dismissal of the complaint, the California Supreme Court had to decide, assuming the facts alleged by the plaintiffs were correct, whether under the state or federal constitution a cause of action had been stated. An initial central question was the choice of a standard of review; two were available. Under the traditional, or old, standard of review in equal protection cases, the plaintiff had the burden of showing the legislation was not rationally related to a legitimate state purpose. Under the newer standard of review, the plaintiff had to establish that the legislation involved a suspect classification or a fundamental interest. If that could be established then the burden shifted to the state to establish that its legislation was necessary to further a compelling state interest. In this case the California Supreme Court decided that the plaintiffs had established that the financial scheme involved both the use of a suspect classification and touched upon a fundamental interest. Hence the court said the burden of proof shifted to the state, and that if the facts alleged by the plaintiff were correct, the state failed to demonstrate why the existing finance scheme was necessary to achieve a compelling state interest. Thus, the court sent the case back to trial for a determination of the facts alleged by the plaintiffs.

Before turning to the trial court's findings, we might elaborate on some of the important points in the opinion of the California Supreme Court. First, as to the question of a suspect classification, the court found that in this case the suspect classification used was one of wealth. Assuming the plaintiff's facts were correct, the court said that the amount of money spent on a child's education was clearly a function of the wealth of the school district in which the child happened to reside. Wealth was the determining factor. Further, assuming for purposes of deciding the dismissal of the complaint that money affects the quality of education, the court concluded that the quality of a child's education depended upon where he happened to live. Whether a child got a high or low quality education was importantly a function of the wealth of the school district.

Additionally, the California Supreme Court found that this scheme affected a fundamental interest of children—their education. Apart from the findings of *this* court that education was important not only from the self-interested viewpoint of the individual child but also from the viewpoint of the best interests of the society, the court noted that in several earlier California cases education had been deemed important for those same reasons. Beyond this, the court took note of Article IX, Section 1, to indicate that the populace of the state had also itself declared education to be of great importance.

With the conclusion that both a suspect classification and a fundamental interest were involved in the case, the court concluded that strict scrutiny of the existing system of educational finance was in order. Unless the state could demonstrate that a compelling state interest was being served by the present finance system and that this present system was necessary to achieve that interest, the system must fall. In response the state argued that local control was the compelling interest being served by the heavy reliance upon the use of the local property tax. In response the court said that, assuming decentralized financial decision making was a compelling state interest, the fact was this state interest was not being served by the present arrangements. Property-poor local districts had no practical free choice in the amount of money they could raise for education. The existing system, assuming the alleged facts were correct, served to deprive local districts of the local choices the state said was such a compelling interest.

Thus, we see that the California State Constitution (as well as the federal Constitution upon which the decision was also based) was read to support the notion that education was such a fundamental interest that the quality of a child's education could not be conditioned by the amount of local property wealth of the district where the child happened to reside. If violin lessons were available in one school district they could not be unavailable in another school district simply because that district had less property wealth.

After the decision by the Supreme Court in California, two things happened. The state legislature amended the finance system so that (1) the minimum level of money assured all districts by the state (based on a combination of local taxes and state aid) was roughly doubled, with a provision for gradual increase in the foundation over the years and (2) a gradually decreasing limit was placed on the revenue that could be raised by a school district through local property taxation, in the absence of approval of increased rates by the districts voters (a voter override).[13] The theory behind these changes was that over a period of years school spending by wealthy and poor districts would converge, provided the voters of the wealthier districts did not approve any overrides.

The second development was the U.S. Supreme Court's decision in *San Antonio Independent School District* v. *Rodriguez*, a case in which the educational finance scheme of Texas had been challenged on the same basis as in *Serrano* (see chap. 2).[14] Only this time the plaintiffs lost when the Supreme Court found that the traditional equal protection test should apply rather than the new equal protection test, and that under the old test the state system of finance was found not be unconstitutional. The U.S. Supreme Court concluded that the old test applied beause neither a suspect classification nor a fundamental interest was involved in the case. More precisely, the Court concluded that classifying children on the basis of *district* wealth, as opposed to their personal family wealth, did not amount to a suspect classification under the Court's precedents and that education when supplied in at least minimally adequate amounts (as all parties agreed was being done in Texas at the time, despite the inequalities in the amount spent per pupil from district to district) was not a fundamental interest. Applying the old test the Court concluded that the system of finance was rationally related to the legitimate state purpose of providing an adequate education while at the same time preserving local control. The existence of some inequalities in the ability of districts to control their own expenditures—inequalities arising out of the differences in local taxable wealth—did not make the system so irrational as to be deemed unconstitutional. These considerations, plus the fears the majority expressed with regard to the chaos that might result if the present system of finance were struck down, plus its sensitivity to the rights of the states to control their own system of taxation and finance, led the Court to refuse to get involved.

Thus when the *Serrano* case went back to the trial court for a determination as to the validity of the facts alleged in the original complaint and assumed to be true for deciding the demurrer by the California Supreme Court, the lower court had to wrestle with two new problems. Did the decision in the *Rodriguez* case in effect nullify the decision by the California Supreme Court? Assuming the original *Serrano* decision remained good law, did the changes in the financial system in California mean that now the system was in compliance with the original *Serrano* decision? Briefly, the trial court concluded that the *Rodriguez* decision did not affect the original *Serrano* decision because that original decision, while in part based upon an interpretation of the U.S. Constitution—an interpretation no longer valid in light of the *Rodriguez* decision—was also based upon the California State Constitution which the U.S. Supreme Court did not purport to construe.[15] (It has to be understood that if the California State Constitution provided less protection to children than did the U.S. Constitution, then the U.S. Constitution would control—to that extent the California Constitution itself would be unconstittional under the U.S. Constitution. But in this instance the California Constitution provided more protection than did the U.S. Constitution—was more royal than the king—and this is permissible. The U.S. Constitution provides the minimum level of protection that must be afforded, not both the minimum and the maximum.)

Thus the trial court concluded it must continue to be guided by the original decision in *Serrano*, and it turned to the impact of the amendments to the financial system. Here the Court found that during the time the amendments had been in effect there was no significant change in the wealth-based spending disparities to be found in the state and, as for the future, that "as long as the voted tax overrides are available to the voters of school districts, there is substantial probability that . . . the present substantial disparities in per pupil expenditures between school districts will never be diminished to any significant extent."[16] In other words, the trial court concluded that the alleged wealth disparities had been proved by the plaintiffs to exist.

The remaining factual issue which had not been decided by the California Supreme Court was the relationship between per pupil expenditures and the quality of the educational program. If there were no relationship between the disparities in money spent per pupil and the quality of the education, there would be no basis for complaint.

The trial court wrestled with two ways of measuring the quality of the school program—an output standard based on using standardized tests to measure how well students were doing in reading and mathematics, and an input standard which measured the kinds and extensiveness of the school district offerings such as class size. The inputs could be viewed as the environmental conditions which provided students with opportunities to learn; unequal offerings meant unequal opportunities to learn. The trial court rejected the use of the output measure because it found that existing statistical methods of determining the extent to which the child's home, social class background, or school factors made a difference in achievement were too unreliable. It was not possible with presently available techniques to determine the precise role these variables played in determining achievement, hence the extent to which money was related to quality in this sense could not be precisely determined.[17] Instead the court accepted the output measure of school district offerings and concluded that disparities in expenditures did account for significant differences in school offerings. Money differences affected such things as (1) class size; (2) teacher quality; (3) curriculur offerings; (4) length of the school day; (5) adequacy of materials and equipment; and (6) supportive services such as counseling services.[18]

In sum, the California Supreme Court and the trial court concluded that the quality of the school program available in local districts was impermissibly a function of local taxable property wealth. More precisely and most significantly the trial court declared that disparities between school districts in per pupil expenditures, apart from the categorical aid, special-needs programs that are not reduced to insignificant differences, which means amounts considerably less than $100 per pupil within a maximum of six years, were unconstitutional. Additionally, variations in tax rates between school districts that are not reduced to nonsubstantial variations within the same maximum period were also unconstitutional. As one commentator noted, these conclusions would seem even to bar the legislature from using any system of school finance that results in differential school spending from district to district which are not based on district wealth. Districts of equal wealth could not spend amounts that varied more than $100 per pupil even if one district wanted to support an elaborate and expensive program and the other district—which could afford to do so—did not want to do so.[19] Thus, the trial court seems to have gone considerably beyond the original decision which only barred wealth-based differences, not both wealth-based and politically based differences. Whether this part of the trial court's opinion will stand on review remains to be seen.

What can be concluded, however, is that chances are the educational programs available in the several districts of California will change. It might further be predicated that the higher quality programs will in all likelihood not be downgraded, but instead those districts whose program is now lower in quality will be improved. Educational offerings in those districts will become more diverse and those programs already in place will be more richly supported. Financial reform will mean curriculum reform.

California is not the only state in which a state court struck down the system for financing education. In the case of *Robinson* v. *Cahill*, the New Jersey State Supreme Court accepted the findings of the trial court that there were great disparities in the amount of money spent per pupil within the state and that state aid did not operate to equalize the sums available per pupil.[20] Given these facts, the court considered whether the educational system in the state met the state constitutional requirement that the legislature provide for the maintenance and support of a "thorough and efficient system of free public schools for the instruction of all the children in this state between the ages of five and eighteen years."[21] The heart of the court's problem was coming to an understanding of what the term "thorough and efficient" meant in more operationalized terms. Judging by the disorganized and ambiguous nature of the opinion, the problem must have been difficult.

Nevertheless it seems possible to cull from the opinion a somewhat coherent understanding of what the court took the thorough-and-efficient requirement to mean. First, the court seemed to be saying that the constitution imposed upon the state the obligation to assure that all children had available a minimally adequate education. Thus there is some minimum, yet to be defined, which must be made equally available to all. Second, that minimum was changeable over time: a century ago failure to provide students with a high school education would not violate the state constitution, said the court, but today a system of public education which did not offer high school education could not be considered to be thorough and efficient. Third, the court seemed to be saying that the constitutionality of the educational program could be determined by measuring the educational achievement of the students—by an output standard. "The Constitution's guarantee must be understood to embrace that educational opportunity which is needed in the contemporary setting to equip a child for his role as a citizen and as a competitor in the labor market."[22] Fourth, the court implied by this standard that students who because of certain background factors—home disadvantages, mental or physical handicaps—could not achieve this output standard without special help, might have to be provided with such help. But then at another point in the opinion, the court seemed to retract this implication when it wrote that nothing it said should imply that the state "may not recognize . . . a need for additional dollar input to equip classes of disadvantaged children for the educational opportunity."[23] This sentence implies such compensatory education is permissible but not required, as previously implied.

There are obvious difficulties in using this output standard for determining if a present educational system is constitutional. Some of the problems are as follows: For what kinds of jobs are students to be assured of being a competitor, the most menial entry-level jobs or jobs requiring greater skill and training? If children are to be assured they will be a competitor what does that mean—some competitors lose—hence, what is to be assured students by this standard? Are even the mentally retarded to be assured of being a competitor? Since that is a literal impossibility, what does this standard require with regard to these students as well as the physically handicapped, the emotionally handicapped, and those who come from homes with severe educational disadvantages?

If the New Jersey courts were to resolve these issues they would be going a long way toward shaping the entire educational program of the public school system. The courts would be setting the minimum goals for the educational system not only by establishing the occupations for which students should be made competitive, but also by establishing the achievements, the skills students would presumably have to have in order to be competitive. Eventually the courts might be called upon to decide if the educational methods used to realize the achievement goals were in fact doing the job, capable of doing the job, and if other methods might not be more effective, all of which assumes that knowledge of these points is available. And from time to time it would seem that courts would be called upon to force and upgrade the output goals as the society changed.

Presumably to avoid all these problems, the court, in *Robinson* v. *Cahill*, despite defining the appropriate constitutional standard in terms of educational outputs, said it was going to review the present system of finance "on the basis of discrepancies in dollar input per pupil . . . We deal with the problem in those terms because dollar input is plainly relevant and because we have been shown no other viable criterion for measuring compliance with the constitutional mandate."[24] Using this approach the court struck the finance system down. "The constitutional mandate could not be said to be satisfied unless we were to suppose the unlikely proposition that the lowest level of dollar performance happens to coincide with the constitutional mandate and that all efforts beyond the lowest level are attributable to local decisions to do more than the State was obliged to do."[25]

Without dwelling on the inadequacies and inconsistencies in the opinion, it should be made clear that this opinion has even more profound implications for the school curriculum and the role of the courts in shaping that program than the two decisions in the *Serrano* case. The basis for an almost complete judicial takeover of the school program was laid in the opinion. The court backed away from the implications of its decision by ultimately relying on only a dollar standard and by turning over to the state legislature, without any guidance on all the issues raised by the opinion, the task of coming up with a finance system to which the court might give its approval. A considerable amount of wrangling between court and legislature ensued with both sides finding it intellectually, practically, and politically impossible to follow through on the implications of the court's output standard. As matters stand in July, 1976 the public schools of New Jersey have closed because the legislature has failed for the moment at least to come up with a method of financing the schools that meets the court's requirements.

In New York State there is now pending yet a different kind of attack on that state's system of educational finance, one that also holds profound implications for the school program.[26] In this suit the plaintiffs are large city school districts, not individual students. The districts begin their argument by asserting that state aid in New York is designed to serve the purpose of easing the burden of school districts less able to finance their public education programs. Second, the plaintiffs argue the present financial aid formula does not in fact serve that purpose for several reasons. By measuring the ability of districts to support their educational program in terms of property wealth per student in average daily attendance, the law provides more financial aid to the district most able to support its educational program and less per-pupil aid to the larger cities which are less able to support their programs. This last statement is so because to measure fiscal capacity simply in terms of property wealth overlooks the fact that urban centers must as a legal and practical matter support massive noneducational services, which leaves these cities with far fewer dollars to support education than the supposedly poorer suburban and rural school districts. The state law also ignores the higher costs of providing the same educational services in the cities. The law penalizes cities by tying aid to average daiy attendance—the urban poor who attend the city schools are highly erratic about attendance; nevertheless full services must be maintained. Finally, the aid formula does not sufficiently take into account the high proportion of children with special educational needs in the cities—needs that are very expensive to service. Third, given the fact the aid formula does not in fact serve its purpose, it must fall pursuant either to the rational basis equal protection test, or to the tests three and four discussed in chap. 2. (The argument rests both on the U.S. Constitution and the equal protection clause to be found in the state constitution, Article I, Section 11.) What is required is a change in the state finance law so that local fiscal capacity is measured fairly to take into account the municipal overburdens and extra education costs that limit the cities' capacity to fund and deliver public education.

While this argument is only suggestive of the fact that state aid ought to be tied to the educational needs of the children in the school districts, the second major set of arguments put forth in the case is explicit on the point. This portion of the argument rests on the New York State constitutional provision which imposes on the state legislature the duty of providing for the maintenance and support of a free common school system "wherein all children of this State may be educated."[27] The plaintiffs argue that the state fails to comply with this requirement by providing less state aid to cities where the educational need is the greatest. Indeed while urban districts could well claim more state aid than other districts, argue the plaintiffs, at the very least they should not suffer under an aid formula that gives them less. Giving cities less has the consequence of failing to meet the higher costs of the educational needs of the larger proportions of disadvantaged students in those cities. It has the further consequence that some students in these cities are not being provided a minimally adequate education. And in a related argument plaintiffs assert that the underfunding of city programs has the effect of functionally excluding many students from public school in that they are not getting a program from which they can benefit. To rectify this situation, educational funding should be given in direct proportion to the educational burdens of school districts.

Although these arguments are mounted by school districts as a way of forcing the state to provide them with more state financial assistance, these same arguments could be used by individual students against their own school districts as well as against the state to argue for an improved educational program "wherein all children [including the individual plaintiff] may be educated." Indeed if accepted by the courts, the arguments of the plaintiffs in this state aid case could lay a basis for a student's challenge not only to the level of financing of his program, but also to its very concept on the ground that it is not well designed to suit his educational needs and he is not being educated. The case, thus, once again seems to open the door to significant judicial involvement in shaping the public school program.

What we may then see emerging in a select number of states is a notion of a right to an education which requires the state either not to make the level of inputs available to the child a function of the wealth of the local district in which the child resides, or, more significantly, requires the state to assure each child of a minimally adequate education. As the discussion of the *Robinson* v. *Cahill* case pointed out, the concept of a minimally adequate education is not without ambiguity, but at the same time lays down a premise for significant judicial involvement in shaping the basic parameters of the public school program.

Other Constitutional Issues

Acceptance by state courts that their state constitutions establish a right to an education on behalf of every student could have wide-ranging implications for a variety of other constitutional issues. First, recognition of a state-created right to an education will affect the kind of test or standard of review used by state courts in equal protection cases. That is, viewing education as a fundamental interest will encourage state courts to adopt one of the stricter equal protection standards of review, which, as was discussed in chap. 2, leads to greater judicial involvement in the operation of schools.[28] For example, if a state court were asked to review school rules for the selection of textbooks and other materials under the equal protection clause of the state constitution, it might be more willing to rely upon a strict standard of review than a federal court would because the state constitution explicitly recognizes education as fundamental.

Second, a state court which accepts education as a fundamental interest is likely to look with greater skepticism upon local school district policies that lead to the exclusion of children from public school on the ground they violated a hair or dress code, exercised rights of free speech, or were married or pregnant.[29] In these areas state courts have not been noted for their liberality in that they have tended to uphold, for example, school hair and dress codes. But once a state supreme court accepts the notion of a right to an education, the viability of these cases must be called into question.

Third, a recognized right to an education lays a solid premise for extension to pupils of procedural due process rights, that is, a right to notice, to a hearing, to present witnesses, to question accusers, before a long-term suspension or expulsion from school may be imposed. At least it is likely that the federal courts would recognize this state-created right as a basis for their extension of U.S. constitutional rights of due process to students.[30]

Thus, acceptance by a state judiciary of a right to an education may force a revision of existing precedent and lays the basis for extensive judicial involvement in a wide range of school policies and activities. At a minimum such a right provides the courts with a rationale for imposing negative limitations in many areas of school policy, if not also providing a premise for requiring affirmative action from the state and localities.

The Right to an Education and Statutory Interpretation

Judicial recognition of a right to an education may have an impact in such nonconstitutional cases as those involving a question of the interpretation of state statutes. To get this point it is first necessary, however, to discuss briefly the work of the state courts in interpreting state statutes, one of the most important functions state courts perform and one which the federal courts for the most part do not get involved with. The kinds of statutory interpretation issues which have arisen and touch upon the school program include the following: whether a state board of education had been given the authority by the legislature to prescribe a state course of study;[31] whether local districts have been delegated the authority by the state legislature to offer programs and courses of study not specifically referred to in the enabling act of the district;[32] what the authority was of the local district in a given state to change textbooks or select textbooks;[33] interpreting what was permitted or required by state laws requiring the adoption of uniform series of books;[34] whether a state statute required a district to provide kindergarten or special education or permitted the district to offer a summer camping program or summer school.[35]

What this list brings out is that neither state boards of education nor local school boards have unlimited authority. Like other agencies of government, school officials only have as much authority as has been delegated to them by the legislature and an action that exceeds that delegated authority is said to be *ultra vires*. Even actions that might be permissible under the U.S. and state constitutions may be illegal if they have not been authorized by the state legislature. The question of whether an action is *ultra vires* must also be distinguished from the question of whether a given action of an official, although within the delegated authority of the official, was nevertheless improper because the action was arbitrary and capricious or abusive of the delegated discretion. These latter sorts of issues will be taken up in the next subsection.

How a state court decides whether an action of a state or local board is *ultra vires* is influenced by many factors: the plain meaning of the words of the statute delegating authority to the agency; the purpose of the law; the legislative history of the law; and such presumptions as whether the law is to be broadly or narrowly construed—whether the law is presumptively permissive or restrictive, that is, whether one presumes the official has the implied authority or whether one assumes lack of authority unless expressly granted in the statute. For example, state courts have ruled that a statute authorizing a local district to offer specifically enumerated courses should be broadly construed so as to permit the offering of courses not listed in the statute: "It cannot be doubted, we think, that the Legislature has given the trustees of the public schools corporations the discretionary power to direct from time to time what branches of learning, in addition to those specified in the statute, shall be taught in the public schools of their respective corporations."[36] In another state the court said offering a foreign language as a course did not violate the state statute requiring English to be the medium of instruction.[37] And in California the attorney general said that local school districts could not offer courses required for graduation, such as automobile driver education, only in the summer.[38] Although the attorney general could find no specific prohibition in the statutes and regulations against such a practice, he decided the California code recognized a distinction between summer and the regular academic year and that there was no explicit legislative authorization for offering such courses only in the summer.

The recent spate of legislative activity recounted in chap. 4 greatly expands the number of issues that may be taken to the state courts. For example, the bilingual education act of Arizona, which authorizes local districts to provide bilingual instruction, is ambiguous as to how authority is shared between state agencies and localities in shaping the content of that program, or, more specifically, how authority is shared in deciding the extent to which the bilingual program will also be bicultural.[39] One section of the new law gives to the state board authority to establish standards students must meet in order to qualify for each grade level prior to and after completion of the program and authority to set the qualifications of teachers in the bilingual programs.[40] The question thus arises whether this provision gives the state authority to push the program toward or away from being bicultural. To answer the question other provisions of the act authorizing the district to establish these programs must be interpreted to see if the grant of authority to the local districts is an implied limitation on state authority.[41] If the grant of authority to local districts is to be broadly construed, then presumably there must be a point at which state regulations could become so detailed as to amount to an intrusion into local authority to control the program. And other more general statutory grants of authority not dealing specifically with bilingual education may have a bearing on how authority is shared. Thus, another provision gives the state board authority to prescribe and enforce a course of study in the common schools and to prescribe the subjects to be taught.[42] Assuming these provisions were sufficiently broad by themselves to control whether bilingual programs could be bicultural—there are yet other complications requiring the review of still other provisions involved in determining whether these provisions should be so broadly construed—the question still arises whether the bilingual act itself modified and narrowed the board's authority with regard to bilingual programs. In sum, state legislatures often enact ambiguous laws which fail to take into account legislation already on the books. The state courts may be asked both to interpret the language of the new laws themselves and to reconcile the new law with the old.

The many problems of statutory interpretation which the state courts have been asked and may be asked to resolve may be influenced by the emerging notions of a right to an education.[43] First, state courts which have recognized a constitutional right to an education may be prone to conclude that a particular statute was enacted by the legislature in order to fulfill its duty to realize the constitutionally mandated right to an education. Having found that implementation of the right to an education is one of the purposes of the legislation, the court may then be willing to give the legislation that sort of interpretation that will best protect the student and his right. Second, even if the court does not conclude the statute was designed to fulfill the right to an education, a court that believed in or accepted such a right might nevertheless exercise what discretion it had at its disposal to resolve any ambiguities in the statute in favor of the student in an effort to further its own conception of what the law should be. Whatever the underlying explanation for the judicial behavior, what we are likely to observe is a stretching by such courts of the statute in new directions not necessarily fully anticipated by the legislature.

Several cases will illustrate these points. In Oregon a state court was asked to rule on whether a local board had the statutory authority to regulate the length of hair of male students.[44] The court began its analysis by recognizing students had a right to attend public school. Thus, the general grant of authority to local districts to discipline students had to be narrowly construed, said the court, otherwise it could be used to destroy the right of students to attend school. Furthermore, school rules might conflict with parental wishes, hence, there exists an additional reason for a limitation of school board power. The court thus decided that all school rules, to be valid, must be reasonably connected with the educational process. In this case the court concluded the school board had failed to show any connection between the rule and the educational process.

There is also some evidence that New York courts have read New

York statutes in a way that promotes the notion of a right to an education. Under Section 232 of the Family Court Act in New York, parents of physically handicapped children may seek an order from the family court charging the county (or a proper subdivision thereof) with the costs of providing private educational services for the child when the child is in need of "special educational training, including transportation, tuition, or maintenance . . . "[45] Courts in construing this provision have stated that the term "special educational training" means that the parent is to obtain a court order for money for private education only if there is no public facility available to meet the child's needs.[46] But in deciding whether such a public facility is available the courts have been especially careful to protect the child. Thus, in one case reimbursement for private school costs was ordered to be paid when it was shown that the child had been doing well in a private school and the public school was only just about to mount its first program capable of serving the child.[47] The court said it would not permit the child's future to be jeopardized by gambling on a special educational program that has yet to prove itself. And in another case the court placed the burden of proving that the public school program could serve the child as well as or better than the private school the child had been attending on the public school officials.[48] The parents ultimately won their claim for reimbursement when the court ruled the public officials had failed to prove their case. Finally, it is important to stress that these liberal interpretations of the New York law not merely protect the child but also constitute a form of collateral attack upon the adequacy of the public school system: parents who seek support for private education are in effect saying the public program is nonexistent or inadequate, and, if the court agrees, the public system is forced to pay a sort of penalty, that is, support the child in private schools.

Courts whose thinking is conditioned by the notion of a right to an education may have an influence upon the content of the school program in another kind of statutory interpretation case. In these cases the general question is the scope of the delegated authority to take an action that limits the educational opportunities of students, and limits the kind and quality of their educational program. For example, the question litigated might be the scope of local authority to classify and label children so as to force them into educational programs they prefer to avoid. Or the question might be whether a local board, pursuant to a general grant of authority to maintain discipline or do that which is necessary for the business management of the schools, could charge fees for textbooks or library privileges or other school related activities and programs. To permit districts to charge such fees might restrict the quality of the educational program of those students who could not afford the fees; therefore, such students could be deprived of access to textbooks, the library, and extracurricular activities and programs. Thus, a court concerned with assuring children of a right to an education might narrowly construe the authority of the local district and conclude the legislature had not delegated the authority to charge such fees.[49] To charge such fees would be an *ultra vires* act.

The Abuse of Discretion

Yet another kind of litigation gives state courts the opportunity to act upon their notions of a right to an education, namely, those cases in which the plaintiff claims a school official has abused his or her discretion. It is important to note that in these cases the claim is not that the legislature did not delegate authority to the official but that this authority was misused. This claim might take any of a number of forms: it might be argued that the action of the official was not rationally related to the purposes he or she was seeking to further, or it might be argued that the action sought to achieve ends irrelevant to an educational system. A related claim is that the ends sought by the action were improper. The complainant might also assert that the means selected to achieve a proper or legitimate educational goal were excessive in that the means chosen unnecessarily trampled upon interests and rights of the student and that other less onerous means were available. The complaint might also rest on notions of fairness and equality of treatment; for example, the school unfairly, without justification, treated some students differently from others. Yet another complainant might claim the purpose sought by the school was not sufficiently important to justify the action taken which gave rise to the grievance. Finally, the issue might be whether the school failed to carry out a duty mandated by statute.

It might be helpful to list some of the kinds of cases in which such claims have been made. For example, with regard to carrying out a mandated duty a state court prohibited a school district from abolishing a music course, whereas in another state the court upheld the discontinuance of a department not mandated by statute.[50] State courts have held that whether kindergarten should be offered was a matter of discretion that should be left to the local district.[51] Other courts have upheld the decision of localities to establish nongraded schools with individualized educational programs;[52] to offer driver education;[53] to offer drama;[54] to offer organized sports and athletics;[55] and to offer many other courses and programs.[56] State courts have also upheld hair length regulations;[57] the assignment of students to particular courses of study;[58] and the use of such materials as *Oliver Twist* and *The Merchant of Venice* despite claims that they were anti-Semitic.[59] The courts have also refused to second-guess schools with regard to their methods of instruction.[60] In general, state courts, when asked to review the exercise of educational expertise, have refrained from interfering, preferring to leave educational decisions to the educators.

Nevertheless, in some cases the courts have stepped in. In New York one lower court refused to permit the school to excuse for the day students who wished to participate in events surrounding Vietnam Moratorium Day in October 1969.[61] Another court barred a school district from lowering its flag to half-mast to memorialize the forty-thousand Americans who died in Vietnam and the four students who died at the hands of the National Guard at Kent State University.[62] Yet another New York court struck down a school rule that prohibited girls from wearing slacks to school, even on the coldest school days.[63] Courts have struck down school rules that resulted in the suspension or expulsion of married students from the regular school program, but have upheld the exclusion of married students from extracurricular activities.[64] A Texas court held a school district lacked the power to adopt a rule excluding mothers from school.[65] However, another court upheld the exclusion of pregnant students from school.[66] The courts have struck down school rules that attempt to regulate out-of-school activities so as to promote study.[67] The courts are split with regard to the authority of schools to compel students to take certain courses over parental objections (to be discussed more fully in chap. 7).

The general restraint state courts have shown, even with regard to such coercive rules as hair and dress codes, the exclusion of married and pregnant students, and the requirement that students take certain courses, is a result of several factors. Deciding whether a given school action is an abuse of discretion is no easy matter as the purposes and methods of education are multifarious, and there are great difficulties in deciding if, for example, methods are rationally related to ends or unnecessarily onerous. Similarly, the courts are likely to feel uncertain in concluding that the purposes being pursued are of insufficient importance to justify the action taken. And when school districts argue that excluding pregnant students or married students is not only a way of educating students in proper behavior but also is needed to avoid disruption and distraction, the courts tend to draw back from second-guessing the school officials.

When courts do step in it appears they do so because they have sensed that an important, even fundamental interest of the students has been affected. Thus, in the Vietnam Moratorium Day case, the court said that giving students the option of staying in school or leaving to participate in various observances forced students to disclose their beliefs on the war, something they should not be forced to do. Similarly, those courts that have stopped districts from forcing students to take courses to which the parents object have done so at least in part on the basis of a parental right to control the education of the child. The slack case noted involved court recognition of unfair or unequal treatment of girls.

Most important for these purposes, courts have been inclined to intervene if they have recognized that a right to get an education has been involved. Thus, those cases barring schools from excluding married students from the regular school program involve this principle. But recognition of a right to an education so as to prevent total exclusion from school is one thing, whereas using such a right as a premise to tackle less coercive school policies, policies that are not tantamount to a form of educational capital punishment, is something else. Yet courts may be getting some encouragement from the state legislatures to intervene in a wider range of discretionary acts on the part of school officials, even with regard to methods of instruction. This can be seen in the laws of California and New York. Not only does the California state constitution require the legislature to encourage by all "suitable means the promotion of intellectual, scientific, moral, and agricultural improvement," but also several California statutes indicate a legislative concern with the adequacy of the programs to be offered with the inclusion of output goals in the statute for the authorized program.[68] Similarly, in New York and North Carolina several state statutes and regulations suggest a state policy of promoting that education which is likely to be effective and of profit to the children.[69] State courts confronted with enactments of this sort may discern nascent legislative support for an output oriented notion of a right to an education, giving the court the political security and intellectual underpinnings to examine actions heretofore deemed wholly within the discretion of local officials, and possibly eventually determining if these actions do in fact promote educational achievement and are rational.

Thus the door may today be slightly ajar to suits claiming an abuse of discretion in the selection of methods of instruction.

Conclusions

Judicial acceptance of the notion of a right to an education means rejection of the older belief that access to the public schools was merely a privilege which the state could extend to whom it wished, in the form it wished, and subject to the conditions it wished to impose. Viewing education as a mere privilege encouraged the courts not to get too deeply involved in reviewing and controlling legislative and school board behavior, but accepting the notion of education as a right encourages a more active judicial role. Furthermore, state courts are likely to be compelled to get more deeply involved in school affairs as state legislatures keep adding new laws to their educational codes—laws that themselves are often vague or ambiguous and that need to be reconciled with the older statutes with which they may conflict and interact. Movement in the states toward holding school districts accountable for output goals also encourages greater judicial involvement. Thus, although state courts have traditionally acted with restraint in the exercise of their powers, we can expect in the future more active involvement of state courts in school affairs generally and in shaping the educational program in particular.

6 Professionals and Their Unions

The legal constraints imposed by the federal and state governments and by the federal and state courts comprise only a portion of the constraints within which the local board must operate when trying to control the local school program. As a practical matter, local boards also lack the time and expertise to get deeply involved in formulating the school program, hence they find they must delegate significant authority to the professionals they employ. Indeed it has become an accepted finding in the literature on school politics that control, at least of the all-important details, of the school curriculum rests in the hands of the professionals, not in those of the board or the community.[1]

During the last dozen years this tendency toward professional take-over of control of the school curriculum has been accelerated by the advent of teachers' collective negotiations. Teachers have pressed at the bargaining table not only for economic concessions but also for concessions directly and indirectly involving the school curriculum. Thus teachers have attempted to force a further reallocation of curricular decision-making authority to the disadvantage of the school board.

The legal question raised by these developments is to what extent does the law either permit or require the local board to give up exclusive control of the school program? (It should be recalled from chapter 4 that the states of Alabama, Arkansas, Oklahoma, and Tennessee require the local school board to establish local textbook selection committees with the power to select books from the list of approved texts. These committees, in Arkansas, Oklahoma, and Tennessee, must be comprised almost exclusively of teachers.) To what extent may local boards delegate their authority to the professionals? Must local boards negotiate with representatives of the teachers over the content of the school program? To what extent does the Constitution protect the academic freedom of teachers to decide what they will teach? These and other related questions will be discussed in this chapter.

The Permissibility of Delegating Authority

The problem of the school board being without the resources—time and expert knowledge—to make curricular decisions is the most important factor in shaping three interrelated developments. First, over time, the domain that is considered to be "basic curriculum policy," which the board says it will keep under its ultimate control, shrinks, and the domain termed "administrative detail," which is in the exclusive discretionary control of the superintendent and staff, increases. Thus, one may find that the selection of most of the instructional materials, perhaps even basic texts, may come to be viewed as an administrative detail within the discretion of the superintendent or even of an assistant superintendent or the principals. Second, over time, the intensity with which the board reviews basic curricular policy recommendations brought to it for final approval may decrease. Thus, the choice of which standardized testing program to use or what method of reading to use in elementary grades may receive only perfunctory review by the board. Only if these decisions become politically controversial is the board likely to examine in any detail the choices made by the superintendent and staff. Third, as time goes on, the superintendent and staff may become more and more cavalier about labeling decisions as administrative details and thereby justifying to themselves not taking the issue to the board for review. They may be encouraged to broaden the definition of what constitutes an administrative detail by the board's already broad definition of the category and by the fact that in their view it matters little whether the board actually formally decides the question, since the board usually merely rubber-stamps their recommendations anyway. Further, the fewer items for decision that have to be taken to the board for approval, the simpler life is for the superintendent and staff. Put more strongly, the natural self-interest of the staff is to avoid the complications involved in seeking board approval for decisions and to increase its autonomy.

But how far, legally, may these developments go? Does the law provide the board with an incentive not to let total control of the curriculum slip into the hands of the staff? Stated differently, may the board leave all curricular decisions to the professionals, or only a portion of those decisions, and if only a portion, which portion?

To answer these questions it is necessary to turn to that not very well developed body of law dealing with the subdelegation of authority. (The subdelegation of authority may involve constitutional issues but this is rare.) Subdelegation is a term used to distinguish grants of authority to subordinates by a board which was the initial recipient of delegated authority. Thus the school board obtains delegated authority from the legislature and it in turn subdelegates authority to its staff. The basic legal question is whether the legislature authorized the school board to subdelegate its decisions; unless the legislature delegated the authority to subdelegate, the school board is without the power to do so. It is basically a question of statutory interpretation. Subdelegations of authority not authorized by the legislature are *ultra vires*.

Deciding whether a school board has the authority to subdelegate is of course an easy matter when the statutes specifically authorize the subdelegation of authority, as does the California Education Code.[2] Similarly the problems of interpretation are lessened when the educational code spells out how authority is to be shared between the board and the staff. For example, the New York code tells us that it is the local superintendent who is to prepare the content of each course of study to be submitted to the board for approval and to recommend suitable textbooks.[3] Here it has been made clear that ultimate control must remain with the board itself. And statutes that impose upon teachers the duty to carry out the approved course of study or to use only approved textbooks also strongly suggest that ultimate control of the curriculum must be at least shared with the board, if not totally under board control.[4]

But when the legislation is ambiguous or silent, deciding how far the board may go in subdelegating its authority becomes more difficult. For example, a statute that authorizes a local board to determine the duties of district employees may or may not be read as an authorization to the board to subdelegate. Or a provision that grants the local board the authority to make all rules necessary to carry out the powers granted to it may or may not be read as permitting the subdelegation of authority.[5]

How the courts might actually interpret these provisions depends of course upon the language of the statutes and their legislative history. Beyond this the courts have said that general grants of authority to officials carry with them the implied authority to employ persons to do work of a clerical or ministerial nature, but not to delegate to these people true discretionary power.[6] How a court responds to a subdelegation of power is also likely to be affected by whether the power can be used to affect important interests of third parties.[7] Other courts have upheld the subdelegation of even discretionary power if the delegation was accompanied by a specification of the standards to be followed. Thus in a New York case the Board of Education authorized principals to assign teachers to "reasonable amounts of" extracurricular duties beyond their responsibilities in the classroom.[8] Principals were also instructed to make sure, as far as practicable, the assignments were equitably distributed. Records of these assignments were to be kept by the principal and, if a teacher felt unfairly treated, he or she could appeal to the assistant superintendent. The court found that these arrangements provided adequate safeguards for the teachers. In sum, the recent trend of cases has been such that courts have tended to uphold subdelegations of authority. They seem to be adopting the advice of commentators who have advocated that subdelegation ought to be permitted when it contributes to the workability of a program. Not to allow the subdelegation of authority could severely cripple the operation of most modern agencies of government, including the schools.

The law of subdelegation of authority thus today does not stand as a major obstacle to increased control of the curriculum by the professional staff. Statutes either explicitly permit such delegations of authority or they have been interpreted by the courts to allow the subdelegation of authority.

The Academic Freedom of Teachers

The other side of the legal coin entails the question of whether local boards must permit teachers to exercise substantial control over what is taught in the classroom because the Constitution bars strong board control of what teachers teach. That is, does the Constitution itself allocate authority to control the curriculum between, on the one hand, the state and local board, and, on the other hand, the teacher, by protecting the teachers' right to academic freedom? The answer to the question is complex and requires that distinctions be made between (1) the rights teachers enjoy as citizens which they may not be asked to forego upon becoming a teacher; (2) the rights of teachers not to be discriminated against on the basis of their political viewpoint; (3) the rights of teachers to control what is presented to students in the classroom; and (4) the procedural due process rights of teachers.

1. The Teacher as Citizen. Upon being hired by the public schools, teachers do not forego outside the classroom the free speech rights they enjoy as citizens; they may publicly criticize the policies of the school district for which they work on matters of public importance if they rely on information generally available to the public and if they do not receive the information on which they base their criticism solely in their capacity as a school employee, and if criticizing the schools does not disrupt their working relationship with their immediate superiors, and if they do not maliciously and untruthfully attack the school district.[9] Additionally, teachers may participate in civil rights demonstrations directed against their own school district, may refuse to disclose the organizations to which they belong, and refuse to reveal their political beliefs to legislative investigative committees.[10] Teachers also need not sign loyalty oaths which have the effect of making them foreswear free speech rights protected by the Constitution.[11] Outside the classroom, teachers, in short, must be allowed to exercise the rights other citizens enjoy.

2. Discrimination on the Basis of Political Viewpoint. Related to these protections is the right of teachers not to be denied (re)employment because of official hostility toward the political viewpoint of the teacher.[12] Discrimination on such a basis would both infringe upon the right of the teacher to speak out and to hold his or her own beliefs and infringe upon his or her interest in not being discriminated against. This kind of discrimination involves serious questions of equal protection in the sensitive area of free expression.[13] Schools may not attempt to keep the curriculum ideologically pure by hiring only those teachers with whom the majority of the school board agrees politically.[14] The board must use other methods of making sure the instructional program carries the messages it prefers to be communicated.

3. Teachers' Rights in the Classroom. Given that teachers may not be excluded from employment on the basis of political viewpoint alone, how far may they go in the classroom? Here the protection afforded teachers begins to lessen. The few cases that have been litigated on the issue support the proposition that while teachers may be free to interject a personal comment into the classroom discussion, or to introduce nonharmful (for example, nonobscene) supplementary materials into the classroom, they do not have the right to pursue their own notion of an educational program when it is in conflict with the prescribed program adopted by the board.

Several cases illustrate this general rule. In one case the teacher converted a high school consumer economics course into a course on political action in which the students learned about school politics by drafting a proposed disciplinary code for the school.[15] The dismissal of the teacher was upheld despite her claim of academic freedom. The dismissal of a college teacher who converted a health course into a sex education course was also sustained.[16] In another college case, where one might have thought the doctrine of academic freedom would have particularly strong protection, the teacher instead of offering students a fundamental survey course in drama covering twenty to twenty-five plays, offered a more complex course which covered only eleven plays and which was designed, in the words of the teacher, to "teach her students how to think".[17] The teacher argued that the First Amendment protected her use of teaching methods and philosophy of education, both of which were well recognized in the profession. The court said, however, that the teacher was attempting to substitute the First Amendment for tenure, and that the notion of academic freedom did not insulate a teacher from review just because the teaching methods used were considered acceptable elsewhere within the teaching profession.

The courts have, however, protected teachers when they merely introduced some nonshocking and nonobscene supplementary materials into the classroom or injected their own personal comments into the classroom. That is, protection is afforded teachers when they have not in effect argued that they had a right to control the total curriculum at taxpayer expense even when the supporting citizenry finds the teacher's version of the program objectionable. Thus teachers have been given judicial protection from dismissal for merely having students read a novel with explicit sexual words and scenes or a magazine article that analyzed the use of the word *mother-fucker* in youth culture.[18] In another case a teacher was dismissed for refusing to comply with school demands which followed parental complaints about the classroom discussion, teaching, materials, and examination methods used by the teacher in a six-day unit on race relations.[19] The court approached the case by noting that a balance needed to be struck between appropriate limits on and rigid regulation of the teacher. The court used several standards of review in reaching a decision; it inquired into any disruption or indoctrination that may have occurred and into the acceptability according to professional standards of the methods used. The court concluded that since the teacher had satisfied all these standards there was no basis for the board's restrictions, that a responsible teacher must have freedom to use the tools of his or her profession as he or she sees fit. If the teacher cannot be trusted to use these tools fairly, he or she should never have been employed in the first place. Finally, as discussed in chapter 2, teachers have been protected from dismissal for wearing black armbands to school in protest against the Vietnam War and for refusing to participate in the flag salute ceremony. If those teachers had materially and substantially disrupted their classrooms, however, the cases would have come out differently.

In sum, the extent to which teachers must be left alone by their school boards can be summarized by the following propositions. (a) A school board is justified in restricting and penalizing a teacher if that teacher ignores or subverts the basic course of study adopted by the board. When teachers introduce supplementary materials into the classroom of their own choosing, a school board is justified in disciplining the teacher if the teacher: (b) materially and substantially disrupted the classroom; (c) introduced obscene materials; (d) used offensive words or materials; (e) engaged in unacceptable indoctrination (see chap. 2); or (f) used teaching methods that were not professionally approved or acceptable.

4. Procedural Due Process Rights. Procedural due process rights protect a teacher from disciplinary action by the board when the teacher was not given fair warning or notice that the activity in which he or she had been engaged was prohibited by school rules or policy. Thus, several of the cases may be read to rest on the proposition that it is unfair to punish someone for actions that were not a punishable offense at the time of the action.[20] For example, it would be improper to dismiss a teacher for having the students read an article with the word "fuck" in the article if there were no school rule prohibiting such an assignment and especially if the school library contained books and magazines using this word: given these circumstances the teacher could fairly conclude use of the article was not contrary to any school rule or policy.

The effect of such a doctrine of fair notice is to leave teachers free to engage in a variety of teaching activities: the silence of the school board may be construed as a practical matter as the delegation of authority to the teacher to control the details of the curriculum in his classroom. Such a conclusion is consistent with another proposition supported by state cases that in the absence of a board rule on the subject, teachers by implication have the delegated authority to issue their own reasonable rules governing student behavior—these teacher initiated rules are valid unless they conflict with state statutes or other rules of the board. In short, unless the board actually does control the school curriculum, teachers are left free to make the decisions for themselves and may not be punished after the fact for making a choice the board decides it does not like.

In sum, the doctrine of academic freedom of teachers does not force the board to leave significant control of the curriculum in the hands of teachers. Boards may impose their own program and require teachers to teach that program. At the margins, however, teachers are free to introduce supplementary materials and comments and if the board does not act, does not preempt the control of the school curriculum, then teachers have the right to fill in the vacuum and make their own decisions.

Teachers' Unions and Control of the Curriculum

With the advent of collective bargaining, teachers have attempted to force boards to share the power to decide what is to be taught, what goes into the schools' programs.[21] This development must be seen in light of the discussion in the first part of the chapter on the natural tendency of the board to give up control of the curriculum to the superintendent and his staff. Indeed, the primary loser in this ongoing struggle over who will control the school curriculum may very well be not the board, but the superintendent, for boards have traditionally relied on the superintendent to see to the school's program design and development.

The central legal question raised by these developments of the last dozen years is whether under state law school boards may refuse to bargain over these curriculum-related demands of teachers' unions and whether boards may bargain over these demands if they want to. And, second, we need to ask what in fact has been the response of school boards in the face of teacher demands to negotiate over the curriculum? But first we turn to a discussion of the policy considerations that shape the legal definition of the scope of negotiations.

1. The Public Interest and the Scope of Negotiations. We begin by distinguishing among the concepts of mandatory subjects of negotiation, permissive subjects, and illegal subjects.[22] Those items that are mandatory subjects of negotiation are those about which the parties must bargain in good faith if one party or the other places a demand on the table—refusal to bargain over the subject constitutes an improper or unfair practice. Furthermore, with regard to mandatory subjects, a party may insist upon agreement on that subject as a condition of an agreement. Mandatory subjects also define those areas on which the employer may not take unilateral action and on which he may not negotiate with individual employees. Permissive subjects are those that may be negotiated if the parties agree to bargain over the subject. Refusal to bargain over a permissive subject as a condition of an agreement is an unfair labor practice tantamount to refusing to bargain on mandatory subjects. Illegal subjects, as the term suggests, are those that the local board is precluded by the U.S. or state constitution or by state or federal law from bargaining over.

Given these definitions we find, not surprisingly, that teachers' associations, and their spokespeople, tend to favor a definition of mandatory subjects of negotiations which is so broad as to encompass any possible subject which either party may want to negotiate over; hence the category of permissive subjects is eliminated and the category of illegal subjects narrowly defined. For example, it is possible to find statements coming from these groups saying such matters as the curriculum, textbooks, extracurricular activities, and class size should all be subject to collective bargaining.[23] Other labor leaders have stated their position to be that "We are seeking no more control over school operations than doctors have over the administration of hospitals."[24] But in a recent statement before the Senate Subcommittee on Labor, Albert Shanker, President of the American Federation of Teachers, seemed to take a somewhat more moderate position:

We have serious reservations about all matters of public policy being subject to collective bargaining. Rather, we think there is a very fine balance between what should be decided in a democracy by the electorate and its representatives and what should be determined by collective bargaining. That which goes beyond should not.

Taking education as a case in point, all conditions of employment should be negotiable. But we should be very uneasy about a situation where collective bargaining could mandate an entire curriculum, for example, and that being voted by 51 percent of the teachers. In other words, insuring meaningful teacher involvement *in the procedures* for deciding such question as textbooks and whether or not there should be homogeneous or heterogeneous groupings is a condition of employment and should be subject to collective bargaining. It would not be good public policy in our view to make the *final* decisions on these matters subject to collective bargaining. (Emphasis added.)[25]

The rationale for a broad definition of negotiable subjects rests on several propositions. First, teachers are the experts with regard to curriculum and ought to be allowed to bargain over the question. Second, it is unproductive for the board to refuse to talk about a subject altogether. A better public service will emerge from discussion, rather than no discussion of the issues. Both sides are educated in the course of negotiations and the result may be a more intelligent and rational decision in the public interest. Third, the broader the range of issues teachers are allowed to bargain over and gain a voice in, the greater will be the job satisfaction of the teachers, the more attractive will teaching be to qualified people, the more people will seek teaching positions, the lower the wage demands as a result of increased competitions for jobs, and the higher the quality of the service provided. Fourth, there is no clear line which can be drawn to distinguish between subjects that are truly "conditions of employment" versus those that are a "management prerogative" or a public policy issue. All aspects of the operation of schools tend to affect each other and are so highly interrelated that they all ought to be on the table. Fifth, everything that goes on in a school directly affects teachers and their terms and conditions of employment; teachers have a right to make demands on all these subjects, demands to which the board must respond. To legally narrow the scope of negotiations is to violate the right of teachers to join unions and to bargain with their employer.[26]

While teachers and their representatives talk in terms of their rights to bargain, others have been concerned with the erosion of public control of public services, with the erosion of governmental sovereignty, with the preservation of managerial prerogatives, with retaining exclusive control in the hands of the public and board control of those matters which go to the heart of the basic mission of the schools.[27] Obviously, this line of thought, when taken to the extreme, leads to the conclusion that virtually no subject is a mandatory topic of negotiation, that there should be no collective negotiations. Those dissatisfied with this kind of rhetorical approach, but who do not accept the teachers' position, have cast about for another approach which would be more useful in drawing a line between mandatory, permissive, and illegal subjects of negotiations.

The current position of the American Association of School Administrators on the scope of negotiations seems to be that salary schedules, hospitalization benefits, reduced class size, compensation for committee work, duty-free lunch periods, and terminal leave pay are the kinds of subjects that should be negotiated. Teachers should be involved through committees on an advisory basis in, among other things, textbook selection and curriculum development. Similarly, the National Association of Secondary School Principals would exclude policy from the bargaining table, preferring to have teacher involvement on such issues as the curriculum through formal councils made up of representatives chosen by teachers, principals, and supervisors.[28]

Professor Clyde Summers approaches the problem from a political perspective.[29] Summers argues that on most issues, especially economic issues, the public employee is politically disadvantaged, absent collective negotiations, in the face of powerful, active, and effective interest groups concerned with the rising cost of government. Hence to rectify the political imbalance, teachers, as well as other public employees, are given the special advantage, vis-à-vis the other interest groups, of exclusive bargaining with the local board. Thus, Summers's general rule seems to be that if the topic is one on which public employees are likely to be outgunned in the political process, it should be made a subject of negotiations. And then he adds a further proviso: the scope of bargaining should be affected by whether or not the employees have the right to strike; if the right to strike is available, then deciding whether a topic is within the scope of bargaining should be based on whether the given topic is amenable to being decided through the play of sheer power. As for making the curriculum a subject of negotiations, Summers, in applying his approach, concludes it should not be. On this topic the union faces no organized, powerful interest groups from which they need special protection, and, in any event, the curriculum is a subject of interest to more than just the school board and teachers; it is also of interest to parents and students who have no representation at the bargaining table. Bargaining between only two parties over the curriculum does not allow for an airing of enough viewpoints and the issue may not be settled with the best interests of the parents and children in mind, but as part of a package agreement in which many items are traded off for other items. Thus, the board might simply give in on the curriculum issue (not because it agreed with the union) as part of a deal in which teachers lowered their demands in another area. The curriculum, Summers seems to be saying, is too important to be decided this way. He would, however, let unions demand that they be consulted on curriculum decisions.

Unlike Summers, Harry Wellington and Ralph Winter assume that public employees are among the most powerful interest groups, even with regard to economic issues, and that giving this group the power to bargain collectively runs an enormous danger of distorting the normal political process for controlling public policy unless that bargaining relationship is carefully controlled.[30]

The basis of the power of the public sector unions is the fact that they are organized and active; public officials are often anxious to avoid the disruption of public services; public officials have an incentive to give away much to unions to gain their political support at election time, especially when much of what is given away may be unknown to the public or only have economic and political implications long after these particular officials have left office; and the fact that other political groups are often not as organized and have fewer political resources than the unions. Thus, given the power of the unions, to broadly define the scope of negotiations runs the risk of permitting unions to determine the nature and quality of the public service to be offered, an issue of great concern to the community at large and especially to parents in the case of public education. Thus, Wellington and Winter seem to argue for excluding from the scope of negotiations such sensitive issues as the curriculum or, in the alternative, establishing one of three kinds of mechanisms to alleviate the problems involved with a broadly defined notion of scope: (a) decentralizing school districts and providing for multiparty bargaining (for example, school officials, union, parents) at the building level on such subjects as the curriculum; or (b) allowing intervention into negotiations of third parties upon the petition of a certain number of citizens and/or holding a public referendum on controversial portions of the final agreement; or (c) establishing commissions which are to recommend to the legislature from time to time special enactments permitting bargaining with respect to specific matters so that in this way the scope of bargaining will be shaped by the interaction of many competing interest groups.

A third approach to defining the scope of negotiations is less overtly political than either the approach of Summers or Wellington and Winter. This approach stresses a host of factors that should be considered in deciding what the scope of negotiations should be and whether a particular item should or should not be within the scope of negotiations.

Thus, in deciding whether a particular issue should be the subject of negotiations, the agency or court charged with deciding the question should ask (a) whether it is a subject likely to cause conflict, (b) whether it is susceptible of resolution by bargaining; (c) whether past practice indicates that other parties have successfully negotiated such an item; (d) whether the union through the bargaining process could contribute to the solution of the particular problem faced by the employer; (e) whether the issue is of vital concern to the employees; and (f) whether the subject is within the core of entrepreneurial control or rather so sensitive and affected with the public interest that it ought not to be a subject of bargaining.[31]

Finally, Derek Bok and John Dunlop offer an argument related to the third approach.[32] They argue that the scope of bargaining will in the end be influenced by the procedures adopted to resolve impasses in negotiations. If strikes by public employees are permitted, they argue, the scope of negotiations should be narrowed as the pressure exerted in the form of disruption of public services is too haphazard a method for deciding issues that affect the public such as the initiation or discontinuance of gov-

ernmental services. But if the strike is illegal and impasses are to be resolved by the more reasoned processes of fact finding and arbitration,
then the scope of negotiations may be somewhat broader. Even in this
case, however, there will be subjects excluded from negotiations on the
ground that they are a managerial prerogative or that they should be settled through the political process. Last, if impasses are to be resolved neither by strikes nor arbitration but by ultimate disposition by a legislative
body, for example, the school board, then the scope of negotiations may
be quite broad. (Before New York's collective bargaining law was amended, impasses that could not be resolved by either mediation or fact finding
were to be settled by a legislative body which in the case of schools meant
the school board. Naturally unions found this arrangement abhorrent as it
encouraged boards not to reach agreement and simply to impose a solution once all the other steps of the negotiation processes were exhuasted.
Today negotiations must continue, indefinitely if necessary.)

In sum, the commentators reviewed here take different positions as to
whether the following items ought to be mandatory subjects of negotiations: (a) the purposes of the instructional program; the courses to be offered; the methods of instruction; the textbooks and other materials to be
used; the doctrinal bias of the courses to be taught; the sequence in the
curriculum; the evaluation of the school program; the audiovisual equipment to be used and made available; the use of multiethnic materials; experimental programs and demonstration projects and schools; the availability of compensatory programs and other special services; the scheduling of classes; the organization of the grade structure; graduation requirements; the grouping and classification of pupils; report cards and grading
of pupils; the use of educational technology such as computer assisted instruction; the choice of extracurricular activities; the evaluation of pupils
with standardized tests; book selection for the school library; student discipline; and academic freedom. There are other topics that have a direct
bearing on the program to be offered in the schools which, it appears all
commentators would agree, should be a subject of negotiations: (b) procedures and standards for promotion and dismissal of teachers; compensation for curriculum development work done during the summer or after
school; in-service training requirements and compensation therefor; the
number of contact hours and work load; the number of teacher preparation hours a week; relief from nonteaching duties; sabbatical leave; and
professional meeting released time. It is less clear how the different commentators reviewed here would react to making the following issues mandatory subjects of negotiations: class size; the school calendar; the length
of class periods; the hiring of additional personnel such as special teachers and supplementary personnel; the definition of the jobs of department
heads; the creation of curriculum committees to advise on curricular poli-

cy; the transfer and assignment of teachers; and the involvement of parents in curricular decision making.

2. The Law and Scope of Negotiations. Legislatures in almost all states have avoided taking a stand on the question of whether the curriculum and related issues are mandatory subjects of negotiations. The typical collective negotiations statute found in the roughly thirty states with collective negotiations laws defines the scope of negotiations simply as "wages, hours, and other conditions of employment," leaving the courts and administrative agencies to settle the question of whether the curriculum falls within those terms.[33] Other state statutes are equally unhelpful. Alaska's law talks in terms of "matters pertaining to their certified employees' employment and the fulfillment of their professional duties".[24] Massachusetts makes wages, hours, and standards of productivity and performance mandatory subjects.[35] Other states establish long lists of management rights that may not be bargained away, for example, "determining the methods and means by which governmental operations are to be conducted."[36] Two states, however—California and Maine—address the problem.[37] For example, California requires negotiations over wages, hours of employment, and other "terms and conditions of employment."[38] "Terms and conditions of employment" is defined to include leave and transfer policies, safety conditions, class size, and procedures to be used for evaluation of employees.[39] Employees are given only the right to confer but not negotiate with the school board over the definition of educational objectives, the determination of the content of courses and curriculum, and the selection of textbooks.[40]

Thus, for the most part, the statutes are of little help in finding the law on the scope of negotiations. When we turn to the opinions of courts and state boards established to administer the state collective negotiation acts we find that an initial problem with which the courts wrestle is whether or not the legislature in defining the scope of negotiations intended the statute to be read expansively. The courts in various states have decided this question differently, with the Court of Appeals in New York taking an expansive approach and the New Jersey Supreme Court deciding differently.[41] But regardless of how the state courts have interpreted their state statutes, at least with regard to the question of whether the curriculum is a mandatory subject of negotiations, all states have said that it is not, apparently because they view the curriculum as a question of policy without significant implications for the working conditions of the teachers. (Not all the issues listed earlier have been specifically decided upon by the courts and public employment boards charged with administering the states' collective negotiations statutes. Also, one study concluded that Michigan has made the selection of textbooks a mandatory subject of negotiations, and that Wisconsin and Nevada have made methods for disciplining pupils mandatory subjects of negotiations. But that same study also concluded that Wisconsin has made the mission and purpose of the schools an impermissible subject of negotiations.[42]

It is interesting to note in this connection that the states have split over whether class size should be a mandatory subject of negotiations. Class size is one of those subjects that can be viewed as both a curricular issue and an issue involving the working conditions of the employees. In states where the courts and public employment boards have found class size to be a mandatory subject of negotiations, the courts have stressed that class size affects the amount of work expected of teachers.[43] In those states where class size was ruled to be only a permissive subject, the policy aspect of the issue was stressed.[44] But even where, as in New York, class size per se is only a permissive subject of negotiations, the impact of class size on working conditions remains a mandatory subject of negotiations.[45] This ruling has the effect of making class size, as a practical matter, a mandatory subject of negotiations, as the following example illustrates: teachers can force a lowering of class size by insisting on bargaining over the work load; the board, in agreeing to a limit on the work load, may, as a practical matter, have to lower class size.

While the states have not made the curriculum a mandatory subject of negotiations, it appears that most states which have decided the question have left the curriculum as a permissive subject, with Wisconsin being a possible exception to the rule.[46] But even as a permissive subject of negotiations there are limits with regard to what the local boards may agree to beyond which they may not go. One possible limitation that boards and unions may face is the law on the subdelegation of authority discussed earlier. Contract negotiations which end in an agreement delegating substantial powers to teachers to control the curriculum may be *ultra vires* if the local board lacks the statutory authority to subdelegate. However, this limitation is not likely to prove to be important, since it seems likely that the very fact that boards have been given the authority to negotiate with teachers' unions may be read as an implied grant to subdelegate authority pursuant to a collective agreement. This conclusion is probably especially true for those states such as New York in which the courts have said the collective negotiations statutes must be broadly construed. Yet even in New York a board that agreed with a union not merely to subdelegate but to give away its entire authority over the curriculum might very well find that such an agreement would be *ultra vires*.

In New Jersey, however, where the courts have tended to narrowly construe the collective negotiations law, a collective agreement provision dealing with the academic freedom of teachers was struck down as *ultra vires*.[47] The provision in question provided:

The Board and the Association agree that academic freedom is essential to the fulfillment of the purposes of the Rockaway Township School District. Free discussion of controversial issues is the heart of the democratic process. Through the study of such issues, political, economic, or social, youth develops those abilities needed for functional citizenship in our democracy. *Whenever appropriate for the maturation level of the group*, controversial issues may be studied in an unprejudiced and dispassionate manner. It shall be the duty of the teacher to foster the study of an issue and not to teach a particular viewpoint in regard to it. [Emphasis added by the court.][48]

Pursuant to this provision, a seventh-grade teacher announced a debate in his class on the subject of abortion. The local superintendent ordered the teacher not to carry out the debate, apparently because he felt the subject was not appropriate for eleven- and twelve-year-old children. The teacher and teachers' association claimed the provision quoted had been violated and sought to have the issue processed as a grievance. The board went to court to seek an injunction to stop the union from prosecuting its complaint as a grievance and to force the issue to be decided by the state commissioner of education. The union counterclaimed, seeking specific enforcement of the arbitration provisions of the contract.

In reaching a decision the court never got to the question of the appropriate interpretation of the contract as it focused on the issue whether the quoted contract provision was itself *ultra vires* and unenforceable. To reach a decision the court took note of the fact that the collective negotiations law in New Jersey specifically said that it was designed *not* to modify any other statute of the state. The relevant other statute was one giving the local board the obligation to provide courses of study suited to the ages and attainments of all pupils. This authority said the court was not affected by the collective negotiations law, could not be delegated or given away, hence the quoted contract provision was *ultra vires*.

Whether other state courts would view a similar contractual provision as exceeding local board authority to subdelegate its power is hard to say. The New Jersey court apparently read the contractual agreement for all it was worth, seeing in it a broad grant of authority to teachers to totally control what was to be taught in the classroom. But the provision could also have been read more narrowly to mean that teachers could supplement the basic curriculum by bringing into class from time to time controversial topics for classroom discussion. Those courts that choose the broader interpretation are more likely to conclude with the New Jersey court that the provision is *ultra vires*.

The dangers that a school board can run into in agreeing on substantive curriculum policy are evidenced by another case. In *Nickels* v. *Board of Education of Imlay City Community Schools,* a local of the AFT sought enforcement of a contract provision requiring the board to take advantage of federal funds available for special and remedial programs.[49] The court found that the local board had in fact contracted to apply for federal funds for a Head Start program and that the decision of whether to start up a Head Start program was a policy matter which the local board had the duty of maintaining under its own discretion and on which it could not bind itself. The court quoted with approval language from another case which said in effect the local board may not abdicate its legislative powers which were given to the local board to be exercised as needed and were not to be straitjacketed by collective bargaining agreements. It was not the intent of the legislature in adopting the collective bargaining law to authorize this kind of self-limitation of authority.

While this court barred negotiations on the curriculum as such, we do find that all states are in agreement that the "impact" of curricular changes must be negotiated if the union so demands.[50] For example, if a new curriculum increases the workload of teachers by increasing the pupil-teacher ratio, that increased workload is a mandatory subject of negotiations. This proviso with regard to the impact of curriculum changes may mean that at least indirectly the curriculum of the public schools is in fact a mandatory subject of negotiations.

Indeed there are many topics that have a direct bearing on how teachers carry out their jobs—how they teach and what is taught the pupils—that are mandatory subjects of negotiation, most notably, the standards and procedures for evaluating teachers and deciding whether to promote or to dismiss (refuse to renew their contracts). Also, whether teachers are to be required to engage in after-school or summer curriculum development sessions, and how much they are to be paid for these services, are mandatory subjects of negotiations. Requiring teachers to engage in in-service training after school hours and perhaps even during school hours also is a mandatory subject in those states which have decided the issue. Rules and regulations with regard to teachers' powers and duties are mandatory subjects, but job assignment and transfer policies have been deemed to be only permissible subjects.[51] The point is, however, there are enough mandatory subjects which have such a direct bearing on what kind of program can be mounted in the public schools that the decisions which exclude the curriculum as a mandatory subject may have less practical import than first appears. Nevertheless it is probably significant that school boards do not have to negotiate, for example, whether art classes will be offered in the school or which textbooks espousing what viewpoint will be adopted. But whether or not boards can make their legal rights stick in the face of strong unions is another question.

3. The Scope of Negotiations in Practice. Assessments of actual collective bargaining contracts have determined that it is common for school districts to negotiate over and agree upon the procedures to be followed by the district in developing and changing the curriculum as well as in selecting the textbooks to be used. Of 978 agreements in effect during the 1968-69 school year, examinations by the National Educational Association show that about 54 percent had provisions dealing with curriculum review and textbook selection. The agreements ranged in specificity and detail but it was common for them at least to establish the committees to be involved, the membership, and responsibilities. The powers of these committees were typically advisory but they did tend to assure teachers of involvement in the curricular decision-making process. Some agreements went so far as to guarantee teachers of notification before any textbooks were changed and the right to meet and discuss these changes with the administration.[52]

A review of the same set of contracts also revealed that roughly 3 percent of these contracts contained provisions relating to pupil testing procedures and programs. These provisions touched upon the testing schedule, the scoring and grading of the tests, the type of tests to be administered, the testing of pupils for purposes of special placement, the review and revision of tests so as to eliminate cultural bias, and, in two contracts, guidelines for interpreting and utilizing the test results were included.

Another study conducted for the National School Boards Association of twenty-eight school districts located throughout the country also revealed the extent to which the curriculum and related topics were included in the contracts. What was found was that all the contracts assessed contained provisions dealing with at least some of the items listed earlier in this chapter. For example, 75 percent of the contracts looked at contained provisions dealing with course content, curriculum change procedures, program development procedures, curriculum committees, curriculum guides, and the evaluation of the curriculum. For another example, 93 percent of the contracts had a provision dealing with some or all of the following items: audiovisual materials, instructional materials, textbook selection, teaching machines, school libraries, materials centers, and other items related to school materials. It was also found, through a questionnaire administered to school board members from these districts, that only on three items did a majority of the board members agree the subject was a "board prerogative": school goals, the setting up of special programs, for example, programs for the handicapped, and the use of multiethnic materials. On all other curricular related items, the board members either said the issue was one that was clearly negotiable or ought to be handled by the administrative staff.[53]

What, more specifically, are the kinds of provisions affecting the curriculum which boards and teachers' unions agree upon? Another study examined collective negotiations contracts from California and New York and made some interesting findings. First, one kind of clause commonly found was one that guaranteed teachers a right to participate in curriculum development matters. Such a provision might simply state that the board and teachers must discuss curricular changes or must work together in developing the school program. Second, another type of common clause addressed itself to the actual committee structure and process for curriculum development. While the typical such clause provided for the creation of committees with both teachers and administrators represented, and with only advisory power, other clauses went further. One clause creating a curriculum committee guaranteed the committee the right to report directly to the school board. Another stated that all curriculum innovation had to be initiated by the committee created by the contract. Another clause assured teachers of the primary voice in curriculum development. Other clauses required the board to show all proposed curricular changes to the teachers' negotiating council before adoption. As for selecting textbooks, various clauses required teachers to be consulted, or actually made text selection primarily the teachers' function.[54] In sum, the contractual agreement between teachers and the local board has become a kind of constitution allocating authority to control the school program.

Finally, we might take note of what can happen in a school district when the board resists negotiating over the curriculum but is faced with a powerful teachers' union that insists upon placing the question on the table. The story begins in 1963 in New York City with a union demand during negotiations for the improvement of "difficult" schools. The union wanted agreement on a plan involving experimental educational policies in schools in low-income areas. The plan included the selection of teachers, principals, and superintendents, with the advice and consent of the union, and joint administration of the pilot schools. The school district charged the union was trying to take over the administration of the schools. The dispute was settled when the union and district agreed to meet and consult once a month during the school year "on matters of educational policy and development."

One of the products of these consultations was the "More Effective Schools Plan" (MES)—a kind of compensatory education program introduced in twenty-one schools. MES, more specifically, involved reduced class size, small group instruction, increased funds for materials and supplies, and frequent consultation between teachers and administrators on teaching and supervision goals and techniques. The target schools also got extra personnel in the form of psychologists, social workers, attendance teachers, speech therapists and community coordinators. Teachers received more preparation periods, release from secretarial tasks and nonteaching duties, and the right to hold conferences during school hours.

During negotiations for the next contract the union demanded that MES be extended to all elementary schools in a ghetto or disadvantaged area of the city. The union also wanted contractual guarantees that MES would not be modified without union concurrence. Again the school board viewed these demands as an intrusion into an area of educational policymaking. The issue was resolved by once again incorporating language in the preamble to the agreement. The board agreed to continue various experimental programs, including MES, and to put aside $10 million for the 1968-69 school years for the development of more new programs. A group to be headed by an outside educator selected by the superintendent and composed of representatives of the union, board, and parents or community groups would make recommendations to the board and superintendent for use of the money. At least half the money was to be used for programs for the reorganization and improvement of yet other schools.[55]

Conclusions

The combined pressure of administrative necessity and union demands already have reallocated power at the local district level so that with regard to the curriculum the employees of the system are the most influential parties in making curriculum policy. All indications are that union pressure to include the curriculum as a subject of negotiations will continue, and as we have seen the law provides but a weak barrier to these trends. While school boards do have the right not to negotiate over the curriculum, they may do so if they wish in most states. In the face of strong unions, schools have negotiated, at least, over the allocation of authority as to who will control the curriculum at the local level. Only if state law were amended to make the curriculum an impermissible subject of negotiations does it appear that these trends could be aborted. All of this means not only that school boards and superintendents have lost the power to act unilaterally with regard to the curriculum, but also that parents are further excluded from a meaningful voice in shaping the program to which their children are exposed. The precise scope of parents' rights with regard to the education of their children is taken up in the next two chapters.

7

The Public and Parents

School district employees are not the only ones interested in obtaining greater influence over the school program. Political organizations, church affiliated groups, community organizations, and parents have also showed a strong interest in controlling the program of the schools. Sometimes this results in conflict, such as arguments over the availability or lack of availability of a particular book in the school library. At other times a dispute may arise over the adoption of a particular course, such as a sex education course, or, more recently, a course using the NSF-funded project, *Man: A Course of Study*. In other places conflict has arisen over the propriety of the system of textbooks adopted by the school board, as in Kanawaha County, West Virginia, where parents and churches launched massive demonstrations and protests to get the school board to revoke its adoption of textbooks claimed to be un-Christian.

These kinds of conflicts raise the question of the authority of citizens generally and parents in particular to control or influence the program to which children are exposed. The chapter begins with an assessment of citizens' rights and then turns to a more detailed analysis of the rights of parents to determine the course offerings, to select materials and books, to give advice, and, participate in curricular decision making, to remove the child from a particular course, to participate in the classification of the child, and to advise the school district formally.

Citizens and the School Board

The authority delegated to local boards by the state legislature to control the program may not be given away by the local board to the public by, for example, agreeing beforehand to abide by the results of public referenda on the important issues before the board.[1] Indeed, the public does not even enjoy a constitutional right to be present when the school board reaches decisions.[2] Even if the public is present it does not have a right to participate in the deliberations of the school board. Direct public participation in the deliberations of legislative bodies is not a right. Excluding the public from any but an observer's role is rationalized in terms of efficiency of the deliberative process and on the grounds that presumably the deliberative body is representative of the public, is open to indirect pressure, and is ultimately accountable to the public through the election process.[3]

What rights, then, does the public enjoy with regard to the school board? Most important is the right to vote either for the board members themselves or for the official, such as the mayor, who appoints the board members. The right to vote is fundamental and may not be denied segments of the local population unless the state has a compelling justification for doing so.[4] But the right to vote has meant little to minority populations, which rarely are able to obtain representation on the school board.[5] And the persistent denial of, for example, black representation on the school board remains constitutional as long as blacks have not also been systematically excluded from participation in the informal political processes that select candidates for public office in the local district, and as long as the district's boundary lines were not deliberately redrawn to dilute the black vote of the district, in an attempt to assure continued denial of representation on the local board.[6] In this regard, it is interesting to note that the law decentralizing New York City's school system requires that the election of the local or community boards of education be carried out by an election procedure called Proportional Representation which is designed to assure minority representation on the local boards.[7] One result of this law has been that in communities with significant numbers of whites, blacks, and Puerto Ricans, all three groups have gained representation on the local board with the result that conflict has emerged over priorities for the local school program: The Puerto Rican representatives are interested in pushing bilingual education whereas, for example, the black representatives are interested in other curricular priorities.[8]

Beyond the right to vote are other legal protections for citizens—other devices that help to maintain the board's accountability to the public. Of great importance are those state statutes that require the board to hold a certain number of public meetings and that require official action to be taken only in public meetings whose deliberations the public may attend. Prohibitions against the taking of formal action in executive sessions, where such sessions are allowed, also help to promote accountability.[9]

Of growing importance is that body of law dealing with public access to government information. New York, for example, has adopted a freedom of information law which requires school districts to make available for inspection and copying statements of policy adopted by the board, minutes of board meetings, materials constituting statistical or factual tabulations that led to policy decisions, internal audits or factual tabulations made by or for the board, administrative staff manuals, and instructions to staff that affect members of the public.[10] This listing of public information touches upon many matters of relevance to control of the school program; for example, test results, studies affecting the adoption of curriculum programs and packages, instructions dealing with the classification and assignment of students to programs and courses. Additionally, the public is protected by those decisions recognizing the constitutional right of employees of a school system, such as teachers, to speak out publicly on school policies including the curriculum of the school.[11] The courts have also struck down overbroad and vague gag rules which public agencies have attempted to place on their employees.[12] Both these sets of opinions help assure a flow to the public of important information about the school program, its theory, method, costs, and effectiveness. Finally, we should not forget the tentative recognition by the Supreme Court of a right on the part of the press to gather information—again an important mechanism for assuring the accountability of government generally and school boards in particular.[13]

This public information not only may affect school board elections but it also provides a basis for petitioning the board and protesting board actions. Here the First Amendment provides important protection against governmental attempts to stop petitioning or protests. If a protest, however, takes the form of a demonstration, march, or picket line outside of school buildings with the result that the operation of the school program is materially and substantially disrupted, then action may be taken to assure the unhindered operation of the school.[14]

In sum, state statutes governing the operation of school boards, the right to vote and protest, and an emerging right to governmentally held information provide the main protections for citizens vis-à-vis the local school board. The educational system is not operated on a participatory democracy model, thus citizens do not have any direct method of controlling the educational program of the schools. And minority groups, which lack the electoral power to obtain significant representation on the local board, may find their educational interests slighted.

The Constitution and Parental Rights

Parents who are citizens enjoy the same rights as those of the citizens discussed in the previous subsection, but as parents they may enjoy some additional rights not enjoyed by citizens generally. Recall the *Pierce* decision, discussed in chapter 2, in which the Supreme Court recognized that parents enjoyed a liberty to direct the upbringing and education of their children. In *Pierce* that liberty formed a basis for striking down a compulsory education law which would have forced all parents to send their children exclusively to public schools. The question here is whether the liberty recognized in *Pierce* provides a basis for a parent to demand a right above and beyond the rights afforded all citizens to participate in formulating the school program.

Until recently it appears that there was a plausible argument in support of such parental right which the Supreme Court would readily accept. The argument, in brief, was that the *Pierce* decision should not be narrowly read as establishing only a right of parents to be free of a state requirement that all children attend public schools, but that instead *Pierce* should be broadly read as establishing a parental right with wider implications for state action within the context of the public school. That is, *Pierce* should stand for the proposition that the parental right to control the upbringing of the child imposes important limits on the state's authority to socialize children. Thus parents who found a portion of the school's program conflicted with their values might under this interpretation of *Pierce* obtain through the courts an exemption for their child from this part of the program. Only if the state had a compelling reason for keeping the child in the course or program could it prevail.

One hint of trouble for this argument is to be found in the *Barnette* decision discussed in chapter 2.[15] In that case the Supreme Court refused to permit schools to require students, on pain of expulsion from school, to participate in a flag salute ceremony; the decision was based upon the First Amendment rights of the pupils. What is significant is the failure of the Court to mention *Pierce* in the case, thereby suggesting that *Pierce* may not be accepted as a basis for limiting public school curricular requirements. Also, a parent recently argued that her rights to control the upbringing of her child were violated when the school administered corporal punishment to her child over her previous objections to that form of discipline.[16] Mrs. Baker premised her argument on the *Pierce* case saying she enjoyed a fundamental right to choose between means of discipline of her children and the school could only override her preferences if there were a compelling reason for doing so. The federal district court rejected her arguments saying that *Pierce* did not ''enshrine parental rights so high in the hierarchy of constitutional values.'' Hence the court concluded it need only examine if several of the cases parents asserted that they alone had the exclusive right to provide their children with sex education and that this was a topic public schools simply could not instruct their children in: courts have summarily rejected this novel proposition in all cases in which this claim was made.[17] Parents have also argued that sex education courses, whether voluntary or not, constituted the establishment of religion, and hence were unconstitutional under the First Amendment. Once again, all courts have rejected this claim.[18] Upon reviewing the content of these courses, the courts found that the courses were taught in such a way as to favor no particular viewpoint. One court noted, for example, that the course materials presented all viewpoints on methods of birth control without bias.[19] In another case, Catholic parents objected to the sentence in the materials "Life comes from life and is nature's greatest miracle." They said the children should be taught that life is God-given. The court rejected the plea but did not comment on the obvious religious viewpoint expressed in the quote.[20] All courts have also rejected the proposition that sex education should be banned from the schools because the possibility exists that an overzealous teacher may not teach the course without bias.[21] The mere possibility of such an occurrence is insufficient, the courts have said, to warrent total prohibition of these courses. And all courts, which have been faced with the argument that sex education courses constitute an unconstitutional invasion of privacy in that students in the courses may reveal personal family matters or be forced to reveal their personal thoughts on sex, have rejected this argument on the basis that it lacked any factual substantiation. [22]

The courts have differed over whether sex education courses may be made compulsory for all students. A Connecticut court upheld a compulsory course in a case in which the plaintiffs did not seek an exemption from the course but only an injunction barring the school from offering the course to anybody.[23] But a New Jersey state court, in the face of objections from parents that the course infringed upon their rights to freely exercise their religion, ruled that a school district could continue to require its students to take a sex education course only if the district could demonstrate that granting the student the exemption would frustrate success of an essential program. The court's opinion did not explore the extent or way in which the course did conflict with the parent's religious beliefs.[24]

Realizing that health and sex education courses are sensitive subjects, state legislatures have taken to requiring districts offering such courses to grant exemptions to parents and students who object to the courses for religious reasons.[25] But even this arrangement was challenged in a California case.[26] The parents made two arguments directed at the exemption provided in the statute: first, they said that their rights of free exercise of religion were not protected by the exemption because, as was the problem in the prayer cases, coercion still existed in the form of peer pressure; second, the exemption violated the Equal Protection clause in that the state laws set up a system whereby those who objected to the course exempted themselves on religious grounds, thereby creating a classification of children based on religion and thereby burdening those children. The California court said in answer to the first argument that this case was not like the prayer cases in which every day, in the immediate presence of all other students, the objecting students had to physically stand up and exempt themselves from the service. Here the students could simply avoid the whole course by seeking an exemption beforehand—the problem of coercion was not nearly so much a problem. In any event, even assuming some modicum of pressure, the court argued there was sufficient justification for the course to warrant rejecting the parents' objections. As for the second argument, the court said that the classification created was not of the school's making, hence there was no state action to complain about.

Other Exemption Cases

Religion has been the basis of other claims for exemptions from particular courses. Thus a student obtained an exemption based on his religious beliefs from a compulsory Reserve Officers' Training Corps (ROTC) course.[27] But even religiously based exemption claims are not always fully honored. In one case the parents objected to the attire students were expected to wear in physical education class, to the performance of certain exercises, and to the fact that their daughter was required to attend the class in the presence of other girls who wore the same prescribed attire.[28] The school was willing to compromise by allowing the plaintiffs' daughter to wear clothing they thought more modest and to exempt the daughter from the immodest exercises. Nevertheless the parents persisted in their suit because the girl was still expected to attend class in the presence of other students and the instructress who were dressed in the prescribed clothing. The court refused to grant the exemption or to require the school to hold a separate physical education class for the plaintiffs' daughter and others who shared the same scruples. To grant the exemption, the court said, could lead to placing an intolerable burden on the schools and would give citizens the power to nullify all state law by simply asserting that the required behavior was contrary to religious beliefs.

But obtaining an exemption from courses based on claims of free exercise of religion should be the easiest kind of case for parents to win because of the central importance in our constitutional scheme of the free exercise of religion. Obtaining an exemption from required courses on other grounds is not likely to be as easily accomplished, yet cases of this sort have also been won by parents. The Supreme Court of Nebraska, without citing a specific constitutional provision, based its decision permitting a parent to pull his child out of a required cooking course on the general right of a parent to control the upbringing of his or her child.[29] In so holding, the court also noted that the "state is more and more taking hold of the private affairs of individuals" and that "we want to be careful lest we carry the doctrine of governmental paternalism too far, for, after all is said and done, the prime factor in our scheme of government is the American home." The court added that as to parental requests for exemptions, "If a reasonable request is made by a parent, it should be heeded." Seven years later, in California, another state court, confronted with a parental demand that his child be exempted from dancing instruction in the school, characterized the case as one involving a religious objection, a moral objection and simply a question of the constitutional right of parents to control their own children. [30] Not to recognize such a parental right or to recognize a power in the state to willy-nilly override reasonable parental desires, said the court, "would be distinctly revolutionary and possibly subversive of that home life so essential to the safety and security of society and the government which regulates it, the very opposite effect of what the public school system is designed to accomplish . . ." The court finally concluded that the exemption must be granted as it would not interfere with the discipline of the school and physical fitness of students could be achieved by means other than dancing lessons. Yet another state court has written, in an opinion upholding a parental request to exempt the child from the school's singing course, that in the absence of proof to the contrary, a parental request must be deemed reasonable, just, in the best interests of the child, and not detrimental to the discipline and efficiency of the school.[31] Following this general rule other courts have allowed parents to exempt their children from courses in geography and domestic science.[32] But parents have not been successful in all states in obtaining exemptions. Thus an Indiana state court has said that a parent's belief that it was in the best interest of the child not to participate in musical studies was insufficient to overrule the governing authorities of the school district.[33]

Demanding That a Course Be Taught

No enormous administrative difficulties are created for school districts by judicially or legislatively created exemptions, hence it is not surprising that in many exemption cases parents have been accommodated. The problems school districts would face would be manyfold more complex if parents were given a right to demand from public schools the provision of courses not available in the school program. If such demands were enforceable the school program could be disrupted, a great deal of trouble might have to be gone through in order to obtain qualified teachers and to purchase necessary materials, not to speak of the problems that might be involved in reorganizing the school schedule and finding available space for carrying on the instruction, and districts could be forced into financial crises. Hence, it should not be surprising that parents have not been very successful in obtaining court orders requiring schools to provide a particular program such as kindergarten when the schools have refused to do so.[34]

But in order to accommodate parental interest in having certain courses taught in the public schools, state legislatures over the years have passed statutes which give to parents the right, if certain conditions are met, to demand of their school board that a program or course be offered. Some of these laws have been narrowly drawn, giving parents, for example, the right to demand that German be taught, or that the local district maintain a kindergarten upon the petition of the parents of at least twenty-five children.[35] Nebraska had at one time a law that permitted parents to petition their local board for instruction in a ''modern European language.''[36] A Rhode Island statute today provides that when twenty students apply for a course in Portuguese, Italian, or Spanish the school must provide the course.[37] The most radical statute is currently in force in Massachusetts:

In every public high school having not less than one hundred and fifty pupils, any course not included in the regular curriculum shall be taught if the parents or guardians of not less than twenty pupils or of a number of pupils equivalent to five percent of the pupil enrollment in the high school, whichever is less, request in writing the teaching thereof, provided said request is made and said enrollment is completed before the preceding August first and provided a qualified teacher is available to teach said course. The teaching of any course as provided by this section may be discontinued if the enrollment of pupils falls below ten. Such courses as may be taught under this section shall be given the same academic credit necessary for a high school, provided that the school committe shall make a determination as to the credit equivalency of such course prior to its being offered.[38]

A provision such as the Massachusetts law raises an interesting constitutional issue which is worth exploring for the light it sheds on the limits, if there are any, on the authority of state legislatures to delegate to parents authority to control the local school educational program.

One way of attacking the Massachusetts law would be to evoke the Equal Protection clause of the Fourteenth Amendment. The starting point for the argument would be *Kramer* v. *Union Free School District No. 1* which challenged a New York state statute which established as eligible voters in school board elections those who owned or leased taxable property in the district, spouses of those who owned or leased property, and parents or guardians of children enrolled in the local district.[39] The plaintiff in the case was a thirty-one-year-old college educated stockbroker, who had no children and who lived in his parents' home; under the New York law he was unable to vote in the school board election. The law also had the effect of disenfranchising other people without children in the public schools, such as senior citizens and others living with children or relatives; clergy; military personnel; those who lived on tax-exempt property; boarders and lodgers; parents who neither owned nor leased qualifying property and whose children were too young to attend school; parents who neither owned nor leased qualifying property and whose children attended private school. Because the law in question affected a fundamental interest, the right to vote, the Supreme Court reviewed the claim of a denial of equal protection under the new equal protection test (see chap. 2). To meet its burden of showing a compelling state interest in the law, the state argued it had a right to allow only those to vote who were primarily affected by the schools (parents and those affected by school taxes). The Supreme Court said the statute was not drafted with sufficient precision to avoid unnecessary injuries. On the one hand, the statute excluded from voting many who had a direct interest in school affairs such as the plaintiff who paid state and federal taxes, but, on the other hand, permitted others with a remote and indirect interest to vote, for example, an uninterested unemployed individual who paid no state or federal taxes but who rented an apartment in the district.

This case shows that it would be unconstitutional for the state to turn all authority of the school board over only to parents, as that would unfairly exclude many interested parties from having a voice in school affairs. Whether the Massachusetts statute quoted violates the ruling laid down in the *Kramer* case is another question. Perhaps not, as those interested in and affected by the schools still retain the right to vote for the school board; they are not disenfranchised by the Massachusetts law. Yet parents are given an advantage, vis-à-vis the school board, not enjoyed by other citizens. Put differently, all other citizens have been denied the advantage given to the parents—Is this deprivation consistent with the Equal Protection clause? Since the disenfranchisement in this case does not affect a recognized fundamental interest, the standard of review would probably be either the rational basis test or tests three or four (see chap. 2). Under these tests the state would seem to have a reasonable chance of justifying the allocation of authority, that is, parents and their children are the ones clearly most directly affected by omissions in the school program, thus giving them the chance to force the provision of new courses is rational and soundly based.

But another constitutional attack remains available. The Massachusetts law may violate the constitutional prohibition against delegation of public authority to private groups.[40] This argument raises an extraordinarily complex question which can only be briefly explored here.

The basic rule is that a delegation of authority to a group or individual will be deemed an improper delegation of authority to a private group or individual if the delegation is viewed by the court as subject to abuse. To determine whether a potential for abuse exists courts seem to explore the following questions: (1) What sort of authority is it that is being delegated?: Is it the power to coerce and harm other individuals or is it merely authority to either confer or not confer a benefit? If the authority is merely the authority to give advice, no real authority has been delegated and there is no problem. (2) Has the likelihood of abuse been reduced because the legislature has imposed standards according to which the authority is to be exercised? Or has the legislature imposed procedures which the delegatee must follow? Or required the delegatee publicly to establish its own standards and procedures as a form of self-restraint? Or subjected the action of the delegatee to review by another agency or the courts? Or is the delegatee ultimately accountable to those over which it exercises authority? (3) To what extent is the recipient group representative, disinterested, accountable, and diverse enough with respect to the subject matter of the authority? That is, is there neither the sense that members have some general dependency upon one another for pursuit of the good life, nor the opportunity for trade and compromise that creates at least the chance of everyone's benefiting from the common enterprise? For example, if licensing authority for positions at the race track is turned over to a private racing association, then the self-interested nature of the group with respect to the authority given raises the possibilities of abuse. In contrast, giving the same licensing authority to the city council avoids self-interested use of the power and, in any event, the city council deals with such a wide range of activities that the possibilities of logrolling helps protect all individuals involved. (4) Do those who may be affected by the authority voluntarily subject themselves to the authority?

If the answers to these questions indicate a likelihood of unfairness or exploitation, then the delegation would be invalidated and the recipient of the authority would be called private. The term *private* does not refer to any fixed universal set of identifying characteristics but to the unsuitability of a group as a recipient of this power. To label the group as private is the conclusion of the analysis not the starting point. Thus letting owners of a majority of the property on a street determine by vote the number of feet houses must be set back from the street has been struck down by the Supreme Court as an improper delegation to a private group.[41] Or, for another example, turning control of the local school board over only to parents might very well be struck down by a court. Such an arrangement would (1) give parents coercive power to harm as well as benefit each other; (2) involve a likelihood of abuse to the extent that the legislature fails to specify the standards and procedures according to which they are to operate; (3) raise problems because the recipient group is narrowly defined with respect to the authority granted and would not be disinterested or accountable to the larger society in its exercise of authority. And any subgroup of parents that found itself in the minority might find itself ruled by a self-interested group of other parents whose self-interest might prompt it never to heed or listen to the minority. Of course all these problems might be avoided with careful drafting of the law so as either to make sure the parents were accountable to the larger public, whom they affect by their actions, or to make sure any actions of the parent group were reviewed by the courts or some broadly based superior governmental unit.

How would the Massachusetts law fare? If given a literal interpretation, the Massachusetts law would probably be unconstitutional in light of the foregoing analysis, since as literally interpreted it could lead to a take-over of the school system by parents. That is, taken to an extreme the Massachusetts law could lead to a rash of parent-initiated courses that could put such demands on the resources of the district as to prevent it from carrying out plans and policies that had been formulated by the majority of the electors in the district. But if an implied limitation were read into the statute to the effect that it may not be used to defeat the basic curricular policies of the school board, or to disrupt and distort the school program, then it probably would survive judicial scrutiny.

The constitutional doctrine against delegating authority to private groups is not the last doctrine standing in the way of turning significant authority to determine the course offering of the local district over to parents. A final major obstacle is the rule that unless a delegatee of authority from the state legislature has been authorized to do so, the delegatee may not in turn delegate its authority to a subdelegatee (see chap. 6). Thus, just as this doctrine may limit school boards in their efforts to delegate their authority to their employees, so they may be limited in handing over their authority to parents.

Selection of Books and Methods of Instruction

Parents have been interested not only in which courses are available in the schools or in exempting their children from particular courses, but also in having a voice in selecting the materials and methods of instruction to be used. Apart from the good chances parents have to obtain from courts orders to stop using for religious instruction religious materials in the classroom, the constitutional and statutory rights of parents in this area are meager. Parents have failed in challenging school requirements that students write certain compositions;[42] failed in challenging methods of instruction in physical education courses,[43] and failed in challenging the fact that single entry bookkeeping was being taught instead of double entry bookkeeping.[44] In one aggravated case a parent challenged the system of correcting papers used by a particular teacher after his daughter was suspended from school for refusing to attend the class in which her rival was rewarded for her top standing in the class by being given the task of grading papers.[45] The facts of the case strongly suggest that the rival abused her authority to grade papers by marking wrong the plaintiff's daughter's answers to problems that were in fact correct. Nevertheless, the court refused to intervene, saying this sort of administrative detail was committed to the discretion of the school officials; that no legal right of the pupil or parent had been violated. And parents have met with no success in challenging the school districts' selection of books for use in the classroom—again the courts have leaned over backwards to avoid interference, as in the challenge brought in New York to the use of the novel by Dickens, *Oliver Twist*, and the play by Shakespeare, *The Merchant of Venice*.[46] The parent argued the books were anti-Semitic, but the court said there was no evidence that the authors' intents were anti-Semitic (as though the intent of authors were a discernible fact).

State statutes do not require parental involvement in the selection of materials of in determining the methods of instruction to be used. In light of this fact the Lawyers' Committee for Civil Rights Under Law has been working on developing model statutes that would require parental, or student, in the case of high schools, approval of materials selected for use. The Lawyers' Committee has also developed model legislation pursuant to which parents and citizens of the community could require the school to engage in a dialogue over possible bias in the educational materials used in the schools. It is the hope of the Lawyers' Committee to persuade state legislatures to adopt these model pieces of legislation. But once again these model laws requiring parental or student approval of materials used in the school raises problems of the delegation of authority to private groups (to be discussed more fully in chapter 9).

Grading and Classification of Pupils

Closely related to the issues of control of course offerings and content and methods of instruction is the problem of assigning students to particular grades and courses of study. It is now black-letter law that school districts in all states have been delegated the authority to establish the grade structure to be used in the schools or even to adopt nongraded instruction and to decide to which grade a child should be assigned.[47] Often the local district establishes standards for promotion and decides if and when a child is to be promoted from one grade to another. Parents have failed through the courts to force school districts to place their children in first grade instead of kindergarten;[48] to force districts to double promote their children even when it has been shown that the student is capable of doing advanced work;[49] to force districts to place their children in a "special progress class" which compresses three years' work into two years.[50] Thus, while in theory courts could overturn such gradation and classification decisions because they were arbitrary and capricious, in practice courts do not interfere in these matters. Of course an alleged discriminatory assignment of pupils on the basis of race or sex raises a host of problems under federal and state constitutions and laws (see chaps. 2 and 3).

While parents have no authority to directly control the assignment of their children to particular grades, courses, or programs, one strategy for involvement in this area remains to be explored. That is, because classification decisions do so importantly affect the kind and quality of education that a child gets, it has been argued that due process procedures ought to be followed by school officials in carrying out the decisions so that erroneous decisions are not made. Thus, before a child may be classified or tracked, the district would have to notify the parent of the pending decision, and provide the student and parent with an opportunity to be heard on the accuracy of the school's classification or tracking of the pupil. Due process would also require that the people making the decision act from substantial evidence and be impartial. Parents would have access to the information relied upon and this would mean access to the child's cumulative records. In particularly sensitive or complex cases parents would be able to bring in their own evidence and expert witnesses to the hearing as well as, possibly, their own lawyer. Once a decision was rendered an avenue for appeal would be available. In short, while parents could not control the placement of their child under these procedures, at least they would have a voice in the decision-making process.

What is the legal status today of such procedures? First, the Supreme Court in *Goss* v. *Lopez* based on the Due Process clause of the Fourteenth Amendment held that rather rudimentary procedural due process requirements must be met in minor school discipline cases which may result in a student's short suspension from school.[51] In such cases the disciplining official must tell the student why he or she might be suspended from school and then give the student a chance to tell his or her side of the story. The whole proceeding need not take very long and obviously falls far short of the complex steps outlined earlier. But the significance of the case is that the Supreme Court has recognized that students must be afforded some degree of procedural due process, and the case lays a premise for extending such rights to the classification of pupils. Second, two lower courts, in conjunction with the exclusion of the mentally retarded from school, as discussed in chapter 2, have extended extensive procedural due process rights to these pupils to assure they are accurately classified and that appropriate treatment is afforded them.[52] Thus, it appears that in situations in which a student may be classifed as mentally retarded, strong protection based on the Constitution may be forthcoming. Such a result is sensible in light of the profound implications for a student of being classified as mentally retarded and in light of the fact that such a judgment may easily be erroneous, as has been demonstrated by the cases in which it was found that large numbers of pupils had in fact been incorrectly labeled (see chap. 2).

But, third, the Constitution has proved to be a weak reed in obtaining due process rights for students caught up in another kind of classification process, namely, one designed to decide whether a student with behavior problems is to be assigned back to the regular class or to some special class or school for such pupils. In one such case a parent wanted a lawyer present at the guidance conference, but the Second Circuit denied the claim saying the conference was only preliminary and that the consequences which were to flow from it were not severe enough to warrant allowing the parent to bring a lawyer into the conference.[53] Although that decision may be undercut by the more recent decision in *Goss* v. *Lopez*, it still seems unlikely that extensive procedural rights will be granted students by the courts when gradation and classification schemes other than those that label children as mentally retarded are involved. It is likely that the courts, in balancing the interests of the pupil against those of the schools, would decide that the interest of the students in normal classification decisions did not sufficiently outweigh the interests of the school to keep procedures simple to warrant the imposition of anything but fairly rudimentary notions of procedural due process.

Fourth, constitutional issues aside, the states have adopted laws that deeply involve parents in the classification of children as mentally retarded or as children in need of special services. The Massachusetts special education law which applies to a whole range of children with special educational needs has some of the most extensive procedural requirements of any state law (see chap. 4). Since the law applies to so many different types of pupils, the law represents a vast extension of procedural rights to many school decisions. Additionally, federal law and a new state statute in California gives parents extensive rights of access to their children's school records, as well as rights to challenge as erroneous materials included in those records.[54] But the kind of statutory protection afforded parents in Massachusetts and California is not widespread; the vast bulk of gradation and classification decisions which schools reach are still immune from either constitutional or statutory guidance.

Advisory Committees

The parent advisory council or local school council in recent years has increasingly come into use, especially in large cities, as a vehicle for parents to obtain some voice in the school program. These councils are usually elected by parents at the building level; if there is a districtwide council it is usually made up of representatives from the building level councils. The size varies from the very small to the very large (some have over one hundred councilors) and it is not clear how representative they are of the communities they serve.[55]

Subject to the limitations of the no-delegation-to-private-groups doctrine and the limitations against subdelegation of authority, these councils could potentially have a meaningful voice in a wide range of issues—the objectives of the school program, the courses to be offered, the methods of teaching, the materials to be used, personnel policy, budgetary decisions, and facilities planning at the district level. In practice, most councils seem to be purely advisory with little impact on the school program, although in concept they are supposed to be more than the sort of merely supportive organization that the PTA has been. This lack of real influence seems to be true even where the councils are required of the local district by law.[56]

There are several legal bases for these councils. Title I of ESEA was recently amended to require a districtwide advisory council as well as a council in each building served by Title I.[57] Under the statute and proposed regulations to implement the law, these councils are to be given information about Title I programs; and they are to advise the local board with regard to planning, implementing, and evaluating the Title I projects. These councils have in the past been able successfully to obtain information through the courts, to force districts to recognize their limited rights to be involved in decision making and to force districts to correct misallocations of Title I funds. Other federal grant programs targeted to children with special needs also carry with them requirements that there be established parent advisory councils.[58] And some states which have established their own grant-in-aid programs for children with special needs have also required the creation of these councils.[59] Thus, a given school building served by several projects may have as many advisory councils, not to speak of those councils that the school districts themselves may have voluntarily established. These developments are part of the more general phenomenon of special governmental programs fostering the creation of organized interest groups benefiting from those programs. The result is a kind of symbiotic relationship between the program and the group served.

There are two other legal sources for parent advisory groups. When the New York legislature adopted legislation decentralizing the New York City school system and thereby creating within New York City a complex federal-type arrangement with a citywide board and chancellor and local elected boards with their own administrative staff, it also required the creation of a parents' association or parent-teachers' association at each building with which the local board, community superintendent, and principals must have regular communication and to which specific information pertaining to pupil achievement must be supplied.[60] Florida has passed a statute that requires all its school districts to establish at least a districtwide school advisory committee to be broadly representative of the community served.[61] The precise functions of these committees is left to the local boards to determine, but the committees must participate in the development of the annual school progress report required by another statutory provision.[62] That report must include, among other things, information on program evaluation, attitudes of students, teachers, administrators, and parents, and financial information. This law is part of a larger legislative effort to encourage the school districts of Florida to decentralize to the building level—to make the principal a more important, perhaps the most important, administrator in the district.

Conclusions

It is not surprising that citizens generally do not have much direct control with regard to what programs are offered at the local school district since participatory democracy is not a commonly followed mode of government found in the United States. It is more surprising that parents have as little voice over the kind of education provided their children in the public schools. Given the basic commitment of the country to parental control of the upbringing of their own children, the present system of public schools (and with little state support for private educational efforts) deeply cuts into the practical control parents have over their child's formal education. Even within the legal limits outlined in the chapter on delegating authority to parents, more could be done to involve parents in curricular decision making. Yet the trends discussed in chapter 6 suggest that just the opposite is occurring, that less and less will parents even have a chance to exercise significant control through the school board as it must now contend with teachers' unions interested in making the curriculum a subject of collective negotiations.

8 State Control of Private Schools

State government controls not only the curriculum of the public schools, but also the program of the seventeen thousand nonpublic elementary and secondary schools which serve five million students.[1] An understanding of the state's interest in controlling begins with seeing the reasons behind compulsory education laws. While it has been argued that compulsory education laws and child labor laws were originally adopted to keep children out of the factories in order to protect the jobs of the adults, those laws serve other purposes as well.[2] They protect the child from parents who might be disinclined to educate their children and in doing so they further the interest of the state in having a literate and law-abiding voting population capable of sustaining itself economically.

Given this rationale for the compulsory education (and given the fact that, as discussed in chapter 2, the states may not prohibit parents from sending their children to private schools but may impose reasonable regulations on those schools), it should come as no surprise that the states seek to assure that the private schools provide the sort of minimally adequate education the compulsory education laws were designed to assure children of receiving. But regulating private schools to make sure the program is minimally adequate is only one reason behind the state's regulation of these schools. States have also sought to regulate private schools to insure that these schools would not become an incubus of culturally and politically divisive ideas and practices.[3] State regulation of private schools thus is a way of trying to maintain political and cultural unity. But as was noted in chapter 2 and will be discussed again, such efforts raise important constitutional issues. Further, the more the states attempt to regulate private schools the greater the likelihood they will stamp out the diversity these schools represent, and the promotion of diversity, the offering of alternative concepts and forms of education, is a central function served by private schools today. Thus the crucial dilemma is how to regulate private schools to assure that they provide a minimally adequate education without at the same time snuffing out educational diversity.

How States Regulate Private Schools

As Figure 8-1 demonstrates, there are many ways in which states regulate private elementary and secondary schools.[4]

Twenty-seven states require private schools to register and seek ap-

153

	Private schools must register	Private schools voluntarily may seek to be registered	No registration either required or voluntarily possible
	1	6	11
Compulsory education law requires that private schools seek prior approval. Short list of required courses.	Kentucky Maine New Hampshire North Carolina North Dakota Pennsylvania Rhode Island South Carolina South Dakota Washington West Virginia	Massachusetts	
	2	7	12
Compulsory education law requires private schools to be comparable to public schools. Long lists of required courses.	Iowa	California	
	3	8	13
Compulsory education law requires comparability. Short list only of required courses.	Alabama Alaska Idaho Michigan[a] Montana Nevada New Jersey Ohio Oregon Vermont	Colorado Connecticut New York	Arizona Arkansas Illinois Missouri

Figure 8-1. Classification of State Laws Affecting Private Schools

proval before they may operate (see squares 1-5). Some states tie the registration requirement to the compulsory education law by requiring attendance either at a public school or at an approved private school (see square 1).[5] The states listed in squares 2 and 3 require approval of the private school but the compulsory education law provisions are satisfied if the private school offers, for example, a program that is substantially equivalent to that offered in the public schools of the district where the

	Private schools must register	Private schools voluntarily may seek to be registered	No registration either required or voluntarily possible
	4	9	14
Compulsory education law requires private education to be regular and thorough.	Maryland		Delaware
	5	10	15
Compulsory education law does not require comparability. Short list of required courses. List sometimes applies to private schools.	Georgia Hawaii Kansas Nebraska	Louisiana Oklahoma Tennessee Wyoming	Florida[b] Indiana Minnesota Texas Utah Virginia Wisconsin

[a] It is not clear from the statutes if Michigan belongs in this category.

[b] Private schools in Florida may voluntarily file certain information with the state.

Figure 8-1. (cont.)

child resides. Maryland says the attendance requirement is satisfied if the private education is regular and thorough. Some states, such as Iowa and South Dakota, go so far as to require private school students to be tested as may be required by the state superintendent. The states listed in square 5 include no such comparability requirements although some, such as Kansas, do assert that for the compulsory education law to be satisfied instruction must be by a competent teacher. The states listed in squares 1 through 5 also differ in the extent to which other statutory provisions list courses that must be offered in the public and private schools of the state. Iowa, in square 2, imposes an unusually long list of required courses on both elementary and secondary public and private schools.

Enforcement of the law in the states listed in squares 1 through 5 can take either of two forms. First, the state may move directly against those private schools that do not register and seek approval to operate. Second, the state may move against the parents who send their children to private schools that have not been approved (square 1) or that do not offer and education substantially equivalent or regular and thorough (squares 2 through 4). Action against parents in the states listed in square 5 is more difficult since the compulsory education law does not set standards as to what sort of education the parents must be providing their children.

Direct state action against private schools themselves cannot be taken in the states listed in squares 6 through 15, since in these states the schools may either voluntarily seek registration if they think it is in their interest to do so (squares 6 through 10) or they are not even given the opportunity to register (squares 11 through 15).[6] In these states, then, control of the private school must take place indirectly by prosecuting parents for violating compulsory education laws. (Note Mississippi is the one state without any compulsory education law.) In Massachusetts the parent may be prosecuted for failing to send the child to a school that either did not seek or failed to get approval. In the states listed in squares 7, 8, 13, and 14, when the parent is prosecuted, the issue in court becomes one of whether, for example, the private school involved is offering a program substantially equivalent to that in public schools. Again prosecution of parents becomes extremely difficult in states listed in squares 10 and 15 as the compulsory education law contains no statement of the standards of education which the parent must provide. As a practical matter, control of private education in these states is almost impossible and indeed nonexistent. In sum, regulation of private schools and private educational efforts ranges from being fairly complete to practically nonexistent.

With these broad outlines in mind it is possible to turn to some of the interesting specific features of this body of law. In those states in which registration of schools is required or voluntary, state officials are typically granted extremely broad authority to set the standards the schools must meet; indeed, the statutory language is typically so broad as to give these officials virtually unfettered authority. With regard to enforcement of the compulsory education laws, this task is often relegated to local school officials who must determine if the private schools in their districts are offering a program that meets the statutory requirements. But these requirements, for example, substantially equivalent, are often difficult to interpret and enforce. Again broad discretionary authority over the private school and private education is given to public officials—authority that can be easily abused.

One form of specific guidance the statutes in some states provide to private schools is to be found in those state statutes prescribing the curriculum for the public schools (sometimes these same laws explicitly refer to the private schools as well). In most states these course listings, as noted in chapter 4, are not very extensive, with Iowa and California being exceptions to this rule. In any event, a private school seeking state approval or wishing to provide an education in compliance with the compulsory education laws can look to these statutes to see what it should be doing.

While most states content themselves with requiring the usual litany of important subjects—reading, writing, spelling, arithmetic, U.S. history, study of the U.S. Constitution, health and drug education, and so forth—some states have imposed requirements on private schools that raise important issues with regard to how different private schools may be. For example, there are many states that require that the language of instruction in private schools be only English.[7] States such as Kansas, Maine, and Nebraska require their private schools to instruct in patriotism to develop a love of country.[8] The Texas compulsory education law permits, attendance only at private schools where good citizenship is taught.[9] In Idaho the state board of education can, if it deems it necessary, prescribe syllabi which private schools must follow.[10] In Michigan, private schools are told they must select their textbooks with a view to using those books that recognize the achievements and accomplishments of ethnic and racial groups.[11] And New Jersey prohibits the use of corporal punishment in private and public schools except that reasonable force may be used to quell a disturbance threatening injury to others, to obtain weapons from students, to defend one's self, and to protect persons and property.[12] More broadly, strict enforcement of equivalency requirements could transform private schools into mere models of the public schools, allowing no diversity. Apparently only one state, Iowa, provides for the possibility of a waiver of state curriculum requirements by the state board upon a request from the private school.[13]

Diversity can also be hampered by the requirement found in the laws of over a dozen states that only certified teachers may teach in private schools.[14] This requirement can impinge upon the schools of such groups as the Amish, who rely on members of their own community to instruct in their schools—members who, because they are Amish, have not gone on to college and hence could not possibly have teachers' certificates. Additionally this requirement can get in the way of experimental schools which call on a whole variety of people in the local community to come into the school to instruct.

Interpreting the Statutes

The general description of the basic approaches used by the states in regulating private education only begins to touch upon the complexities of these laws. For example, when state laws grant to the state board of education the authority to set reasonable standards or minimum academic standards, or to set standards that will assure a curriculum "sufficient to meet the needs of the pupils in every community"; or more generally, when state laws give the state board of education power to approve and accredit private schools, what precisely are those powers?[15] May state officials regulate every detail of the program of private schools, and if not, what are the limits of the state board's authority? In states that require the registration of private schools, only three states spell out in any detail the procedures to be followed if a license to operate is revoked—Iowa, Maryland, and Nevada. And only one state, Maryland, establishes the procedures to be followed in case the initial application for a license is denied. What procedure is to be followed in the other twenty-six states? There are no cases that shed any light on how these statutes are to be interpreted, but presumably courts asked to interpret them will do so in ways that protect the private school and its patrons. That is, for example, the statutory power of the state board to set standards for private schools would be interpreted broadly enough to permit the state board to protect certain basic interests of the public but not so broadly as to permit state boards to stamp out all diversity that private schools may bring to the educational scene. As will be discussed later, this approach to the interpretation of the statutes may be required in order to preserve their constitutionality.

The compulsory education laws raise a different set of problems, the first one being, Who has the burden of proof in a case in which the parent is charged with failing to comply with the compulsory education law? The statutes do not say expressly, but where the violation of the compulsory education law is a criminal offense, as is the case in many states, the burden of proof must rest on the state. It would be highly inconsistent with basic principles to force the parent to prove his or her innocence rather than to require the state to establish guilt. And this is the approach taken in most cases. The New Jersey Supreme Court has held that litigation concerning a compulsory education statute should proceed as follows:[16] (1) The state must make a complaint which alleges that the child is in attendance in public schools; (2) the parent is obliged to provide evidence that the child is being instructed according to one of the exceptions to the compulsory education law (that is, is attending a private school with equivalent instruction); (3) the state must then disprove that the child is receiving instruction equivalent to that of the public schools. As the New Jersey court said, the ultimate burden of proof remains with the state in accordance with the usual rule applicable in penal cases. Other cases have also held that for an indictment against parents to be legally satisfactory it must not merely allege that the parent has not enrolled the child in the public schools; it must also negate the inference that the parent is nevertheless in compliance with the compulsory education law by providing equivalent instruction elsewhere.[17] One state court, however, has said that if parents prefer home instruction they "have the burden of showing that they have in good faith provided an adequate course of instruction in the prescribed branches of learning."[18] Thus state courts are not in total agreement on who has the burden of proof.

The next question raised by compulsory education laws is, What sort of private education satisfies the statutory requirements? This question may be broken down into several closely related questions: (1) May a parent remain in compliance by providing a substantially equivalent education in the home, or does the statute prohibit home instruction even if substantially equivalent? (2) When do compulsory education laws require that the private educational effort be given prior approval for the parent to be in compliance with the law? (3) In states that excuse children from attendance at the public schools if they are receiving instruction elsewhere, which has been approved by the state, may parents avoid conviction under these laws by showing in court that even though the educational program had not been given prior approval by the state, nevertheless it was substantially equivalent to the programs in the public schools? (4) Whether the education is provided in the home or in private schools, what must that educational program look like in order for it to be substantially equivalent, or to be regular and thorough, or to be comparable or offered by a competent instructor, or to be in compliance with standards for public schools "in every respect," or to be a program in which all common branches are taught by instructors whose qualifications are essentially equivalent to those of teachers in the public schools? Note the fourth question is closely related to the first question in the following way: it may be that the state compulsory education law does not prohibit home instruction per se but that the courts have interpreted such requirements to mean that private education must be substantially equivalent in such a way that home instruction can never be deemed to satisfy the requirement—that is, although home instruction remains theoretically permissible under the law, as a practical matter the courts may never agree that it satisfies the standard of the statute.

The first question arises in those states in which the compulsory education law makes no reference to excusing children from attendance at the public schools if they are receiving appropriate education at home. For example, the law might simply state that children are excused from attendance at the public schools if they are provided equivalent instruction in a private school. The question thus becomes one of whether parents who instruct their children at home are maintaining a private school within the meaning of the law. State courts have split on this issue. A state court in Washington said a child attending home instruction was not attending a private school.[19] "Such a requirement means more than home instruction; it means the same character of school as the public school, a regular, organized, and existing institution making a business of instructing children of school age in the required studies and for the full time required by the laws of this state. . . . The parent who teaches his children at home, whatever be his reason for desiring to do so, does not maintain such a school. Undoubtedly a private school may be maintained in a private home in which the children of the instructor may be pupils. This provision of the law is not to be determined by the place where the school is maintained, nor the individuality or number of the pupils who attend it. It is to be determined by the purpose, intent, and character of the endeavor."[20] One reason given by another court for interpreting the state statute as barring home instruction is that permitting home instruction would place an intolerable burden on the state in supervising these educational efforts.[21] Clearly states that prevent home instruction reduce the chances of educational diversity. As will be discussed later, prohibiting home instruction may be unconstitutional.

Other state courts have, however, interpreted similar statutory provisions to permit home instruction as long as it met the statutory requirement that the education be, for example, equivalent to that in the public schools. Thus in one case Clarence Peterman withdrew his child from public school and hired a tutor because of a disagreement with the teacher and school authorities.[22] The tutor had been a successful public school teacher for several years and instructed the child for the same number of hours and in the same subjects as the child had been experiencing in public school, but she did not call her activity a private school, she had no facilities other than a desk and blackboard, and she did not establish a tuition. The state prosecuted Peterman for disobeying the compulsory attendance law, alleging his child was not in any school. The court affirmed the acquittal of Peterman saying that "A school, in the ordinary acceptation of its meaning, is a place where instruction is imparted to the young," so that home instruction satisfied the statute.[23] Further, the court added that the purpose of the compulsory education law was to secure the child the opportunity to acquire an education and "The result to be obtained, and not the means or manner of obtaining it, was the goal which the lawmakers were attempting to reach."[24] The same result has been reached in other cases.

The second question is usually easily answered in that the compulsory education law explicitly requires tha the private educational activity must be approved by the state if the parent is to be in compliance with the law.[25] However, sometimes these statutes merely say that attendance is required at the public schools unless the child has been excused by the superintendent for various reasons listed in the statute.[26] There thus exists an implication that the parent has the burden of going to the local official to obtain the necessary permission to excuse the child from the public school. There seem to be no cases probing this question, but in one case, noted earlier, the court could have upheld the parent's conviction on the ground that he had not obtained the approval of the superintendent, but instead the court decided the case on the ground that home instruction did not satisfy the requirement of attending a private school.[27] In yet another case, the court treated the compulsory education statute as though it required prior approval.[28] The Virginia statute in question required that children attend public school, private school, or be taught by a tutor "of qualifications approved by the State Board of Education and approved by the division superintendent." While there was no mention of advance approval in the statute, the court held the parents could not raise the question of the adequacy of the teaching they were giving their children as a defense to their refusal either to send their children to school "or to have their qualifications as tutors, as teachers in the home approved by the division superintendent of schools."[29] Thus the court read the statute to require some form of prior approval, and failure to obtain prior approval of the parents' qualifications as tutors was a sufficient basis to convict the parents even if they could prove that their instruction was equivalent to that in the public schools. In short, when prior approval is required by the statutes, it is not always discernible from the words of the statute, and, as we have seen, even when prior approval is required, courts may not require it, and when it seems not to be required, courts may nevertheless require it.

As for the third question, when prior approval is required either explicitly or implicitly, failure to obtain prior approval means the parent is barred from attempting to avoid conviction by showing that nevertheless the instruction being offered was equivalent to that in the public schools. The immediately preceding Virginia case and a Massachusetts state court decision support this conclusion.[30] Once again there are constitutional issues involved here to be discussed later.

The fourth question raises a large number of complex problems with which several state courts have wrestled. Preliminarily it should be noted that not every standard quoted in question four has been the subject of a court decision, thus the comments which follow may not be relevant to each of the quoted standards. In determining whether a private educational effort is equivalent to the public program the courts may behave differently depending on whether the instruction is in a home or in a private school. Some state statutes force such a distinction in that they require home instruction or tutoring to be by certified teachers, whereas instruction in private schools need not be by certified teachers.[31] A California court has upheld this distinction on the ground that there are institutional forces that tend to maintain the quality of education in private schools, such as the interest of supervisors in demanding good performance of the teachers in order to keep up the reputation of the school.[32] In states that do not require that home instruction be by certified teacher, the courts have tended to behave in such a way that if the parent can show he or she is certified, that helps his case, but the absence of certification does not mean the education provided is not equivalent.[33] The courts look beyond certification to see if the parent is in fact qualified in terms of his or her own education and competence.

Home instruction may also not satisfy the compulsory education statute if equivalence means that children must always be educated as part of large groups, in classes of large numbers of pupils. New Jersey state courts have split on this question with the most recent decision, saying the statute should not be read to imply such a requirement.[34] Indeed, if large group instruction were required as part of a process of educating the child in social adjustment, it would effectively mean the end of home instruction. However the court said only academic equivalence was to be examined.[35]

As for the substance of the educational program, both the state and the parents submit evidence, but usually it is the state that must carry the burden of showing that the education provided in the home or at private school was inadequate. In reaching this decision the judge and/or jury typically are asked to consider evidence on the number of hours of instruction; its regularity; the nature of the materials used; the subjects covered; the methods of instruction; and in some cases the educational achievement of the pupils.[36] With regard to the last point, what the courts seem to examine is the question of how well these particular children are doing under private instruction compared to how they might be doing under public instruction—a question almost impossible to answer.[37] In any event, what the cases taken together show is that instruction will not be deemed inadequate merely because, for example, the math books used in the home were not so up to date as those in the public schools or that all the equipment available in the public schools was not available at home.[38] Home and private school instruction have been viewed as not equivalent if courses or subjects prescribed by state statute and required in the public schools are ignored in the private educational effort.[39] In one of the New Jersey cases the court cited the absence of examination, grades, and tests; the failure to observe patriotic holidays; the lack of discipline and a planned approach to teaching health and hygiene; and the irregularity of the instructional day, as evidence of lack of equivalency.[40] In several New York cases parents were successfully prosecuted who sent their children to Jewish parochial schools devoted exclusively to the study of Jewish law, the Talmud, and the Bible.[41]

In sum, the equivalency of private education raises difficult problems of statutory interpretation and the standard opens the door to state and local officials forcing all private education to be exactly like public education, thereby eliminating educational diversity and parental freedom of choice. Courts interpreting these provisions should be mindful of the principle that the purpose of the compulsory education laws is that "all children will be educated, not that they shall be educated in any particular way."

Delegation, Due Process, and Prior Approval

The review and analysis of the state laws affecting private education brought out that in those states in which state officials have been given authority to establish standards for private schools or authority to approve or accredit private schools, it is common for the statutes to grant this authority without laying down the parameters within which this authority must be exercised. In New York a statute that granted this wide-ranging authority to the State Commissioner of Education was struck down as an unconstitutional delegation of authority.[42] The highest court in New York said that "Private schools have a constitutional right to exist, and parents have a constitutional right to send their children to such schools. [Citing *Pierce* (see chap. 2).] The legislature under the police power has a limited right to regulate such schools in the public interest. [Citing *Pierce* (see chap. 2).] Such being the fundamental law of the subject, it would be intolerable for the Legislature to hand over to any official or group of officials a unlimited, unrestrained, undefined power to make such regulations as he or they should desire, and to grant or refuse licenses to such schools, depending on their compliance with such regulations."[43] Clearly the New York court is correct, in that without standards to guide the discretion of the commissioner, inconsistent and arbitrary decisions could be reached in the licensing of schools, for the commissioner's own biases might end up being the basis for these decisions rather than considered legislative policy and legitimate state interests. What are needed are either legislatively promulgated standards (which in turn must be subject to the limitations of the U.S. Constitution, to be discussed later) or standards for licensing promulgated by the commissioner himself (also subject to constitutional limitations) which are consistent with some general policy laid down by the legislature. In this way the potential for arbitrary decisions would be minimized and licensing would be based on considered state interests, not administrative whim.[44]

Also of importance in this area are administrative procedures to be followed in the licensing of private schools, but some states neither include within their educational codes nor as part of an administrative procedure act any procedures that must be followed by state officials in granting or revoking licenses. (Administrative procedure acts are general acts applicable to administrative agencies and sometimes municipalities and school districts. These acts specify the procedures that these agencies must follow in issuing rules and regulations and in carrying out such quasi-judicial functions as granting and denying licenses. These acts also usually spell out the conditions under which judicial review of the agency's action may be obtained and the standards of review the courts must follow in reviewing the actions of agencies.) The absence of any statutorily determined procedures raises serious problems since, without procedural safeguards, such as the opportunity to be heard, abuse of discretion is more likely. For example, having a hearing at which people seeking to gain or hold onto a license may present their side of the case, coupled with the requirement that the official base his decision only on the evidence of record, is another way—along with having standards officials must follow—of protecting individuals who plan to or do operate alternative or experimental private schools against arbitrary and biased governmental officials. But state courts have been notorious in saying that licenses of any sort are privileges, hence state agencies need not follow any special procedures in granting or denying them. Nevertheless there is some movement in both state courts and federal courts toward the view that licenses are sufficiently important interests that the requirements of due process must be followed in granting and denying them.[45]

The emerging view is most certainly the correct view, especially if one understands that the licensing procedure required by twenty-eight states is a form of prior restraint on freedom of speech. That is, the licensing procedures and the compulsory education requirement that parents send their children only to schools that have prior state approval is a form of prior censorship of the private educational effort with all the entailing risks for free speech. Prior restraint prevents speech before it can take place and suppression by a bureaucrat is more likely to be applied than suppression through after-the-fact criminal prosecutions. The licensing procedures, even if a hearing is granted, provide less protection than those of a criminal trial in an after-the-fact prosecution of a violation of the compulsory education laws; the prior approval system allows less chance for public scrutiny; and the dynamics of a bureaucracy move toward ever-broadening control.[46] Furthermore, a prior approval system for education raises special problems. What is it, after all, that the state officials are asked to approve of? The answer is, basically, a plan for a child's education; hence state officials are asked to predict if a particular educational program will adequately educate the child.[47] The possibilities for arbitrary decisions based on personal prejudice and bias are obvious in this situation.

For these reasons the Supreme Court has tended to examine closely all systems of prior restraint and has said that unless special procedural safeguards are provided prior restraint is not permissible. These safeguards have been stated to be: (1) proving that the form of speech involved should not go forward rests with the censor; (2) since only a judicial determination suffices to impose a valid final restraint, the censor must either grant the license or go to court to obtain the restraining order; and (3) the system of review must assure a prompt final judicial decision.[48]

Even in those states that establish procedures for granting and denying licenses to private schools, those procedures do not conform to these requirements as nothing in the statutes either places the burden of proof on the state or gives to the judiciary the final authority to grant or issue the license. Prior approval of private educational efforts as implemented by states today thus remains highly suspect and may very well be unconstitutional.

But even if states were to change their procedures so as to be in accord with what the Supreme Court has required in other prior restraint cases, the question remains as to whether prior restraint is a good idea. Could the courts do any better at determining the adequacy of the private educational plan up for review, or of predicting the educational outcomes of the methods to be used?: It is highly improbable that they could. All in all, it would seem that after-the-fact review would be the wiser course—to prosecute schools and parents once they undertook the educational effort, after the fruits of that effort could be discerned. This approach is less speculative in nature and provides better protection for the parents, students, and teachers.

Prohibiting Home Instruction

Another threat to educational diversity are those compulsory education laws that prohibit home instruction. Such a restriction raises a serious constitutional issue as it severely cuts into the recognized constitutional right of parents to control the upbringing of their children (see chaps. 2 and 7). Since this right today is likely to be viewed by the courts not as an ordinary liberty but as a liberty akin to such other fundamental liberties as freedom of speech and the free exercise of religion, only a compelling state justification would probably save such a prohibition from a ruling striking it down as unconstitutional.[49] States might offer two arguments in support of the prohibition: first, that it is administratively more convenient for the state to regulate the private educational efforts of schools as opposed to what goes on in numerous living rooms around the state, and, second, private schools are likely, because of the need to maintain their public reputations, to assure children of a better quality education. But it would seem that neither of these arguments would be sufficiently compelling to overcome the parent's right to educate his or her own child so long as that education in fact met the reasonable standards for private education established by the state. It cannot be said that home instruction is per se inferior or inadequate unless the state can convince a court that only large group instruction is to be allowed because of the lessons learned from attending schools as part of a large group, for example, lessons in social adjustment. If the state made this argument it would be imposing a concept of an adequate education on parent and child which itself would need justification. This is a value judgment of the most intrusive kind and hardly one sufficiently important to warrant this kind of state control. Finally, mere administrative convenience has never been deemed to be a compelling enough reason for the state to trample on fundamental rights.[50]

Private Teachers Must Be Certified

The requirement of some seventeen states that private teachers must hold state certification may also be constitutionally suspect.[51] Once again this restriction places an enormous obstacle in the way of parents interested in controlling the upbringing of their children by educating them at home. A state might be justified in placing such a prior condition on private educational efforts if it could be established that teaching was a profession like medicine or law in which special training is obviously needed if the practitioner is to be able to provide even minimally adequate services. But there is no evidence that adequate teaching can be provided only by those who have gone through teacher education programs and obtained a state certificate. Thus, the requirement may in fact only serve to bar most home instruction without significantly advancing an important state interest: the infringement on individual liberty is not justified by the proved benefits of the requirement.

Beyond these problems, certification requirements can significantly impinge upon the free exercise of religion. For example, a certification requirement would make illegal the private religious schools of the Amish since these schools are taught by Amish teachers who, as part of their religion and culture, have not gone on to college and consequently have not obtained a certificate to teach.[52] This is a problem that has been confronted and not finally legally resolved in Iowa, where all private school teachers must be certified and where a large number of Amish live. Any constitutional resolution to the question would probably be undertaken in the analytical framework established by the *Wisconsin* v. *Yoder* case discussed in chapter 2. In brief, it would seem the Amish would have to be granted an exemption from the certification requirement if it were established that the requirement severely impinged upon their free exercise of religion (which it probably does) and if the state cannot establish that granting an exemption would frustrate the realization of a compelling state interest (which the state probably cannot do.)

The Imposition of Curriculum Requirements

As the review of the state laws reveals, state statutes in a variety of ways impose specific curricular requirements on private schools. But, as discussed in chapter 2, we know that the state may only impose reasonable regulations on private schools, that those regulations may not be so detailed as either to deny parents a reasonable choice with respect to teachers, curriculum, and textbooks or to deny parents a fair opportunity to choose for their children instruction which they want and which the state cannot show is harmful. Beyond this we know that the Supreme Court has struck down a law that would have barred private schools from instructing children by using a classroom language other than English and would have even barred teaching children a language other than English before the eighth grade. The Court viewed the law as an unwarranted infringement upon the rights of parents and private school teachers. And lastly we know that curricular requirements may not abridge the free exercise of religion without there being a compelling reason for the restriction. In sum, because private education does involve fundamental rights of parents to educate their children, free speech, and the free exercise of religion, it would appear that only those curricular requirements that were necessary to achieve a compelling state interest would withstand judicial scrutiny.

With this general proposition in mind we can turn to a brief examination of several of the curricular requirements that states today impose upon private schools. First, some states today still require that all instruction be in English.[53] In light of the case striking down a law prohibiting instruction in a language other than English, the question becomes whether there is a difference between a state statute that prohibits certain instruction and a state statute that requires a certain form of instruction. In this instance the two would seem to be identical and the current laws appear unconstitutional.

Second, states also require that children be taught patriotism, love of country, and even to be moral. Such requirements as these compel private school teachers to espouse values and beliefs with which they may disagree. In light of *West Virginia* v. *Barnette* (see chap. 2) it is doubtful that states could compel private school teachers to confess belief in these values. Further, such requirements by implication prohibit instructing children in contrary viewpoints, a clear infringement of the free speech rights of parents and teachers. A related question is whether the state could prohibit parents and private schools from teaching certain doctrines, such as Marxism, communism, or racism. Traditionally, First

Amendment doctrine tells us that such rules would be unconstitutional unless the instruction of the pupils posed a clear and present danger to society or if the instruction incited pupils to violent action for which they had been primed and prepared to carry out once given the word. It is highly doubtful that politically radical or racist instruction of elementary and secondary pupils would meet these tests which stress the immediacy of danger to society.[54]

For these same reasons it would appear that the Michigan statute that requires private schools to select textbooks that recognize the achievements and accomplishments of ethnic and racial groups is not constitutional.[55] But specific course requirements such as that all private school children be taught English, arithmetic, and U.S. history are probably constitutional in that they serve a substantial state interest and only minimally interfere with the freedoms of parents and teachers. Yet how far might the state go with such requirements—could it constitutionally go so far as to force private education to be identical to public education? Note that the compulsory education law requirements that private education be substantially equivalent tends to impose such uniformity upon private education.

The answer to these questions seems to be that it would be unconstitutional if the state tried to eliminate all diversity in educational offerings by forcing the private school to be exactly like the public schools. As some state courts have said, the purpose behind the compulsory education laws is that children be educated, not that they all be educated in the same way.[56] And any state which tried to act to the contrary would run afoul of the Court's language in *Farrington* v. *Tokushige* (see chap. 2) that parents may not be denied a "reasonable choice in respect of teachers, curriculum, and textbooks." And the degree of this protection of parental choice is likely to rise as the state curricular requirements impinge upon the free exercise of religion. In brief, while the precise extent of power that states have in forcing private schools to offer a certain kind of educational program cannot be stated, we do know that the power does not include making the private school over into a model of the public schools so that parental choice is eliminated. Private schools must be permitted to be different, and this probably means significantly different, even radical. And in light of this standard the possibility exists that current state laws that require private education to be substantially equivalent may be unconsitutional if the natural meaning of those words is fully imposed upon private educational efforts.

9

Conclusions and Policy Recommendations

Who has the authority to control the school curriculum? The short answer to the question is that today control of the school curriculum is shared by all three levels of government, by the state and federal courts, by the teachers' union, and in a minor way, by parents. What are the policy consequences of this shared control? Again the short answer is that today the curriculum is supposed to be purged of much of older America's culture and is increasingly being directed toward the improvement of the learning of children as measured by standardized tests. What further changes in the system for controlling the school's program ought to be considered? Briefly, there are two kinds of changes—those involving modifications in the present system and those involving more drastic changes that would place primary control of a child's education back in the hands of parents. Each of these points will be further elaborated on in this chapter. But one word of caution is in order at this point. The conclusions that follow have been presented in broad strokes to bring out what appears to have been the general trend of development over the past twenty years. The picture which emerges from these pages will not be wholly accurate for all states but, rather, will aim at representing current trends.

Sharing Control of the Curriculum

We are now in a position to elaborate on the new models for governmental control of the school program sketched in the first chapter so as to bring out some additional features. It will be recalled that in the first chapter we noted that the control of the curriculum had become increasingly legalized, centralized, bureaucratized, and diversified in terms of the number of participants in the decision-making process. One factor that has made these developments possible is the fact that even in states that have prized local control of the school program, the principle of local control of education no longer seems to count heavily in the formation of educational policy. While lip service is still paid to this doctrine, in actual practice it does not seem to stop new state and federal efforts to influence what goes on at the local level. To the extent that the principle still counts in political debates in Congress and in state legislatures, it serves merely as a weapon to force modifications of proposed initiatives. For example, the design of

169

grant-in-aid programs may be affected by arguments couched in terms of the preservation of local control of education, as occurred in 1974 when Congress consolidated several existing grant-in-aid programs as a way of simplifying the grant-in-aid system and providing a modest increase in local discretion.[1] Additionally, the doctrine of local control seems to continue to play a role in the course of administering grant-in-aid programs by weakening the political position of federal and some state officials interested in seeking strong enforcement of federal and state regulations.

Related to that point is the further finding that today there seems to be a widespread agreement on the proposition that the federal and state governments may legitimately attempt to shape the priorities and nature of the local program. What goes on at the local level is today viewed as of national and statewide concern and should not be left solely to the control of local administrators who lack the more general perspectives.

Similarly, the traditional barrier against judicial involvement in school affairs has been breached. At one time courts strongly held to the view that educators were experts who should be left free of judicial supervision especially when the judiciary could claim no special expertise in the area. But increasingly, not only has the expertise of the educator come to be doubted, but also courts have come to believe that expertise, even assuming it is genuine, must be confined by the principles adumbrated in the U.S. and state constitutions. This development has been compounded by the expansion in the hands of the courts of these legal principles. The most important development has been the steps taken toward recognition of a state-created right to an education with wide ramifications for most of what goes on in the schools. In the federal courts the expansion and use of the Equal Protection clause has also meant greater judicial intrusion into the affairs of the schools.

The lowering of these political and psychological barriers to greater control of the school program by units of government other than the local distict has been accompanied by a change in how control is shared among the three levels of government over the school program. While measuring the degree of change from the older models is difficult in that the terms *control* and *authority* and *power* are difficult to state in measurable terms, we do have one significant way of indicating the degree of the change, and that is by noting the number of new federal and state statutes, federal and state regulations, and federal and state cases bearing on the school program. There has been a virtual explosion in the size of this body of law over the past twenty years. The vast bulk of the legal materials discussed in this book is the product of the last twenty years alone.

The new involvement of the federal and state legislatures has resulted not only in increased control by these bodies but also in the creation of federal and state bureaucracies with significant authority to interpret the new legislation. And since the legislative mandate often is ambiguous, requiring further interpretation by the bureaus charged with enforcement, these agencies often develop policies of great import for local districts that are at best only logical deductions from the statutory language, rather than policies based expressly on legislatively approved positions. Thus a new and not wholly predictable participant has been introduced into the process for decisions about the public schools' programs. And while these agencies may often feel politically vulnerable and lacking a solid political base, they nevertheless have enough power at a minimum to force local districts into dissembling compliance with their requirements, if not to bring about something more than mere token compliance.

The kinds of demands being placed on the districts are both negative and positive. The negative prohibitions usually are directed toward eliminating some form of discrimination. But negative prohibitions by themselves do not represent the most sweeping control by state and federal agencies and courts since negative restraints leave local districts free to develop many policies of their own choosing. Negative restraints, however, can be converted into positive requirements, and since this conversion can be accomplished by an administrative agency, this point underscores the power of these agencies in education. All this is brought out most dramatically by OCR's reading of Title VI's negative prohibition against race discrimination to require that affirmative steps be taken to provide special instruction in English to non-English-speaking students (see chap. 3). In addition to negative requirements, positive requirements have been imposed by the state legislatures. The new special education laws impose such positive duties on local districts which, as with other such new duties, significantly reduce the discretion of local boards.

The combination of negative prohibitions and positive requirements has meant significant involvement of the state and federal levels of government in the following tasks which make up the policymaking process (see app. 1A): the establishment of educational priorities; the establishment of minimum educational standards; the creation of pupil classification systems; the determination of the cultural bias of courses; and the methods of program evaluation. State and federal influence have also reached the development of new materials and approaches. Indeed there is almost no role in the policymaking process that state and federal agencies as well as courts do not share with local districts.

The degree of federal and state involvement and judicial involvement in the schools seems likely to increase over time and not abate. This seems to be true for several reasons. First, as noted earlier, the barriers against such involvement have been breached if not surmounted. Second, there appears to be a logic to reform movements brought about from the top down that leads to more control: since each state or federal requirement imposed on districts is not self-enforcing and pressures at the local level encourage noncompliance, the result is a perceived need for more rules and requirements to check the ways that the local districts have found for circumventing the original rules. All of this is compounded by the likelihood that districts will continue trying to circumvent the rules laid down by courts and state and federal agencies. This is so because the demands of these laws and regulations are often so far-reaching in their implications, for example, the special education laws, that districts have no way, at least in the foreseeable future, of achieving full compliance. Money alone is a central problem; as it is typical of reform legislation to make demands without providing all the funds needed to fully carry out the reform. Furthermore, the changes asked often may entail changes throughout the local system that, if doable without other legal and political complications, take time to work out; but often the required changes conflict with other constraints within which the district feels it must also work and a compromise is struck resulting in only partial compliance with the new reform requirements.

A third reason state and federal control is likely to expand is that tackling one educational problem, such as the problem of children from disadvantaged homes, points to the need to tackle others, such as the learning problems of the mentally retarded, the learning disabled, and the extremely bright child. And each new piece of legislation increases the control of either or both the federal and state governments. The recently adopted federal grant-in-aid program for the handicapped has prompted the legislative chairman of the Council of Chief State School Officers, Pennsylvania Education Secretary John Pittenger, to say "This new bill will increase federal aid to special education by 5 percent but federal regulation in that area by 50 percent."[2] Regulations for enforcement of that act are still in the draft stage, but indications are they will be sweeping and will have profound implications for districts accepting federal aid for handicapped children. For example, these regulations may call for the mainstreaming of handicapped students which will affect the entire school program, and the regulations are likely to lead to a large number of complaints having to do with school architecture and affirmative action for handicapped students.

Fourth, the federal statutes such as Title VI and IX can be the basis for individual court suits which seek enforcement of those laws in ways not yet contemplated by federal regulations. Thus the courts may be asked to extend these statutes to deal with sexism and racism in textual materials. And the courts may take the opportunities given them by the state and federal statutes to extend the protection of those statutes in ways that go beyond what was originally intended by Congress or the state legislatures, thus further entangling the local boards in requirements.

The upshot of these developments is that it is no longer accurate to speak of local control of the educational program. School boards must engage in a continuous dialogue, must continuously bargain with federal and state officials over the school's program. The point may even have been reached that we should characterize the local board not as a local unit of government with some power to establish basic educational policy, but as a governmental agency charged with carrying out the details of the basic policies established by higher units of government and the courts.

The Professionals

As if all this were not sufficient, we have also noted that as regards the curriculum, most observers of public schools agree that the professionals employed by the schools already have the dominant voice vis-à-vis the school board. (Recall from chapter 4 that Alabama, Arkansas, Oklahoma, Tennessee, and Utah have by statute turned the selection of textbooks over to professionals who operate statewide textbook commissions and/-or local textbook selection committees.) That is, the school boards tend to delegate what authority they have, given the constraints of federal and state laws and court rulings, to the superintendent and his staff as well as teachers, to determine the details of the school program. With the rise of teachers' unions demanding to negotiate both over the allocation of authority to control the curriculum and the content of the school program itself, the authority of the school board has been further eroded. It might not even be wholly accurate to talk of codetermination of the curriculum by the board and professionals. Perhaps the more accurate statement is codetermination by state, federal, and local professionals with the local board serving as an advisory or sounding board.

Parental Authority

The decline in the authority of the local school board has direct implications for the chances of parents to obtain from the public schools their preferred educational program: the less the authority of the school board, the lower are the chances of parents obtaining what they want through the school board. Additionally, actual legal rights of parents vis-à-vis the public schools are meager. The problems parents face in the exercise of their *Pierce*-created right are enhanced by the rising costs of private school and the strong barriers established by the Supreme Court against aid to religious schools, the predominant form of private school (see chap. 2).

We have also seen that there are in some states efforts to regulate private schools in such a way as to make them like the public schools, thereby further reducing the reasonable choice even of those parents with the money to afford private schooling. The content of formal education at the elementary and secondary levels is today largely in the hands of people remote from parents and not susceptible to parental influence.

Beyond these formal aspects of the curriculum, parents also lack authority to control whether their child is placed in a traditional classroom or in an "open classroom," and whether traditional ways of grouping students will be used versus the use of nongraded approaches. Parents have no influence over the type of report cards issued, the methods of assessing pupils' achievement and progress, or even the method of discipline used in the school. Parents cannot determine whether the school stresses competition for grades or plays down this aspect of schooling and stresses individualized progress. There is, in short, much that happens to their children in school which parents have no right to influence.

The kind of curriculum to which parents are today being impelled to expose their children is nonreligious, secular, but not militantly secular. It is oriented toward achievement as measured by standardized tests. The program is more diverse in that it must now be designed to take into account the differing needs of pupils and may not be simply directed to the average and normal English-speaking child. The program is to be purged of the prejudices of an older America—sexism and racism—but may be a program in which children are exposed to strong statements on behalf of newer attitudes toward the appropriate roles of, for example, women and men in our society. Thus, schools may introduce students to ideas strongly in conflict with parental viewpoints. And merely informing the child that such viewpoints exist carries the implied message that there are many people who believe that the viewpoint of the child's parents may be wrong. This phenomenon produces the greatest controversy in health or sex education courses. For some people this opening up of options for the child, this liberating of the child from the parents' educational domination is what education should be all about; for others, however, this function of the school undermines the family and creates the risk of confusion and anxiety in the child. But, at least with regard to sex education courses, parents usually have the option of obtaining an exemption for their child. When it comes to political education, parents have not been given that option and there are fewer restraints on political bias in schools than on any other value-laden portion of the school program. Schools today may require the children of communistic parents to take courses in the evil of communism or the children of socialistic parents to study the benefits of the free enterprise system. Schools may and do present distorted accounts of the Civil War, the civil rights movement, and the problems of racial discrimination in the country. This last point is brought out most clearly by the occurrences in Virginia between 1950 and 1972.

In 1950, the politics of Virginia were dominated by a political organization or machine headed by Senator Harry F. Byrd, Sr.[3] During the state legislative session of that year the organization obtained from the legislature, with little opposition, a resolution creating the "Virginia History and Government Textbook Commission" whose task it was to see to the writing of suitable texts on Virginia history. These texts were then to be required for use in all districts in the state. Three textbooks were commissioned for grades four, seven, and eleven, and after many rewritings to fit the requirements of the Byrd-dominated textbook commission, the books were published and used in the public schools until January 1972. The distortions found in these texts are exemplified by the high school text entitled *Cavalier Commonwealth*. This book described slavery as "comprehensive social security" and suggested that the Negroes themselves had instituted segregation to protect their own institutions. All statements that appeared in original drafts of the manuscripts on the Byrd organization were deleted and no reference was permitted in the text to the "massive resistance" to desegregation adopted as official state policy following the 1954 Supreme Court segregation decision. Only with the weakening of the Byrd organization and the rise of black voting power and criticism from the press was action finally taken to remove the books from the approved state textbook lists.

What occurred in Virginia is only a more extreme example of what occurs in many school districts throughout the country. Scholar after scholar has discovered that the textbooks used in the public schools carry messages not all parents would agree with.[4] The general message to American students about the United States is that we are the most powerful, peace-loving, and benevolent society in the world. And it is no small part of the school curriculum that is affected with this kind of political bias. It has been estimated that American schools spend more time and effort on political education than do the Soviet Russian schools.[5] Another study shows that in grades ten to twelve alone, the number of political courses (for example, American history; civics; social studies; problems of democracy) available in school averages at 4.8 with a standard deviation of 1.5. That same study also shows that a significant percentage of students takes between two and three such courses during only the last three years of high school.[6]

An Assessment

What is the justification for the recent increase in the centralization of authority controlling the school program? To answer the question it is necessary to return to the principles listed in chapter 1 that have played a role in deciding how authority should be allocated. The principles which seem to have been given the greatest weight in shaping the present system are the principles of state and national interests; the principle of affected interests; the principle of equality; and the principle of efficiency and effectiveness. But in each case each principle has been given a special interpretation to justify the increasing centralization of the control of the school program.

Thus the justification of the newer models for controlling the school program probably goes as follows. The vaunted benefits of local control of education seem not to have materialized; namely, that local control provides a training ground for democracy and a means by which self-reliance and initiative can be developed. Data tends to show that few people participate in local governmental affairs and those who do tend to be from upper social classes only.[7] Neither does local control per se enhance a sense of community or belonging as people tend more to identify themselves with the nation or the total urban area in which they live, rather than with their particular local school district.[8] Local control has not produced a more legitimate form of government, for the fact is that many minorities have failed to gain representation and influence at the local level.[9] For them the legitimacy of the public schools is subject to severe question. Indeed the costs of local control have been quite high: the trampling of minority interests and the neglect of the educational needs of many children—those from disadvantaged homes, the mentally and physically handicapped, and the non-English-speaking. Notions of equality and fairness demand that these children by given protection and apparently the only way this seems possible is through action by the federal and state governments and through the courts.

Beyond the problem of equality is the fact that with the high mobility of this society the educational failures of one district spell trouble for those other parts of the country to which these failures travel. Education is a matter of interest to the nation and state, not just the locality. For this reason and because of the increasing costs in providing education, we need to make sure the educational program is efficient and effective and the way to do this is through improved efforts at educational testing and evaluation.

Finally, the principles of affected interests and efficiency provide support for the increased professional control of the school program. There are thus powerful arguments that justify the teachers' unions demands for negotiations over the curriculum.

Of course what this rationale for increasing centralization overlooks or plays down is the principle of parental rights to control the education of their children. What we seem to be saying is that there is no way the other principles can be satisfied while at the same time protecting parental rights. Furthermore, the argument on behalf of increased centralization assumes that increased centralization does not itself produce inefficiencies and waste. There is also an implication that because all the benefits of local control were not fully realized, it makes sense to eliminate totally what benefits there are: that the lost opportunities for local and parental control are a small price, a price of little significance. Further, it seems that the argument for more centralization assumes, without saying so, that the separation of politics and education can be maintained under a centralized system. But the materials in chapter 4 and the Virginia example recounted earlier show that such a separation is not so easily maintained. And if one is tempted to say that Virginia represents a unique example one need only turn to recent educational history in Arizona to disconfirm that belief. Arizona, one of the more centralized states in the union, has just concluded three long and rancorous political struggles arising out of an effort by state officials to control education at the local level. One of these episodes was discussed in chapter 4. Another involved the adoption and implementation of a statute requiring students to take a course in the benefits of the free enterprise system. The third involved an effort on the part of the state board, through its power to control textbook selection, to require all school districts in the state to teach reading only by the phonics approach. In all three instances full state control was ultimately beaten back, but these incidents show centralized authority can be used to impose controversial viewpoints.

The dilemma we face is that, in attempting to maximize one principle or set of principles, we invariably end up violating other principles. To maximize local control has in the past meant the neglect of certain children in violation of the principle of equality. To stress equality as well as several other principles seems to result in an undermining of parental control, the separation of education from politics, and several other principles. Is there anything that can be done to help mitigate these terrible trade-offs?

Modifications of the System

One way of increasing local control would simply be to dismantle some of the main features of the present system for controlling the school program, for example, state textbook adoption laws, the federal grant-in-aid effort, and state laws designed to protect handicapped and non-English-speaking pupils. And indeed President Ford's effort to move toward block grants seems to represent just this sort of reform (see chap. 3). But while reducing the federal role in local educational efforts is at least thinkable and perhaps politically possible there are no indications that the political power or will exists to roll back the increasing state involvement in local educational efforts. In such an event, cutting back on the state and federal role could once again expose the disadvantaged and handicapped and non-English-speaking pupils to the indifference of the earlier period.

But some reduction in federal and state involvement, when coupled with other reforms, may make more sense. For example, if school boards could be made more representative of the various constituencies trapped within the boundaries of local districts, then it might be safe to reduce somewhat the power of the federal and state governments which is now needed to protect those groups. Election of school boards by wards or by the methods of proportional representation could serve to obtain for minority groups representation on the school board; thus these groups could protect themselves at the local level by insisting upon the programs that serve their interests. But this kind of reform will tend to protect only certain kinds of groups, namely, groups defined in terms of race, ethnicity, religion, and social class as it is in these terms that political participation and voting take place. Likely to be excluded from representation are those parents of children with mental and physical handicaps, since they do not tend to live and act together as a political unit. Also, small minority groups that comprise only a small percentage of the local population will fail to be protected. Hence, *total* elimination of the federal and state presence is not warranted, even with the electoral reforms suggested here.

Related to the change in how board members are elected are such reforms as assurance of access to information relied upon by the district in shaping its educational program. Freedom of information laws, which are free of the ambiguities and the vagueness of the New York law, would be of great help in this regard. As an additional requirement state law could require school districts to document major curricular changes so that there would be information to check up on the wisdom of the local decision.

It also seems clear that steps need to be taken to stop the increasing tendency of school boards to negotiate with teachers over the substance of the school curriculum, since the inclusion of the curriculum as a subject of negotiations leads to and involves the following kinds of complications. If the curriculum is a permissive subject of negotiations, let alone being a mandatory subject, it would be possible for a school board and union to negotiate over, for example, how the history of unionism is to be presented in American history courses, with the union insisting upon an interpretation favorable to it and unfavorable to employers. Other doctrinal issues might wind up being the subject of negotiations, for example, the position taken on the Democratic and Republican parties; the attitude to be taken toward racism in schools, including teachers' unions, and so on. Thus 51 percent of the teachers could insist upon doctrinal viewpoints that could end up being imposed upon the other 49 percent because the school board was willing to go along to obtain a wage concession from the union. More broadly, it seems clearly not to be in most people's interest to have the curriculum shaped by the haphazard exigencies of the bargaining process. Is it proper for agreement on whether or not there will be a compensatory education program to hinge on the board's willingness to concede to, for example, a union demand for increased health benefits? To put the point somewhat differently, it does not seem to serve the interests of most people in society to make continued board control of the curriculum contingent on the board's willingness to agree to higher economic benefits. To make the curriculum a subject of negotiations means the board may end up having to pay for the right to continue to decide curriculum policy by paying higher wages and other benefits. Should government be in the position of having to pay an economic price to a private group in order to continue to keep control of what it was established to do? The answer clearly seems to be "no."

Thus, one needed reform is legislation that attempts to draw a line between, on the one hand, the curriculum and related items, and, on the other hand, those rewards and protections employees traditionally have sought as preconditions to the continued provision of their services. Such legislation would make the curriculum and closely related items illegal subjects of negotiations so as to bar school boards even voluntarily bargaining over the curriculm. But if this kind of legislation is not adopted, other measures designed to protect parents and other interested groups should be considered—other measures such as requiring a referendum on those aspects of the agreement dealing with the curriculum; multiparty bargaining with regard to curricular issues; open "fishbowl" bargaining; and requiring the parties to publicly declare their bargaining positions at the start of negotiations. With regard to the last point note should be made of the following provsion from California's collective bargaining law:

(a) All initial proposals of exclusive representatives and of public school employers, which relate to matters within the scope of representation, shall be presented at a public meeting of the public school employer and thereafter shall be public records.

(b) Meeting and negotiating shall not take place on any proposal until a reasonable time has elapsed after the submission of the proposal to enable the public to become informed and the public has the opportunity to express itself regarding the proposal at a meeting of the public school employer.

(c) After the public has had the opportunity to express itself, the public school employer shall, at a meeting which is open to the public, adopt its initial proposal.

(d) New subjects of meeting and negotiating arising after the presentation of initial proposals shall be made public within 24 hours. If a vote is taken on such subject by the public school employer, the vote thereon by each member voting shall also be made public within 24 hours.

(e) The board may adopt regulations for the purpose of implementing this section, which are consistent with the intent of the section; namely that the public be informed of the issues that are being negotiated upon and have full opportunity to express their views on the issues to the public school employer, and to know of the positions of their elected representatives.[10]

These kinds of proposals provide some protection for parents and other groups in the society, but still more needs to be done. Schools today enjoy sufficient discretion to impose upon students politically biased courses and materials. One way to elevate this problem would be to give parents the right to seek an exemption from those political education courses that present a viewpoint with which the parent strongly disagrees. Such a statutory remedy, however, has certain problems with it. First, merely to allow the exemption seems to create the presumption that schools have the right to use public resources to mount nonrequired, elective, politically biased courses. But what is the justification for forcing taxpayers to pay for courses, for example, in the benefits of the free enterprise system when they may disagree with the content of the course— when the course is designed to produce citizens who will form a large and stable political group permanently opposed to the viewpoint of the objecting taxpayers who are forced to support their own political powerlessness? Such a political education effort hardly seems justified in a society in which public opinion is supposed to control government, not government public opinion. Second, merely to allow an exemption means unequal treatment of parents and pupils. Some parents will find the political education program serves to support their biases whereas others, who have sought the exemption, find the schools hardly provide them with the same supportive attention.

As an alternative solution to the problem of political bias, legislatures should consider the promulgation of a statute requiring of schools a duty of fairness.[11] This duty might be specified as follows: when a school provides instruction with regard to matters of a political nature then it must adequately and objectively cover the issues both explicitly and implicitly touched upon by the materials: the coverage must be fair in that it accurately and objectively reflects the opposing views on the issues; and reasonable attention must be paid to the significant major opposing views. This rule would not apply to each class session but to the work in a course of an entire semester or perhaps at most of a year, hence over such a period of time the materials in the course would have to be sufficiently balanced to meet the rule's requirement.

In general terms, the rule would function to prevent forcing taxpayers to support political views with which they disagree. It would prevent the schools from playing a role in determining the number of adherents to a political viewpoint or policy. The rule assumes that inequalities in the number of people supporting a given political position should not be a function of the intentional political educational activities of the public schools. The rule also assumes it is not the function of public schools purposefully to attempt to positively reinforce some political views and negatively reinforce others. Finally the rule assumes that it is appropriate for the schools to promote consideration of important political issues and the opposing viewpoints: schools should provide opportunities for students to sort out their own thinking and this means assuring a rich flow of information and viewpoints—the creation of a marketplace of ideas. The rule, thus, attempts to preclude governmental control of public opinion.

The rule would apply, we suggest, not to each class session but to the work in a course of an entire semester or perhaps at most of a year, hence over the semester or year the materials in the course must be sufficiently balanced to meet the rules requirement. The requirement in the rule that there must be a fair presentation not only of the issues explicitly raised but also those implicitly raised is to avoid the following sort of problem. What if the school, in taking up the riots that occurred in Watts, Detroit, Newark, Washington, D.C., and other cities, simply approached the topic in terms of the adequacy of the training and equipment of the police and military forces brought onto the scene? Certainly such an issue was involved in these riots but to view the riots only in these terms is a distortion. The implicit message of such an approach, *even if* the school's discussion of the issue of the management of the police and National Guard is informed and balanced, is that the only issue placed on the public agenda by the riots was this question of police and military management.

Next, the kind of issue to which the rule applies would not simply be those issues currently being debated in the media, Congress, and state legislatures or local deliberative bodies. School take up issues that are academic or theoretical or historical, and balance would be expected in the treatment of those issues as well. It would make little sense to impose upon a school a requirement of balance when discussing whether Congress should adopt some form of national health care plan, but not require balance when discussing the free enterprise system or socialism.

The limitation of the rule to the presentation of significant and major opposing views is to avoid the problem of forcing schools to present every possible position that may be or has been adopted with regard to an issue. Clearly this term leaves room for dispute, but what this part of the obligation entails might best be worked out on a case-by-case basis.

The rule would also require that the viewpoints taken up be accurately presented and objectively treated. The idea here is that the views not be caricatured or distorted in order to encourage rejection by the students, but this would not preclude a critical and reasoned examination of the views as long as all views are subject to the same critical analysis, so as to reveal the premises, assumptions, logic, and consequences of each view. And the requirement that reasonable attention be paid to the views taken up is designed to allow some leeway to school officials to take into account the importance of a view, its complexity, and the interest of the students in the view being explored.

Finally, the rule of fairness would apply to both required and elective courses, as it imposes a general duty to be fair in presenting materials, not merely to be fair to those students who form a captive audience. The rule is directed not merely against school practices which might be termed indoctrination but also to those school programs that are merely severely biased or unfair.

Complaints with regard to violations of the rule might be turned over to an administrative agency established to handle such complaints or to the chief state school officer. The decision of the agency or the chief state school officer would in turn be subject to judicial review. In any event, the idea of the duty of fairness is to protect parents and other interested groups from schools becoming the vehicle for propagating particular political viewpoints.

Yet a different approach for addressing the problem of stereotyping and bias in educational materials has been suggested by the Lawyers' Committee for Civil Rights Under Law.[12] The proposed statute imposes on teachers a duty to present alternative views to the bias found in the materials already in use in the classroom. Additionally, the students, parents, and citizens would be guaranteed access to all materials used by the students and the right of the students, parents, and citizens to seek a conference with regard to the materials and to request the opportunity to observe the use of the materials in the classroom would be established. The statute specifies certain steps to be followed with regard to the observation to minimize class disruption. At the conference, the student, parent, or citizen may present a plan with regard to what they think will bring about compliance with the duty imposed by the statute on the teacher. In case the teacher disagrees, he or she may request that a three-person panel decide whether the request should be granted or denied. The panel is to be made up of two teachers employed by the system but appointed by the students or parents or citizens, and the third panel member by the teacher. The panel would be given considerable discretion by the state to fashion the appropriate remedy.

A different kind of protection is afforded parents and students by the Massachusetts law giving parents and students the right to demand, under certain conditions, the provision of a course by the local school board (see chap. 4). As suggested in that chapter, such a law could be redrafted or interpreted in such a way as to avoid running afoul of the doctrine against delegating public power to private groups. The advantage of this kind of a law is that it returns to parents and students some degree of affirmative power to shape the educational program to which the student is exposed. Parents and students are given, by this law, a power that goes beyond a mere veto or negative power.

Just as the Massachusetts law gives parents an affirmative voice in shaping school program, not just a veto, so other reforms with regard to the selection of textbooks and other materials seem warranted. In states with statewide adoption of textbooks, those laws could be abolished or, if that is not politically feasible, substantially modified. The modifications could include requirements for greater parental involvement in the selection of materials at all stages of the selection process. Also, the laws could be changed to give local districts more leeway in the selection of materials. Thus, the laws might be changed in the way they have been in California to require lists of at least five books per subject/grade. Generous opportunities to obtain waivers should be permitted. Supplementary materials should go unregulated and no listings should be required for courses not mandated by statute.

Another kind of reform that might be adopted either in states using state textbook adoption systems or relying on local adoption would be one that would require school districts to place proposed materials, whether it be books or audiovisual materials, on public display for a period of time, say, ninety days, coupled with an invitation to parents and others to submit written comments, to be followed by a public hearing if necessary.[13]

A related but more sweeping reform has been suggested by the Lawyers' Committee for Civil Rights Under Law.[14] The proposed statute would, with regard to materials required for use by students, place primary responsibility for the initial selection in the hands of the teachers, subject to approval or disapproval by a parent-elected board in elementary schools and student-elected boards in high schools. For nonrequired materials, the law would permit the decision to be turned over to either the teachers, a student-elected committee, or individual students. The proposed statute also outlines the procedures to be followed in electing these committees and for their operation. But the central thrust of the new law is to give to parents and students a veto power over those materials required for use in the schools without any possibility of the teachers appealing and obtaining a reversal of that veto. Hence, the likely effect of such a law would be to force collaboration between teachers and parents or students in the initial selection of the materials.

Additional protection for parents and students could be obtained by legislative extension in all states of procedural due process rights to the mentally retarded as already has occurred in such states as California and Massachusetts (see chap. 4). Procedural protections should also be given to other students exposed to school classification decisions that are liable to have a significant impact upon their school careers. For example, decisions to place students in the slow or bottom tracks in high schools should be governed by procedures under which the student and his or her parents may seek to challenge the evidence upon which the decision was based and to present evidence of their own. While it may appear that such protections could greatly complicate the running of schools, such a prediction does not seem well founded in light of the general indifference most students and parents show with regard to what schools do in this area. Chances are only a few students and parents would seek enforcement of their procedural rights.

The effectiveness of many of these proposed reforms importantly depends upon the school district having sufficient financial capacity to mount new courses and to change its educational materials. Indeed, whether any school district has meaningful control over its curriculum and whether in turn parents can have a meaningful voice, depends upon having the money available to change and adopt new programs. Today, as the finance reform court cases discussed in chapters 5 and 2 bring out so clearly, meaningful choice with regard to the school program does not exist in many poor school districts. Thus, a further important reform is revision of the prevailing methods of financing public elementary and secondary education. Such a reform would be designed at least to equalize the fiscal capacity of school districts so that each district would have the same meaningful choices as other districts. Absent such a reform, the notion of local control of the educational program will continue to be more an abstract doctrine than a reality for many school systems.

Educational Vouchers

The kinds of reforms outlined in the previous section leave intact the basic structures of the governing system for education. But perhaps more radical change is needed if we are fully to implement the promise of *Pierce* that each parent has the right to control the upbringing of his or her child. One approach is the educational voucher.[15] Under such an arrangement a marketplace would be set up in which schools would compete for students. Once a student and his or her parents have chosen a school to attend, they turn into that school a chit or voucher obtained from the state and worth to the school a certain amount of money; the school in turn redeems the voucher from the state to obtain its funds. The central effect of a voucher system is that it creates a wider choice for families than now exists with regard to the kind of education they prefer. That is, the voucher system tends to maximize the principle of parental control of the child's education. At the same time it seems possible to design the voucher system so that in maximizing parental control one does not end up neglecting the other principles for the allocation of authority.

There is no room here to explore all the different possible variations of a voucher system that have been and could be discussed, which would simultaneously tend to maximize many of the principles listed in chapter 1. Providing, in rough outline, the description of one such voucher system would assist in reaching an understanding of how vouchers might serve as a remedy for some of the problems found in the present arrangement for controlling the program of the schools. Reasonable parental choice under a voucher system would be enhanced by providing all parents with state aid in the form of a voucher so as to enable all parents to send their child to the school of their choice, whether it be a private or publicly operated school. In this way parents could seek out for their children a school that emphasized, for example, a scientific curriculum, or a religious school, or a school with a distinct political viewpoint. This means the state would not so regulate these voucher schools as to reduce their diversity or as to reduce the choice available to parents. Naturally, the state might still want to require that certain subjects be taught. For example, English, arithmetic, American history. If there is a lack of diversity, a lack of choice, it would be because of the results of the operation of the market and not because the state, through its authority to attach conditions to the voucher funds and to regulate private schools, purposefully eliminated those choices.

A sensitive question in this regard is the issue of the rules surrounding the selection of students for admission by the voucher schools. Under this scheme a school specializing in science educaton could select students with a view to their abilities in science. However, it would be wise and probably legally required for the states to bar the participating school from selecting students on the basis of race.[16] The selection of students on the basis of wealth could be minimized by preventing schools from charging tuition above and beyond the value of the voucher. Thus, rich parents could not buy their way into more expensive participating schools by supplementing the state voucher with funds from their own bank accounts.

The voucher system could also be arranged so that children with special education needs are protected. One way this could be done would be to give to parents of handicapped children and educationally disadvantaged children a voucher worth more than the normal voucher and requiring schools admitting such pupils to provide special educational services for these children. Further, the voucher given these children might be worth enough to provide schools admitting them with a somewhat higher profit, thereby creating an incentive for schools to admit such pupils. Finally, state law could guarantee every child access to some school, so that even if a child were turned down at all schools to which he or she applied, steps would then be taken to place that child in an appropriate school. State regulations could also be established with regard to the expulsion of students from school.

As a further protection of the consuming parents, participating schools could be required to publish annual reports and other documents covering such matters as the nature of the program, the kinds of students served, the background of the teaching staff, the educational achievement of the students attending the school, the governing system, the financial status of the school, and the like. This sort of information should help parents make an informed and reasoned choice and would help to assure the accountability of the school to parents and state officials.

While other aspects of any full-fledged voucher system could be discussed—mechanisms for monitoring and regulating the participating schools, their governing structure, their liability to suit for educational malpractice, and the like—what has been presented here should be sufficient to show that an entirely new system for providing education could be provided which serves the many principles outlined in chapter 1. Indeed, this system not only would be designed to enhance parental choice and the protection of pupils with special needs, it would in the view of many be a more efficient and educationally more effective system because of the competition created between schools for students. At the same time, the schools could be regulated to prevent racial discrimination and to require some minimum level of a common program so as to reduce the political and cultural divisiveness which might otherwise occur and which looms as such a threat in pluralist America. But the state's hand in this regard should not be so heavy as to eliminate reasonable parental choice.

Notes

Chapter 1
Introduction

1. John Rawls, *A Theory of Justice* (Cambridge, Mass.: Harvard University Press, 1971), pp. 248-250.

2. *Wisconsin v. Yoder,* 406 U.S. 205 (1972).

3. Stephen Arons, "The Separation of School and State: *Pierce* Reconsidered," *Harvard Educational Review* 46 (February 1976): 76.

4. *Wisconsin v. Yoder, 406 U.S. 205 (1972);* Michael B. Katz, *Class, Bureaucracy, and Schools* (New York: Praeger, 1975), chap. 1; Sidney W. Tiedt, *The Role of the Federal Government in Education* (New York: Oxford University Press, 1966), chap. 3; W. Norton Grubb and Stephan Michelson, *States and Schools* (Lexington, Mass.: D. C. Heath, 1974), pp. 17-24.

5. Alexis de Tocqueville, *Democracy in America* (Bradley ed. 1956) (New York: Alfred A. Knopf, 1956), pp. 86-97; J. S. Mill, "On Liberty," in *Utilitarianism, Liberty, and Representative Government* (Everyman's Library) (New York: J.M. Dent & Sons, n.d.), pp. 167-170; J.S. Mill, "On Representative Government," in ibid., chap. 15; John E. Coons, William H. Clune III, and Stephan D. Sugarman, *Private Wealth and Public Education,* (Cambridge, Mass.: Harvard University Press, Belknap Press, 1970), pp. 14-20.

6. Robert Dahl, *After the Revolution?* (New Haven: Yale University Press, 1970), p. 64; R. Reischauer and R. Hartman, *Reforming School Finance* (Washington, D.C.: Brookings Institution, 1973), pp. 147-148.

7. Kenneth Culp Davis, *Administrative Law Text*, 3d ed. (St. Paul, Minn.: West Publishing, 1972), Chapter Two.

8. See, generally, Alan A. Altshuler, *Community Control* (New York: Pegasus, 1970); Leonard J. Fein, *The Ecology of the Public Schools* (New York: Pegasus, 1971).

9. Katz, *Class, Bureaucracy and Schools,* chap. 1.

10. This kind of argument provides one of the justifications for local control of education. See materials cited in *supra* note 5.

11. Statement by Senator Wayne E. Morse printed in Tiedt, *Role of the Federal Government in Education,* pp. 59-69.

12. Dahl, *After the Revolution?*, pp. 28-40.

13. J.S. Mill offers such an argument. See J.S. Mill, "On Representative Government."

14. Joseph M. Cronin, *The Control of Urban Schools* (New York: Free Press, 1973); Edward C. Banfield and James Q. Wilson, *City Politics* (New York: Vintage Books, 1963), pt. III.

Chapter 2
The Federal Courts and the U.S. Constitution

1. William R. Hazard, "Courts in the Saddle: School Boards Out," *Phi Delta Kappan* (December 1974): 259, 261.

2. Nathan Glazer, "Towards an Imperial Judiciary," 41 *The Public Interest* (Fall 1975): 104, 106.

3. For a brief review of the work of the Supreme Court between 1937 and 1953, see Robert G. McCloskey, *The American Supreme Court* (Chicago: University of Chicago Press, 1960). For general assessments of the work of the Warren Court, see Alexander M. Bickel, *The Least Dangerous Branch* (Indianapolis: Bobbs-Merrill, 1962); Alexander M. Bickel, *The Supreme Court and the Idea of Progress,* Harper Torchbook ed. (New York: Harper & Row, 1970); Archibald Cox, *The Warren Court,* (Cambridge, Mass.: Harvard University Press, 1968); Phillip B. Kurland, *Politics, The Constitution, and the Warren Court* (Chicago: University of Chicago Press, 1970); Robert G. McCloskey, *The Modern Supreme Court* (Cambridge, Mass.: Harvard University Press, 1972); Martin Shapiro, *Law and Politics in the Supreme Court* (New York: Free Press of Glencoe, 1964).

4. Plato, *Republic,* in Edith Hamilton and Huntington Cairns, eds., *Plato: The Collected Dialogues,* Bollingen Series LXXI.(New York: Pantheon Books, 1961), p. 575; Ernest Barker, *Greek Political Theory* (London: Methuen, 1970), p. 209.

5. *Pierce* v. *Society of Sisters*, 268 U.S. 510 (1925).

6. *Wisconsin* v. *Yoder*, 406 U.S. 205 (1972).

7. See *March* v. *Earle*, 24 F. Supp. 385 (D.C., Pa. 1938); *Stephens* v. *Bongart*, 189 A. 131, 15 N.J. Misc. 80 (1937).

8. *Farrington* v. *Tokushige*, 273 U.S. 284 (1926).

9. *Meyer* v. *Nebraska*, 262 U.S. 390 (1923).

10. The Supreme Court specifically allowed for the reasonable regulation of private schools in *Pierce* v. *Society of Sisters*.

11. Stephen Arons, "The Separation of School and State: *Pierce* Reconsidered," *Harvard Educational Review* 46 (February 1976): 76.

12. Alexander Mieklejohn, *Political Freedom*, (New York: Harper & Brothers, 1960), pp. 10, 12; Laurent B. Frantz, "The First Amendment in

the Balance,'' *Yale Law Journal* 71 (July 1962): 1424; *West Virginia Board of Education* v. *Barnette*, 319 U.S. 624, 641 (1943).

13. *Meek* v. *Pittenger*, 95 S. Ct. 1753 (1975); *Committee for Public Education and Religious Liberty* v. *Nyquist*, 413 U.S. 756 (1973); *Lemon* v. *Kurtzman*, 403 U.S. 602 (1971); *Board of Education* v. *Allen*, 392 U.S. 236 (1968); *Everson* v. *Board of Education*, 330 U.S. 1 (1947).

14. *Brusca* v. *State Board of Education*, 332 F. Supp. 275 (E.D. Mo. 1971), *aff'd mem.*, 405 U.S. 1050 (1972).

15. *School District of Abington* v. *Schempp*, 374 U.S. 203 (1963); *Engle* v. *Vitale*, 370 U.S. 421 (1962).

16. *McCollum* v. *Board of Education*, 333 U.S. 203 (1948).

17. *Epperson* v. *Arkansas*, 393 U.S. 97 (1968).

18. *Daniel* v. *Waters*, 515 F.2d 485 (6 Cir. 1975).

19. *Wright* v. *Houston Independent School District*, 486 F.2d 137 (5 Cir. 1973), *cert. denied*, 417 U.S. 969 (1974).

20. *School District of Abington* v. *Schempp*, p. 225.

21. Ibid., p. 225.

22. The Supreme Court in *Wisconsin* v. *Yoder* drew this distinction between religion and philosophical beliefs.

23. Ibid.

24. See Fredrick A. Olafson, ''Teaching About Religion: Some Reservations,'' in Theodore R. Sizer, ed., *Religion and Public Education* (Boston: Houghton Mifflin, 1967), p. 84.

25. J.S. Mill, ''On Liberty,'' in *Utilitarianism, Liberty, and Representative Government* (Everyman Library Edition) (New York: J.M. Dent, n.d.), pp. 161.

26. John L. Childs, *Education and Morals* (New York: Appleton-Century-Crofts, 1950), pp. 270-271.

27. This is a requirement virtually every state imposes: see, for example, Arizona Rev. Stat. Ann. §15-1021 (1974), Code of Ala. tit. 52 §545 (1973 Cum. Supp.); New York Educ. Law, §801 (McKinney's 1969); Tenn. Code Ann. §49-1902, §49-1908, §49-1307 (1975 Cum. Supp.); Rev. Code Wash. Ann. §28A-02-080 (1970).

28. Code of Ala. tit. 52 §545(1)(Cum. Supp. 1973); Fla. School Law §233.064 (West Supp. 1976); Miss. Code Ann. §37-13-13 (1973); Utah Code Ann. §53-14-7.5 (1975 Supp.); Arizona Rev. Stat. §15-1025 (1975); Texas Code Ann. §21-1031 (1972).

29. *West Virginia Board of Education* v. *Barnette*, 319 U.S. 624 (1943).

30. Ibid., p. 631.

31. Compare *Sapp* v. *Renfroe*, 511 F. 2d 172 (5 Cir. 1975), with *Spence* v. *Bailey*, 465 F. 2d 797 (6 Cir. 1972).

32. *Augustus* v. *Sch. Bd. of Escamba County*, 507 F. 2d 152 (5 Cir. 1975), *Tate* v. *Board of Education of Jonesboro, Ark., Special School District*, 453 F. 2d 975 (8 Cir. 1972); *Melton* v. *Young*, 465 F. 2d 1332 (6 Cir. 1972); *Smith* v. *St. Tammany Parish School Bd.*, 448 F. 2d 414 (5 Cir. 1971); *Caldwell* v. *Craighead*, 432 F. 2d 213 (6 Cir. 1970), *cert. denied*, 402 U.S. 953 (1971).

33. See, for example, California Education Code, Section 9031 (1975); New York Education Law, §704 (McKinney's 1969).

34. *Epperson* v. *Arkansas*, p. 276.

35. *McDonald* v. *Board of Election Comm'rs,* 394 U.S. 802, 809 (1969); *McGowan* v. *Maryland*, 366 U.S. 420, 425-426 (1961); *F.S. Royster Guano Co.* v. *Virginia*, 253 U.S. 412 (1920).

36. "Developments in the Law—Equal Protection," *Harvard Law Review*, 82 (March, 1969): 1065, 1087.

37. *Shapiro* v. *Thompson*, 394 U.S. 618, 634 (1969). The interests the Court has declared to be fundamental include voting, criminal appeals, and the right of interstate travel. *Harper* v. *Virginia Board of Elections*, 383 U.S. 663 (1966); *Griffin* v. *Illinois*, 351 U.S. 12 (1956); *Shapiro* v. *Thompson*, 394 U.S. 618 (1969). Classifications based on race, alienage, or nationality have been declared to be suspect classifications. *Brown* v. *Board of Education*, 347 U.S. 483 (1954); *Korematsu* v. *United States*, 323 U.S. 214 (1944); *Graham* v. *Richardson*, 403 U.S. 365 (1971). For a discussion of the new equal protection test, see "Developments in the Law—Equal Protection," *Harvard Law Review* p. 1087 *et seq*. The Supreme Court has flirted with making classifications on the basis of sex a suspect classification but has not quite taken the final step in this direction. For a discussion of recent cases, see "The Supreme Court, 1974 Term," *Harvard Law Review* 89 (November 1975): 47, 95.

38. Gerald Gunther, "Foreword: In Search of Evolving Doctrine on a Changing Court," *Harvard Law Review* 86 (November 1972):1, 8.

39. Ibid., p. 20.

40. John E. Nowak, "Realigning the Standards of Review Under the Equal Protection Guarantee—Prohibited, Neutral, and Permissive Classifications," *Georgetown Law Journal* 62 (March 1974): 1071, 1093-1094.

41. Gunther, "Foreword," p. 24.

42. *San Antonio Independent School District* v. *Rodriguez*, 411 U.S. 1 (1973).

43. See John Hart Ely, "Legislative and Administrative Motivation," *Yale Law Journal* 79 (June 1970): 1205, 1242-1245.

191

44. See, for example, *Keyishian* v. *Board of Regents*, 385 U.S. 589 (1967).

45. *Cole* v. *Richardson*, 405 U.S. 676 (1972); *Connell* v. *Higginbotham*, 403 U.S. 207 (1971).

46. "Notes: Aliens' Right to Teach: Political Socialization and the Public Schools," *Yale Law Journal* 85 (November 1975): 90; and see *Hampton* v. *Mow Sun Wong*, 44 U.S.L.W. 4737 (1976).

47. *Russo* v. *Central School District No. 1*, 469 F.2d 623 (2 Cir. 1972), *cert. denied* 411 U.S. 932 (1973) (flag salute case); *James* v. *Board of Education*, 461 F.2d 566 (2 Cir. 1972) *cert. denied*, 409 U.S. 1042 (1972) (armband case).

48. *Tinker* v. *Des Moines Independent Community School District*, 393 U.S. 503 (1969).

49. See quotation from Brief for Petitioners in the *Farrington* v. *Tukushige* case in David L. Kirp and Mark G. Yudof, *Educational Policy and the Law* (Berkeley, Cal.: McCutchan, 1974), pp. 35-36; also David Tyack, "The Perils of Pluralism: The Background of the Pierce Case," *American Historical Review* 74 (October 1968): 74; Michael B. Katz, *Class, Bureaucracy, and Schools* (New York: Praeger 1975), p. 48.

50. See for example, Maine Rev. Stat. Ann. tit. 20 § 102.7 (West Supp. 1976); Wash. Rev. Code Ann. § 28A.05.015 (1972).

51. New York Education Law, § 3204 (McKinney's 1969).

52. *Meyer* v. *Nebraska*.

53. U.S. Commission on Civil Rights, *The Excluded Student: Educational Practices Affecting Mexican-Americans in the Southwest*, Report III (Washington, D.C.: Government Printing Office, May 1972), p. 14.

54. Sex has not yet been termed a "suspect classification" by the Supreme Court hence the new equal protection could only apply if education were deemed a fundamental interest, which it is not. "The Supreme Court, 1974 Term," *Harvard Law Review* 89 (November 1975): 47, 95; *San Antonio Independent School District* v. *Rodriguez*.

55. *New Rider* v. *Board of Education of Independent School District No. 1, Oklahoma*, 480 F. 2d 693 (10 Cir. 1973) *cert. denied* 414 U.S. 1097 1973).

56. *Zeller* v. *Donegal School District Board of Education*, 517 F. 2d 600 (3 Cir. 1975) (en banc), and cases cited therein.

57. *Kelley* v. *Johnson*, 44 U.S.L.W. 4469 (April 5, 1976).

58. *Ordway* v. *Hargraves*, 323 F. Supp. 1155 (D. Mass. 1971).

59. *Cleveland Board of Education* v. *LaFleur* 414 U.S. 632 (1974); *Andrews* v. *Drew Municipal Separate School District*, 507 F. 2d 611 (5 Cir. 1975).

192

60. *Presidents Council, Dist. No. 25* v. *Community School Board No. 25,* 457 F. 2d 289 (2 Cir. 1972).

61. *Brown* v. *Board of Education,* 347 U.S. 483 (1954).

62. *Jackson* v. *Godwin,* 400 F. 2d 529 (5 Cir. 1968).

63. Ibid., p. 536.

64. Such programs have been undertaken in the public schools. "Comment, Alternative Schools for Minority Students: The Constitution, the Civil Rights Act, and the Berkeley Experiment," *California Law Review* 61 (May, 1973): 858.

65. *Green* v. *County Scool Board,* 391 U.S. 430 (1968).

66. *Pennsylvania Ass'n for Retarded Children* v. *Commonwealth,* 334 F. Supp. 1257 (E.D. Pa. 1971), *modified,* 343 F. Supp. 279 (E.D. Pa. 1972).

67. *Mills* v. *Board of Education,* 348 F. Supp. 866 (D.D.C. 1972).

68. *Lau* v. *Nichols,* 414 U.S. 563 (1974).

69. The decision rested in 42 U.S.C. 2000d (1970).

70. *Frederick L.* v. *Thomas et al.,* Memorandum and Order Dated Jan. 7, 1976, Civ. Action No. 74-42 (E.D. D.C. Pa. 1976).

71. *Larry P.* v. *Riles,* 343 F. Supp. 1306 (N.D. Cal. 1972).

72. *Hobson* v. *Hansen,* 269 F. Supp. 401 (D.D.C. 1967), *aff'd sub nom, Smuck* v. *Hobson* 408 F. 2d 175 (D.C. Cir. 1969) (en banc).

73. David L. Kirp, "Schools as Sorters: The Constitutional and Policy Implications of Student Classification," *University of Pennsylvania Law Review* 121 (April 1973): 705, 731, 749.

74. See Jay Katz, "The Right to Treatment—an Enchanting Legal Fiction?" *University of Chicago Law Review* 36 (Summer 1969): 755, 780.

75. *San Antonio Independent School District* v. *Rodriguez.* John Coons.

76. *San Antonio Independent School District* v. *Rodriguez.*

77. *Brown* v. *Board of Education.*

78. Ibid., p. 494.

79. See, generally, Betsy Levin and Philip Moise, "School Desegregation Litigation in the Seventies and the Use of Social Evidence: An Annotated Guide," *Law and Contemporary Problems* 39 (Winter 1975): 50.

80. See, for example, *Hart* v. *Community School Board,* 383 F. Supp. 699, 728-37 (E.D. N.Y. 1974), *aff'd,* 512 F. 2d 37 (2 Cir. 1975).

81. See Meyer Weinberg, "The Relationship Between School Desegregation and Academic Achievement: A Review of the Research," *Law and Contemporary Problems* 39 (Spring, 1975): 241.

82. Derrick A. Bell, "Waiting on the Promise of *Brown*," *Law and Contemporary Problems, 39* (Spring, 1975): 341.

83. *Graves* v. *Walton Cty. Bd. Ed.,* 300 F. Supp. 188 (D.C.Ga.), *aff'd* 410 F. 2d 1152 (5 Cir. 1968); *Miller* v. *School Dist. No. 2, Clarendon Cty., S.C.,* 256 F. Supp. 370 (S.C. 1966).

84. See, for example, *Lemon* v. *Bossier Parish School Board,* 444 F. 2d 1400 (5 Cir. 1971).

85. *Knight* v. *Board of Education of City of New York,* 48 F.R.D. 108 (E.D. N.Y. 1969); and also 48 F.R.D. 115 (E.D. N.Y. 1969).

86. See Gary Orfield, "How to Make Desegregation Work: The Adaptation of Schools to Their Newly-Integrated Student Bodies," *Law and Contemporary Problems* 39 (Spring 1975): 314.

87. Levin and Moise, "School Desegregation Litigation in the Seventies" p. 114.

Chapter 3
The Federal Government

1. H.R. Rep. No. 93-805, (93rd Congress, 2d Sess. (1974), reprinted in *U.S. Congressional and Administrative News*, 3 (St. Paul, Minn.: West Publishing, 1975), pp. 4093, 4095.

2. National Defense Education Act, 20 U.S.C.A. §401 et seq. 1974); Smith-Hughes Vocational Education Act, 20 U.S.C.A. §11-15, 16-28 (1974); Vocational Education Act of 1963 and Vocational Education Amendments of 1968, 20 U.S.C.A. §1241 et seq. (1974); National Science Foundation Act of 1950, 42 U.S.C.A. §1861 et seq. (1969).

3. Sidney W. Tiedt, *The Role of the Federal Government in Education,* (New York: Oxford University Press, 1966), p. 162; John F. and Anne O. Hughes, *Equal Education* (Bloomington: Indiana University Press, 1972), pp. 58-62.

4. 20 U.S.C.A. §241a et seq. (1974) as amended by Education Amendments of 1974, 20 U.S.C. 821 c 1974).

5. 20 U.S.C.A § 1232a (1974).

6. P. Michael Timpane, "Federal Aid to Schools: Its Limited Future," *Law and Contemporary Problems,* 38 (Winter-Spring 1974): 493, 495.

7. H.R. Rep. 93-805 in *U.S. Congressional and Administrative News,,* p. 4095.

8. Michael W. Kirst, "The Growth of Federal Influence in Education," in C. Wayne Gordon, ed., *Uses of the Sociology of Education* (The

Seventy-third Yearbook of the National Society for the Study of Education, Part II), (Chicago: National Society for the Study of Education, 1974), p. 448.

9. Title VI of the Civil Rights Act of 1964, 42 U.S.C.A. §2000d (1974); Title IX of the Educational Amendment of 1972, 20 U.S.C.A. §1681 et seq. as amended (1974; Supp. 1976).

10. *United States* v. *Butler*, 297 U.S. 1 (1936); *Steward Machine Co.* v. *Davis*, 301 U.S.548 (1937); *Helvering* v. *Davis*, 301 U.S. 619 (1937).

11. *Steward Machine Co.* v. *Davis*.

12. Bishop Hoadley in a sermon before George the First, 1717, quoted in Learned Hand, *The Bill of Rights* (New York: Atheneum, 1972), p. 8.

13. *Morning* v. *Family Publications Service, Co.*, 411 U.S. 356, 369 (1973).

14. 20 U.S.C.A. §241a (1974) as amended by the Educational Amendments of 1974, 20 U.S.C. §821 (1974).

15. See, generally, Hughes and Hughes, *Equal Education*.

16. Ibid., p. 57.

17. 20 U.S.C.A. §241e (1974); 45 C.F.R. 116.17(d) (1975); ESEA Title I Program Guide No. 44, Guideline 1.1, March 18, 1968; and proposed regulation 40 Fed. Reg. 11481, 16a.20 (1975).

18. 20 U.S.C.A. §241e (1974); 45 C.F.R. §116.17 (a) and (g) (1975); ESEA Title I Program Guide No. 44, Guideline 1.1, 2.1, March 18, 1968; and proposed regulation 40 Fed. Reg. 11481, 116a.20 (1975).

19. 20 U.S.C.A. §241(e)(b) (1976 Supp.)

20. 40 Fed. Reg. 11482, 116a.22(f) (1975).

21. 20 U.S.C.A. §241e(a)(1)(1976 Supp.); 45 C.F.R. §116.17(f) and 116.18 (1975); ESEA Title I Program Guide No. 44, Guideline 4.2, March 18, 1968; and 40 Fed. Reg. 11482, 116a.22 (1975).

22. ESEA Title I Program Guide no. 44, Guideline 4.7, March 18, 1968; 40 Fed. Reg. 11482, 116a.22(e) (1975).

23. 20 U.S.C.A. §241e(a)(1)(1976 Supp.); 45 C.F.R. §116.24 (1975); ESEA Title I Program Guide No. 44, Guideline no. 3.1; and proosed regulation 40 Fed. Reg. 11476, 116.31 (1975).

24. 20 U.S.C.A. §241e(a)(3)(c)(1976 Supp.); 45 C.F.R. §116.26 (1975); and proposed regulation 40 Fed. Reg. 11485, §116a.26 (1975).

25. 20 U.S.C.A. §241e(a)(3)(B)(i) and (ii)(1976 Supp.); 45 C.F.R. §116.17(h) (1975); ESEA Title I Program Guide No. 44, Guideline 7.1, March 18, 1968; and proposed regulation 40 Fed. Reg. 11476, §116.30 (1975).

26. 20 U.S.C. 241e(a)(6) and 241o(1976 Supp.); 45 C.F.R. 116.22

(1975); ESEA Title I Program Guide no. 44, Guideline no. 6.1, March 18, 1968; and proposed regulation 116.33 in 40 Fed. Reg. 11476 (1975).

27. All Title I projects were to be well planned, to assure effectiveness. 45 C.F.R. 116.18 (b)(1975); ESEA Title I Program Guide No. 44, Guidelines, nos. 2.1, 3.1, 4.1, 4.3, 5.1, and 5.6; and proposed regulation 116a.22 in 40 Fed. Reg. 11482 (1975).

28. *Hobson* v. *Hansen*, 269 F. Supp. 401 (DDC 1967), *aff'd en banc sub nom; Smuck* v. *Hobson*, 408 F. 2d 175 (D.C. Cir. 1969); Frank Levy, Arnold J. Meltsher, and Aaron Wildavsky, *Urban Outcomes* (Berkeley: University of California Press, 1974), chap. 1.

29. Title I of ESEA, *Is It Helping Poor Children*? (A Report by the Washington Research Project of the Southern Center for Studies in Public Policy and the NAACP Legal Defense and Educational Fund, Inc., 1969).

30. Ibid.; Hughes and Hughes, *Equal Education,* pp. 51-52.

31. H.R. Rep. No. 93-805 in *U.S. Congressional and Administrative News,* p. 4096.

32. Hughes and Hughes, *Equal Education*, pp. 99-101.

33. Ibid., p. 52.

34. David O. Porter and David C. Warner, "How Effective Are Grantor Controls?" in Kenneth E. Boulding, Martin Pfaff, and Anita Pfaff, eds., *Tax Transfer in an Urbanized Economy,* (Belmont, Cal.: Wadsworth, 1973), p. 276.

35. R. Stephan Browning and Jack Costello, Jr., "Title I: More of the Same?" *Inequality in Education* 17 (June 1974): 23, 31-40; Hughes and Hughes, *Equal Education*, pp. 78, 82, 84, 56.

36. Hughes and Hughes, *Equal Education*, pp. 78-80.

37. H.R. Rep. 93-805 in *U.S. Congressional and Administrative News*, p. 4097; Assessment of Reading Activities Funded Under the Federal Program of Aid for Educationally Deprived Children" (Report to the Congress, by the Controller General of the United States, December 12, 1975), p. 12; David K. Cohen and Tyll van Geel, "Public Education," in Samuel H. Beer and Richard E. Barringer, eds., *The State and the Poor*, (Cambridge, Mass.: Winthrop, 1970), p. 231.

38. Assessment of Reading Activities Funded Under the Federal Program of Aid for Educationally Deprived Children, p. Chapter Two; H.R. Rep. No. 93-805 in *U.S. Congressional and Administrative News*, pp. 4097-4099.

39. Hughes and Hughes, *Equal Education,* pp. 86, 90.

40. "1975 Annual Report to the President and the Congress" (Washington, D.C.: National Advisory Coucil on the Education of Disadvantaged Children, 1975), pp. 79-103.

41. See Hughes and Hughes, *Equal Education;* Jerome T. Murphy,

"Title I of ESEA: The Politics of Implementing Federal Education Reform," *Harvard Educational Review* 41 (February 1971): 35; David O. Porter and David G. Warner, "How Effective Are Grantor Controls?"; Milbery Wallin McLaughlin, "Implementation of ESEA Title I: A Problem of Compliance," *Teachers College Record* 77 (February 1976): 397; David K. Cohen and Tyll van Geel, "Public Education"; Michael W. Kirst, "The Growth of Federal Influence in Education"; Tyll van Geel, "Evaluation and Federalism," Special Qualifying Paper, Harvard Graduate School of Education, April, 1970.

42. 42 U.S.C.A. §2000d (1974).

43. Frank T. Read, "Judicial Evolution of the Law of School Integration Since *Brown* v. *Board of Education*," *Law and Contemporary Problems* 39 (Winter 1975): 7, 17-32; Gary Orfield, *The Reconstruction of Southern Education* (New York: Wiley-Interscience, 1969); Fredrick M. Wirt, *Politics of Southern Equality: Law and Social Change in a Mississippi County* (Chicago: Aldine, 1970); Fredrick M. Wirt and Michael W. Kirst, *The Political Web of American Schools* (Boston: Little Brown, 1972), Chapter Nine; "Note, 'The Courts,' HEW and Southern School Desegregation," *Yale Law Journal* 77 (December 1967): 321.

44. 45 C.F.R. 80.3 (b)(1) (1975).

45. Ibid., 80.5(b) (1975).

46. Ibid., 80.3(b)(2) (1975).

47. Memorandum dated July 10, 1970, Identification of Discrimination and Denial of Services on the Basis of National Origin, 35 Fed. Reg. 11595 (1970).

48. *Lau* v. *Nichols*, 483 F. 2d 791, 792-3 (9 Cir. 1973) (en banc).

49. San Francisco Unified School District, *Bilingual Education in the San Francisco Unified School District 1* November 1, 1967), Appendix at 61 *Lau* v. *Nichols*, 414 U.S. 563 (1974).

50. Ibid., pp. 101, 103-104.

51. *Lau* v. *Nichols*, 483 F.2d 791 (9 Cir. 1973) (en banc), *rev.* 414 U.S. 563 (1974).

52. *Lau* v. *Nichols*, 414 U.S. p. 571.

53. Telephone conversation with Dr. John Molina, Director of Bilingual Education Programs, Department of Health, Education, and Welfare, April 5, 1974.

54. U.S. Bureau of the Census, Current Population Reports, P-20, No. 250, Persons of Spanish Origin in the United States: March 1972 and 1971, pp. 1-2 (Table A), p. 16 (Table 4); U.S. Bureau of the Census, Census of Population: 1970, American Indians p. 192, (Table 18); U.S. Bureau of the Census, Census of Population: 1970, Japanese, Chinese, and Filipi-

nos in the United States, p. 68. Table 18; U.S. Bureau of the Census, Census of Population: 1970, National Origin and Language, p. 492, Table 19.

55. Telephone conversation with Dr. John Molina.

56. John Molina, "ESEA Title VII Bilingual Education: State of the Art," *Linguistic Reporter* 15 (November 1973):4.

57. U.S. Commission on Civil Rights, *The Excluded Student: Educational Practices Affecting Mexican-Americans in the Southwest*, Report no. 111 (Washington, D.C.: Government Printing Office, May, 1972), p. 14; Select Committee on Equal Educational Opportunity, *Toward Equal Educational Opportunity*, S. Rep. No. 92-000, 92nd Cong., 2d Sess (1970), pp. 286-287.

58. U.S. Commission on Civil Rights, *The Excluded Student*, pp. 68, 14.

59. Hearings on Equal Educational Opportunity Before the Select Committee on Equal Educational Opportunity of the Senate, 91st Cong., 2d Sess. (1970), p. 3817; Select Committee on Equal Educational Opportunity, *Toward Equal Educational Opportunity*, pp. 286-87.

60. Children's Defense Fund of the Washington Research Project, Inc., *Children Out of School* (Cambridge, Mass.: Children's Defense Fund, 1974), p. 78.

61. Statement of Martin H. Gerry, Dep. Dir., Office for Civil Rights, before General Subcommittee on Education, Committee on Education and Labor, March 12, 1974, Summary Sheet Attachment.

62. Ibid., p. 9.

63. Ibid., pp. 9-14.

64. *Education U.S.A.*, March 15, 1976, p. 173. Also see Children's Defense Fund of the Washington Research Project, Inc., *Children Out of School*, p. 78.

65. Much of this evidence is reviewed in United States Commission on Civil Rights, *A Better Chance to Learn. Bilingual-Bicultural Education* (Clearinghouse Publication 51), May 1975.

66. V. John and V. Horner, *Early Childhood Bilingual Education Project* (New York: Modern Language Association, 1971), p. 171; James Bossard and Eleanor Boll, *The Sociology of Child Development,* 3d ed. (New York: Harper, 1960), chap. 15.

67. United States Commission on Civil Rights, *A Better Chance to Learn: Bilingual-Bicultural Education,* p. 25.

68. Ibid., pp. 25, 27.

69. Ibid., pp. 79-80.

70. Ibid., pp. 29-83.

71. 42 U.S.C.A. §2000(d)(2) 1974 provides for judicial review of agency enforcement of the Civil Rights Act of 1964, and provides for the application of the Administrative Procedure Act, 5 U.S.C.A. §701-06 (1970). In particular 5 U.S.C.A. §706(2)(e) requires a court to set aside an agency action that is not supported by substantial evidence.

72. Kenneth Culp Daivs, *Administrative Law Text,* 3d ed. (St. Paul, Minn.: West, 1972), Sections 29.01-29.10.

73. Ibid., p. 528; *Corn Prod. Co.* v. *Department of Health, Education, and Welfare,* 427 F. 2d 511 (3 Cir. 1970).

74. *Consolidated Edison Co.* v. *NLRB,* 305 U.S. 197, 229 (1938).

75. *FPC* v. *Florida Power & Light Co.,* 404 U.S. 453, 463-64 (1972).

76. See "Comment, Teaching Woman Her Place: The Role of Public Education in the Development of Sex Roles," *Hastings Law Journal* 24 (May 1973): 1191.

77. 20 U.S.C. §1681(a)(Supp. 11, 1972).

78. 20 U.S.C. §1681(a)(1) through (5); 20 U.S.C. §1686 (Supp. II, 1972).

79. 20 U.S.C. §1681(b).

80. Ibid., §1682.

81. But see *Board of Public Instruction of Taylor County, Fla.* v. *Finch,* 414 F. 2d 1068 (5 Cir. 1969), in which the definition of "program" as the term is used in Title VI is discussed.

82. *Morning* v. *Family Publications Service,* Co., 411 U.S. 356, 369 (1973); relied on by Justice Stewart in *Lau* v. *Nichols,* 414 U.S. 563, 571 (1974), concurring opinion of Justice Stewart.

83. 40 Fed. Reg. 24141, §86.34 (1975).

84. 40 Fed. Reg. 24141, §86.34(e) (1975).

85. Ibid., §86.21(b).

86. Ibid., §86.21(b)(2).

87. 40 Fed. Reg. 24141-2, §86.36 (1975).

88. Ibid., §86.36(c).

89. 40 Fed. Reg. 24140, §86.31(a)(1975).

90. 40 Fed. Reg. 24141, §86.3.(b)(7) (1975).

91. Ibid., §86.31(a) (1975).

92. Ibid., §86.34 (1975).

93. Ibid., §86.33.

94. 40 Fed. Reg. 24142 §86.41(a) (1975).

95. Ibid., §86.41(b).

96. Ibid.

97. Ibid.

98. 40 Fed. Reg. 24143, §86.41(c) (1975).

99. 40 Fed. Reg. 24142, §86.41(c)(1975).

100. 40 Fed. Reg. 24143, §86.41(c)(1975).

101. 40 Fed. Reg. 24142, §86.41(b) (1975).

102. "Comment, Implementing Title IX: The HEW Regulations," *University of Pennsylvania Law Review* 124 (January 1976): 806, 837-841.

103. 40 Fed. Reg. 24141, §86.31(b)(5) (1975).

104. Ibid., §86.31(b)(4).

105. 40 Fed. Reg. 24142, §86.40(a) (1975).

106. Ibid., §86.40(b)(1).

107. Ibid., §86.40(b)(2).

108. Ibid., §86.40(b)(3).

109. Ibid., §86.40(b)(4)-(5).

110. 40 Fed. Reg. 24135 (1975).

111. 40 Fed. Reg. 24143, §86.42 (1975).

112. Compare *Lehman* v. *City of Shaker Heights,* 418 U.S. 298 (1974).

113. There have been many studies of sexual bias in curriculum materials, e.g., J. Land, "Sex Role Stereotyping in Elementary School Readers, Grades 1-6, Adopted by the State of Indiana for the Years 1973-78," dissertation, Ball State University, 1974; W. Jay, "Sex Stereotyping in Selected Mathematics Textbooks for Grades Two, Four, and Six," dissertation, University of Oregon, 1973; Gwyneth E. Britton, "Why Jane Can't Win: Sex Stereotyping and Career Role Assignments in Reading Materials," ERIC, ED 092-919, May 1974; Lenore J. Weitzman and Diane Rizzo, ' "Biased Textbooks," (Washington, D.C.: National Foundation for the Improvement of Education, 1974) (Pamphlet).

114. A good book on racial bias in textbooks is: D. MacCann and G. Woodard, *The Black American in Books for Children: Readings in Racism* (Metuchen, N.J.: Scarecrow Press, 1972).

115. National Science Foundation Act of 1950, 42 U.S.C.A. §1861 et seq. (1969).

116. For a history of NSF's involvement in curriculum development see, Science Curriculum Review Team, "Pre-College Science Curriculum Activities of the National Science Foundation," vol. II, app. 2, in U.S. Congress, House, Committee on Science and Technology, "National Science Foundation Curriculum Development and Implementation for Pre-College Science Education," 94th Cong., 1st Sess., 1975, p. 157; NIE Curriculum Development Task Force, "Current Issues, Problems, and Concerns in Curriculum Development," January 15, 1976 (processed).

117. Controller General of the United States, "Administration of the

Science Education Project 'Man: A Course of Stuuy,'" in U.S. Congress, House Committee on Science and Technology, "National Science Foundation Curriculum Development and Implementation for Pre-College Science Education," pp. 39, 74. For a complete list of NSF-funded projects see Science Curriculum Review Team, "Pre-College Science Curriculum Activities" pp. 303-308.

118. For a review of the curriculum development process see, generally, Science Curriculum Review Team, "Pre-College Science Curriculum Activities."

119. For statements claiming NSF has promoted a national curriculum, see Minority Report of Joanne McAuley to accompany Report of the Science Curriculum Implementation Review Group to the Chairman, Committee on Science and Technology, U.S. House of Representatives, October 1, 1975, in U.S. Congress, House, Committee on Science and Technology, "National Science Foundation Curriculum Development and Implementation for Pre-College Science Education," pp. 16, 18-19; Statement of Hon. John B. Conlan, Representative from Arizona before the Subcommittee on Science Research and Technology of the U.S. House of Representatives, February 10, 1976 (National Science Foundation Press Release, No. PR76-16, February 10, 1976.

120. Science Curriculum Review Team, "Pre-College Science Curriculum Activities of the National Science Foundation," p. 126.

121. Ibid., p. 115.

122. F.R. Schlessinger et al., *A Survey of Science Teaching in Public Schools of the United States* (Columbus: Center for Science and Mathematics Education, Ohio State University, 1971).

123. Information supplied by Suzanne K. Quick, Rand Corporation, 2100 M Street, N.W., Washington, D.C. 20037, based on information obtained from the National Science Foundation,

124. Ibid.

125. Science Curriculum Review Team, "Pre-College Science Curriculum Activities of the National Science Foundation," p. 120; Report of the Science Curriculum Implementation Review Group to the Chairman, Committee on Science and Technology, U.S. House of Representatives, October 1, 1975, in U.S. Congress, House, Committee on Science and Technology, "National Science Foundation Curriculum Development and Implementation for Pre-College Science Education," p. 8.

126. "National Science Foundation Curriculum Development and Implementation for Pre-College Science Education," a report prepared for the Committee on Science and Technology, U.S. House of Representatives, 94th Cong., 1st Sess. (1975), 7-8.

127. Information supplied by Suzanne K. Quick.

128. Science Curriculum Review Team, "Pre-College Science Curriculum Activities of National Science Foundation," pp. 303-308.

129. Ibid., p. 164-165, Table 1.

130. Ibid., p. 303.

131. Ibid., p. 183.

132. Statement of Hon. John B. Conlan; and see Peter B. Dow, "MACOS: The Study of Human Behavior as One Road to Survival," and George Weber, "The Case Against *Man: A Course of Study*," Phi Delta Kappan 57 (October 1975), pp. 79, 81.

133. Science Curriculum Review Team, "Pre-College Science Curriculum Activities of National Science Foundation," pp. 303-308.

134. 20 U.S.C.A. 241c-1 et seq. (1976 Supp.); 20 U.S.C.A. 880(b) et seq. (1976 Supp.)

135. 20 U.S.C.A. 1865 et seq. (1976 Supp.); W. Norton Grubb and Marvin Lazerson, "Rally 'Round the Workplace: Continuities and Fallacies in Career Education," *Harvard Educational Review* 45 (November 1975): 451; and see criticism of the previous article by Kenneth Hoyt, Director of Career Education Office, United States Office of Education, *Education U.S.A.*, February 2, 1976, p. 135.

136. 20 U.S.C.A. §331 (1976 Supp.)

137. *New York Times*, Tuesday, March 2, 1976, p. 14.

Chapter 4
The Changing State Role

1. Edward C. Bolmeier, The School in the Legal Structure, 2d ed. (Cincinnati: W. H. Anderson, 1973), pp. 89-97.

2. Sample provisions cited in LeRoy J. Peterson, Richard A. Rossmiller, and Marlin M. Volz, *The Law and Public Education* (New York: Harper & Row, 1969), p. 373.

3. Ibid., pp. 11-40; 375-380; California State Constitution, Article IX, Section 7.5.

4. Peterson et al., *Law and Public Education*, pp. 375-30.

5. See, for example, Iowa Code Ann. §257.25 (1972).

6. See, for example, Mich. Stat. Ann. §15.3363-§15.3365 (1975).

7. See materials cited in note 27 of chapter 2.

8. See Pa. Stat. Ann. tit. 24 §7-771 (1962).

9. Mass. Gen. Laws Ann. c. 71 §30 (1971).

10. For example, Rev. Code Wash. Ann. §28A.05.030 (1970).

11. For example, Cal. Educ. Code §8502 (1975).

12. The statutes draw distinctions between what must be taught in elementary and secondary schools. See, for example, Iowa Code Ann. §275.25 (1976 Supp.).

13. Compulsory education laws in many states exempt those who may not be able to benefit from the regular program. See Children's Defense Fund of the Washington Research Project, *Children Out of School* (Cambridge, Mass.: Children's Defense Fund, 1974), pp. 224-225.

14. Ibid.

15. See, for example, Rev. Code Wash. Ann. §28A.04.120 (1972); Gen. Laws R.I. §16-1-4 (1970); Wis. Stats. Ann. §39.02 (1966).

16. Pa. Stat. Ann. tit. 24 §15-1512 (1962).

17. For example, Iowa Code Ann. §257.25 (1976 Supp.).

18. Information derived from, Roald F. Campbell and Tim B. Mazzoni, Jr., *State Policy Making for the Public Schools* (Berkeley, Cal.: McCutchan, 1976), Table IX-2, and IX-4, pp. 288-290, 293-296.

19. Oregon Rev. Stat. §337.141 (1975).

20. S.D. Laws Ann. §13-34-11 (1975).

21. N.J. Stat. Ann. §18A:4-25 (1968); Maine Rev. Stat. Ann. tit. 20 §102.7 (West. Supp. 1976).

22. N.Y. Commissioner's Rules and Reg. §100.2(b).

23. N.J. Stat. Ann. §18A:6-9(1968); New York Educ. Law §310 (McKinney's 1969); N.D. Century Code §15-21-07 (1971); Wyo. Stat. Ann. §21.1-10(e) (1975 Cum. Supp.).

24. Del. Code Ann. tit. 14 §121 (1953); and the New Jersey state board has quasi-judicial authority in cases involving the dismissal of teachers, N.J. Stat. Ann. §18A:6-10 (1968).

25. New York Educ. Law §207 (McKinney's 1969).

26. New York Educ. Law §208, 209 (McKinney's 1969).

27. New York Educ. Law §3204 (McKinney's 1969).

28. *Rochester Democrat and Chronicle*, Saturday, March 27, 1976, p. 5A.

29. N.Y. Commissioner's Rules and Reg. §100.2, Part III, Part 200.

30. N.Y. Regents' Rules and Regulations §6.4, 3.35 (a)(1).

31. N.Y. Educ. Law §408 (McKinney's 1975 Supp.).

32. Derived from Campbell and Mazzoni, *State Policy Making for the Public Schools*, Tables IX-2 and IX-4, pp. 288-290, 293-296.

33. Cal. Educ. Code §9400 et seq. (West 1975); Cal. Educ. Code §461, 493, 494, 1085, 5761, 5986, 6750.1, 6802, 6902.5, 6931, and 8055 (1969, 1975).

34. The extent of legislative control of the school program is reflected in, Cal. Educ. Code §8551, 8553, 8571, 8572, 8576, 8573, 8503-4, 8571, 9240-44 (1975). Another section of the code says these provisions are to be construed liberally, Cal. Educ. Code, §2 (1969). But the provisions have been construed strictly: 53 Cal. Ops. Atty. Gen. 230 (1970); 43 Cal. Ops. Atty. Gen. 322 (1964).

35. See, for example, Nev. Rev. Stat. §385.110 (1973); Ariz. Rev. Stat. Ann. §15-102(15) and (16) (1975).

36. Arthur Block and Tyll van Geel, "State of Arizona Curriculum Law," in Tyll van Geel, with assistance of Arthur Block, "Authority to Control the School Curriculum: An Assessment of Rights in Conflict," A study completed under a grant from the National Institute of Education to be published in ERIC, pp. 112-120.

37. Campbell and Mazzoni, *State Policy Making for the Public Schools,* p. 48.

38. Dinah Shelton and Daniel A. Clune, "The Politics of Morality: A History of California's Guidelines for Moral Instruction," Childhood and Government Project, University of California, Berkeley (n.d.) (processed).

39. Cal. Educ. Code §9400, 9231, 9323 (1975).

40. Ariz. Rev. Stat. Ann. §15-102(18) (1975); Cal. Educ. Code §9400, 9221-9225 (1975); Fla. School Law §233.07 (West's Supp. 1976).

41. Miss. Code Ann. §37-43-1 (1973); Gen. Stat. N.C. §115.206.1 and 115.206.3 (1975).

42. Code of Ala. tit. 52 §433(19) (1973 Cum. Supp.)

43. Ky. Rev. Stat. §156.405 (1974 Cum. Supp.); Okla. Stat. tit. 70 § 16.101 (1971); Tenn. Code Ann. §49-2001 (1966); Utah Code Ann. (53 13-1)(1970).

44. Texas Code Ann. §12.11-12.16 (1972).

45. N. Mex. Stat. Ann. §77-13-1 (1975 Supp.).

46. Ariz. Rev. Stat. Ann 15-102(18) 15-442(A)(2) (1975); and see, for example, Ky, Rev. Stat, Ann. §156.435(1) (Cum. Supp. 1974).

47. Cal. Educ. Code §9400(a)(1975).

48. Miss. Code Ann. §37-13-3(1973); Ariz. Rev. Stat. Ann. §15-442(5) and 15-450B(s)(1975).

49. Cal. Educ. Code §9240-9244 (1975); Fla. School Law §233.09(4)(a) as amended by chapter 74-337 and §233.09(4)(d) as amended by chapter 74-337 (West Supp. 1976).

50. See, for example, Code of Ala. tit. 52 §433(2) and §433(23) (Cum. Supp. 1973).

51. Fla. School Law §233.07 et seq. as amended by chapter 74-337 (West Supp. 1976).

52. Local boards in Texas must select only from approved lists, Texas Code Ann. §12.62 (1972).

53. Ark. Stat. Ann §80-1711; Okla. S. tit. 70 §16-111 (1971); Tenn. Code Ann. §49-2021 (1966).

54. Code of Ala. §433(25) and (26)(1973 Cum. Supp.).

55. Cal. Educ. Code §9400(a) and 9221.5 (1975).

56. This point raises complex problems with regard to some statutes. See Block and van Geel, "State of Arizona Curriculum Law," pp. 121-134.

57. Cal. Educ. Code §9221.5(1975).

58. Derived from Campbell and Mazzoni, *State Policy Making for the Public Schools,* Tables IX-2 and IX-4, pp. 288-290, 293-296.

59. Cal. Educ. Code §8571, 8572 (1975).

60. Ariz. Rev. Stat. Ann. 15-119 (Career education (1975); Fla. School Law §233.068 (West Supp. 1976); Ariz. Rev. Stat. Ann §15-102(17), 15-1015, 15-1051, 15-1199 (1975).

61. New York Educ. Law §804-a; (McKinney's 1969); Ill. Ann. Stat. c.122 §10-27.1, 27-9.1 (1962); Cal. Educ. Code 8751, 8506-8507 (1975).

62. Code of Aka. tit. 52 §545(1)(1973 Cum. Supp.); Fla. School Law §233.064 (1961); Miss. Code Ann. §37-13-13 (1973).

63. Ariz. Rev. Stat. Ann. §15-1025 (1975) Texas Code Ann. §21-1031 (1972).

64. Cal. Educ. Code §9031 (1975).

65. N.J. Stat. Ann §18A:35-1 (1968); S.D. Laws Ann. §13-33-6 (1975); Tenn. Code Ann. §49-1927 (1966); Cal. Educ. Code §8553, 8576 (1975).

66. Fla. School Law §229.8055 (West Supp. 1976).

67. Ill. Ann. Stat. §22 art. 27-1 (West Supp. 1976); N.Y. Educ. Law. 3201-a (McKinney's Supp. 1975).

68. Cal. Educ. Code §91 (West Supp. 1976).

69. See note 50.

70. Carol Amyx, "Comment: Sex Discrimination: The Textbook Case," *California Law Review* 62 (July-September 1974): 1312, 1330-1331.

71. New York Board of Regents, Position Paper No. 14, quoted in Division of Curriculum Development, "Reviewing Curriculum for Sexism" (Albany, N.Y.: N.Y. State Education Department, 1975), p. 1 (booklet).

72. Division of Curriculum Development, "Reviewing Curriculum for Sexism."

73. Amyx, "Comment: Sex Discrimination: The Textbook Case," p. 1332-1333.

74. Cal. Educ. Code §9400 et seq. (1975); Florida School Law §233.07 et seq. (West Supp. 1976).

75. Fla. School Law §233.25(3)(b) as amended by Chap. 74-337 (West Supp. 1976); Cal. Educ. Code §9426, 9234 (1975).

76. Members of Harvard Graduate School of Education Seminar, "Quality Control for Instructional Materials: Legislative Mandates of Learner Verification and Implications for Public Education, *Harvard Journal on Legislation* 12 (June 1975); 511.

77. Cal. Educ. Code §5771, 6445.1 (1975); New York Educ. Law §4404(4), 4404(2)(a), 3208(2)(McKinney's 1970), Gen. Stat. N.C. §115.1.1(4) (1975 Supp.).

78. Ariz. State Board of Education Rules and Regulations, §2-D.

79. Cal. Educ. Code §6201 (1975).

80. Oregon Rev. Stat. §339.030 (1975).

81. Miriam Clasby, Maureen Webster, and Naomi White, *Laws, Tests, and Schooling* (Syracuse, N.Y.: Educational Policy Research Center, October 1973), p. 64, Table 2.1 (processed).

82. Ibid., Table 2.4, p. 66.

83. Ibid., Table 2.9, p. 86.

84. Cal. Educ. Code §5779 (1975); Fla. School Law §229.57(3)(b)(West Supp. 1976).

85. Clasby, et al., *Laws, Tests, and Schooling,* Table 2.6, pp. 75-76.

86. Public Act No. 78, §1(b) (1970).

87. Fla. School Law §230:22(b), 228.165(3)(West Supp. 1976).

88. Jerome T. Murphy and David K. Cohen, "Accountability in Education—The Michigan Experience," *The Public Interest* 36 (Summer 1974): 53; Ernest R. House, Wendell Rivers, and Daniel L. Stufflebeam, "An Assessment of the Michigan Accountability System," *Phi Delta Kappan* 55 (June 1974): 663; C. Phillip Kearney, David L. Donovan, and Thomas H. Fisher, "In Defense of Michigan's Accountability Program," *Phi Delta Kappan* 56 (September 1974): 14; Ernest R. House, Wendell Rivers and Daniel L. Stufflebeam, "A Counter-Response to Kearney, Donovan, and Fisher," *Phi Delta Kappan* 56 (September 1974): 19.

89. Discussion based on, van Geel, "State of Florida Curriculum Law," pp. 38-51; and van Geel, "State of California Curriculum Law," pp. 69-76, in van Geel, "Authority to Control the School Curriculum."

90. Gen. Stat. N.C. §115.1.1 (1975 Supp.).

91. Gene Hensley, C. D. Jones, and Nancy Ellen Cain, "Questions and Answers: The Education of Exceptional Children," Report no. 73 (Denver, Colo.: Education Commission of the States, September 1975): 2-3; Fredrick J. Weintraub and Alan Abeson, "New Education Policies for the Handicapped: The Quiet Revolution," *Phi Delta Kappan* 55 (April 1974): 526.

92. Robert L. Flanagan, "Note: The Right of Handicapped Children to an Education: The Phoenix of *Rodriguez,*" *Cornell Law Review* 59 (March 1974): 519, 520; Stanley Herr, "Retarded Children and the Law," *Syracuse Law Review* 23 (1972); 995, 996.

93. Children's Defense Fund of the Washington Research Project, *Children Out of School*, p. 100.

94. James J. Gallagher, "Phenomenal Growth and New Problems Characterize Special Education," *Phi Delta Kappan* 55 (April 1974): 516.

95. Hensley et al., "Questions and Answers: The Education of Exceptional Children," pp. 4, 10; National Advisory Council on the Education of Disadvantaged Children, 1975 Annual Report to the President and the Congress (Washington, D.C.: 1975), app. B, pp. 116-119.

96. Cal. Educ. Code §6901 et seq. (1975).

97. Mass. Gen. Laws Ann. c. 71B (1975 Cum. Supp.). The following analysis draws heavily on Milton Budoff, "Engendering Change in Special Education Practices," *Harvard Educational Review* 45 (November 1975): 507.

98. Ibid.: Carl D. Milofsky, "Why Special Education Isn't Special," *Harvard Educational Review* 44 (November 1974): 437; David Kirp, William Buss, and Peter Kuriloff, "Legal Reform of Special Education: Empirical Studies and Procedural Proposals," *California Law Review* 62 (January 1974): 40.

99. National Advisory Council on Education of Disadvantaged Children, *1975 Annual Report to the President and the Congress* (Washington, D.C., 1975), pp. 126-130.

100. N.Y. Educ. Law §3204.2-a(b)(McKinney's 1969); Ariz. Rev. Stat. Ann. §15-1098 (1975).

101. National Advisory Council on Education of Disadvantaged Children, *1975 Annual Report to the President and Congress*, pp. 126-30.

102. Mass. Gen. Law Ann. c. 71A (1975 Cum. Supp.).

103. See, for example, Fla. School Law 231.15 (West Supp. 1976); Cal. Educ. Code §13133 (1975).

104. Cal. Educ. Code §6307, 5986 (1975).

105. Cal. Educ. Code §5801; also see §8058 (1975).

106. Mass. Gen. Laws Ann. c 15 § 16 (1973).

107. Cal. Educ. Code §31175 et seq. (West Supp. 1976).

108. For a short discussion of the Alum Rock experiment, see Stephen D. Sugarman, "Family Choice: The Next Step in the Quest for Equal Educational Opportunity?" *Law and Contemporary Problems* 38 (Winter-Spring, 1974): 513, 555-563.

109. Cal. Educ. Code §5811 et seq. (West Supp. 1976).

110. Compact 9 (June 1975): 2.

111. John F. Hughes and Anne O. Hughes, *Equal Education* (Bloomington, Ind.: Indiana University Press, 1972), p. 70.

112. Michael W. Kirst, "The Politics of Federal Aid to Education in California," in Joel S. Berke and Michael W. Kirst, *Federal Aid to Education* (Lexington, Mass.: D. C. Heath, 1972), p. 77-109.

113. Jay D. Scribner, "The Politics of Federal Aid to Education in Michigan," in Berke and Kirst, *Federal Aid to Education*, pp. 131, 156.

114. Fredrick M. Wirt, with assistance of Anthony M. Cresswell and Paul M. Irwin, "The Politics of Federal Aid to Education in New York," in Berke and Kirst, *Federal Aid to Education*, pp. 325, 348.

115. Hughes and Hughes, *Equal Education*, chap. 4.

116. Laurence Iannaccone, "The Politics of Federal Aid to Education in Massachusetts," in Berke and Kirst, *Federal Aid to Education*, pp. 193-233; Jerome T. Murphy, "Title I of ESEA: The Politics of Implementing Federal Education Reform," *Harvard Educational Review* 41 (February 1971): 35, 52-60.

Chapter 5
The State Courts

1. The following book contains a long list of sample provisions from state constitutions: Edward C. Bolmeier, *The School in the Legal Structure*, 2d ed. (Cincinnati: The W.H. Anderson Co., 1973), pp. 89-97.

2. Florida State Constitution, Article IX, Section 1; New York State Constitution, Article XI, Section 1.

3. See, for example, *Piper* v. *Big Pine School District of Inyo Coun-*

ty, 193 C. 664, 226 P. 926 (1924); *Maddox* v. *Neal,* 45 Ark. 121 (1885); *People* v. *School Board,* 161 N.Y. 598, 56 N.E. 81 (1900); *Ward* v. *Flood,* 48 C. 36, 17 Am. R. 405 (1874).

4. *Illinois Dept. of Public Welfare* v. *Haas,* 15 Ill. 2d 204, 154 N.E. 2d 265 (1958).

5. Almost all states have provisions exempting the handicapped from compliance with the compulsory education laws. Children's Defense Fund of the Washington Research Project, Inc., *"Children Out of School"* (Cambridge, Mass.: Children's Defense Fund, 1974), p. 93, app. 1.

6. New York Family Court Act, §232 (McKinney's 1975).

7. *Bond* v. *Public Schools of Ann Arbor School District,* 383 Mich. 693, 178 N.W. 2d 484 (1970).

8. *Paulson* v. *Minidonka County School Dist.,* 93 Idaho 469, 463 P. 2d 935 (1970); also, in *Special School Dist. No. 65* v. *Bangs,* 144 Ark. 34, 221 S.W. 1060 (1920), the court struck down tuition charges, saying the constitutional guarantee of a free public school system precluded such charges.

9. *Carpio* v. *Tucson,* 21 Ariz. App. 241, 517 P. 2d 1288 (1974).

10. Ibid., 517 P. 2d p. 1295.

11. *Hamer* v. *Board of Education,* 292 N.E. 2d 569 (1973).

12. *Serrano* v. *Priest,* 5 Cal. 3d 584, 487 P. 2d 1241, 96 Cal. Rptr. 601 (1971).

13. Cal. Educ. Code Sections 176555.5-17665.5 (West Supp. 1976); Kenneth L. Karst, "California, *Serrano* v. *Priest's* Inputs and Outputs," *Law and Contemporary Problems* 38 (Winter-Spring 1974): 333, 335.

14. *San Antonio Independent School District* v. *Rodriguez,* 411 U.S. 1(1973).

15. Memorandum Opinion re Intended Decision at 33, *Serrano* v. *Priest,* Civil No. 938,254 (Cal. Super. Ct., April 10, 1974).

16. Ibid., p. 74.

17. Ibid., p. 89.

18. Ibid., p. 95.

19. Karst, "California, *Serrano* v. *Priest's* Inputs and Outputs," p. 347.

20. *Robinson* v. *Cahill,* 118 N.J. Super. 223, 287 A.2d 187 (1972), *modified and aff'd on other grounds,* 62 N.J. 473, 303 A.2d 273 (1973).

21. New Jersey State Constitution, art. IV, sec. 7, para. 6.

22. *Robinson* v. *Cahill,* 303 A.2d p. 295.

23. Ibid., pp. 297-298.

24. Ibid., p. 295.

25. Ibid.

26. *Board of Education, Levittown Union Free School District, Nassau County* v. *Nyquist*, No. 8208/74 (Supreme Court, Nassau County, N.Y.).

27. New York State Constitution, art. XI, sec. 1.

28. This happened in the *Serrano* v. *Priest* decision.

29. *Neuhaus* v. *Federico*, 505 P. 2d 939 (1973).

30. *Goss* v. *Lopez*, 419 U.S. 565 (1975).

31. *Wagner* v. *Royal*, 78 Pac. 1094 (1904).

32. See cases cited in LeRoy J. Peterson, Richard A. Rossmiller, and Marlin M. Volz, *The Law and Public School Operation* (New York: Harper & Row, 1969), p. 380.

33. See cases cited in Evelyn R. Fulbright and Edward C. Bolmeier, *Courts and the Curriculum*, (Cincinnati: W. H. Anderson, 1964), pp. 136-138, 145-148; Peterson et al., *The Law and Public School Operation*, pp. 387-88.

34. Ibid., pp. 139-145.

35. See cases cited in Fulbright and Bolmeier, *Courts and the Curriculum*, pp. 24-28; 29-31; 33-37.

36. *Myers Publishing Co.* v. *White River School Township*, 28 Ind. App. 91, 93, 62 N.E. 66, 67 (1901).

37. *Board of Education of Topeka* v. *Welch*, 51 Kan. 792, 33 P. 654 (1893).

38. 43 Cal. Ops. Atty. Gen. 322 (1964).

39. Ariz. Rev. Stat. §15-1098(A)(1), and (2) (1975).

40. Ariz. Rev. Stat. §15-1097 (1975).

41. Ariz. Rev. Stat. §15-1098 (1975); Ariz. Rev. Stat. 15 448 (1975) authorizing local districts to offer "special subjects."

42. Ariz. Rev. Stat. §15-102(15) and (16) (1975).

43. See Frank I. Michelman, "In Pursuit of Constitutional Welfare Rights: One View of Rawl's Theory of Justice," *University of Pennsylvania Law Review* 121 (May 1973); 962, 1010-1015.

44. *Neuhaus* v. *Federico*, 505 P.2d 939 (1973).

45. New York Family Court Act §232 (McKinney's 1975).

46. *Matter of Richard C.*, 75 Misc. 2d 517, 348 N.Y.S. 2d 42 (1973).

47. *Matter of Peter H.*, 66 Misc. 2d 1097, 323 N.Y.S. 2d 302 (1971).

48. *Matter of Hilary M.,* 73 Misc. 2d 513, 342 N.Y.S. 2d 12 (1972).

49. *Young* v. *Trustees of Fountain in Grade School,* 64 S.C. 131, 41 So. 824 (1902).; *Morris* v. *Vandiver,* 164 Miss. 476, 145 So. 228 (1933).

50. *Jones* v. *Board of Trustees of Culver City School District* 8 Cal. App. 2d 146, 47 P. 2d 804 (1935); *Ehert* v. *School District of Borough of Kulpmont,* 333 Pa. 518, 5 A. 2d 188 (1939); also *State ex. rel. Brewton* v. *Board of Education of St. Louis,* 361 Mo. 86, 233 S.W. 2d 697 (1950).

51. *State ex. rel. Shineman* v. *Board of Education,* 152 Neb. 644, 42 N.W. 2d 168 (1950); *Talbot* v. *Board of Education of New York,* 171 Misc. 974, 14 N.Y.S. 2d 340 (1939).

52. *State* v. *Ghrist,* 222 Iowa 1069, 270 N.W. 376 (1936).

53. *Acorn Auto Driving School* v. *Board of Education,* 187 N.E. 2d 722 (1963).

54. *Cross* v. *Trustees of Walton Graded School,* 129 Ky. 35, 110 S.W. 346 (1908).

55. Many cases have been decided on this question. See Fulbright and Bolmeier, *Courts and the Curriculum,* pp. 54-61; Peterson et al., *Law and Public School Operations,* p. 381.

56. See Fulbright and Bolmeier, *Courts and the Curriculum,* chap. 3.

57. *Leonard* v. *School Committee,* 349 Mass. 704, 212 N.E. 2d 468 (1965); *Blaine* v. *Board of Education,* 502 P. 2d 643 (1972); but see *Murphy* v. *Pocatello School Dist. No. 25,* 95 Idaho 32, 480 P.2d 878 (1971).

58. *Realy* v. *Caine,* 16 A.D. 2d 976, 230 N.Y.S.2d 453 (1962); *Ackerman* v. *Rubin,* 231 N.Y.S. 2d 112, (1962); *Isquith* v. *Levitt,* 285 A.D. 833, 137 N.Y.S. 2d 497 (1955); *Board of Education of Sycamore ex. rel. Wickham* v. *State,* 80 Ohio St. 133, 88 N.E. 412 (1909).

59. *Rosenberg* v. *Board of Education of City of New York,* 196 Misc. 542, 92 N.Y.S. 2d 344 (1949).

60. *State* v. *Avoyelles Parish School Board,* 147 So. 2d 729 (1962); *Alexander* v. *Phillips,* 31 Ariz. 503, 254 P. 1056 (1927); *Neilan* v. *Board of Directors of Independent School District of Sioux City,* 200 Iowa 860, 205 N.W. 506 (1925).

61. *Nistad* v. *Board of Education of City of New York,* 61 Misc. 2d 60, 304 N.Y.S. 2d 971 (1969).

62. *Lapolla* v. *Dullaghan,* 63 Misc. 2d 157, 313 N.Y.S. 2d 435 (1970).

63. *Scott* v. *Board of Education of Union Free School District No. 17, Hicksville;* 61 Misc. 2d 333, 305 N.Y.S. 2d 601 (1969); *Johnson* v. *Joint School Dist.,* 95 Idaho 317, 508 P. 2d 547 (1973).

64. *Carrollton-Farmers Branch Independent School Dist.* v. *Knight,* 418 S.W. 2d 535 (1967); *Alvin Independent School Dust.* v. *Cooper,* 404

S.W. 2d 76 (1966); *Board of Education* v. *Bentley*, 383 S.W. 2d 677 (1964); *McLeod* v. *State ex. rel. Colmer*, 154 Miss. 468, 122 So. 737 (1929) (cases barring exclusion of married students from the regular program); *Board of Directors* v. *Green*, 259 Iowa 1260, 147 N.W. 2d 854 (1967); *State ex. rel. Barker* v. *Stevenson*, 27 Ohio Op. 2d 223, 189 N.E. 2d 181 (1962); *Kissick* v. *Garland Independent School District*, 330 S.W. 2d 708 (1959); *Starkey* v. *Board of Education,* 14 Utah 2d 227, 381 P. 2d 718 (1963) (cases upholding the exclusion of married students from extracurricular activities).

65. *Alvin Independent School District* v. *Cooper*, 404 S.W. 2d 76 (1966); also *Nutt* v. *Board of Education,* 128 Kan. 507, 278 P. 1065 (1929).

66. *State ex. rel. Idle* v. *Chamberlin*, 12 Ohio Misc. 44, 175 N.E. 2d 539 (1961).

67. *Dritt.* v. *Snodgrass*, 66 Mo. 286 (1877); *Hobbs* v. *Germany*, 94 Misc. 469, 49 So. 515 (1909), *State ex. rel. Clark* v. *Osborne*, 24 Mo. App. 309 (1887); but compare *Magnum* v. *Keith*, 147 Ga. 603, 95 S.E.1 (1918).

68. California State Constitution, art. IX, sec. 1; Cal. Educ. Code §5771, 6445.1 (1975); and Title 5 Cal. Ad. Code, §3220(d)(1975).

69. New York Education Law §4404(4), 4404(2)(a), 3208(2)(McKinney's 1969); G.S.N.C. Ann. §115.1.1(4) (1975 Supp.).

Chapter 6
Professionals and Their Unions

1. A good review of the literature on educational politics can be found in Paul E. Peterson, "The Politics of American Education," in F.N. Kerlinger and J.B. Carroll, eds., *Review of Research in Education,* 2 (Itasco, Ill.: F.E. Peacock 1974): 348, 354; and William Boyd, "The Public, the Professionals, and Educational Policymaking: Who Governs," *Teachers College Record* 77 (May 1976): 539.

2. Cal. Educ. Code §7 (1975).

3. N.Y. Educ. Law §1711, 2508, 2566 (McKinney's 1969).

4. See, for example, Cal. Educ. Code §13556, 13204, 23404, 13443(d) (1975).

5. See, for example, Arizona Rev. Stat. §15-441 and 442 (1975).

6. LeRoy J. Peterson, Richard Rossmiller, and Marlin V. Volz, *The Law and Public Education* (New York: Harper & Row, 1969), p. 231.

7. See *Permeter* v. *Young*, 31 So. 2d 387 (1947).

8. *Parrish* v. *Moss*, 200 Misc. 375, 106 N.Y.S. 2d 577 (1951), *aff'd* 279 A.D. 608, 107 N.Y.S. 2d 580 (1951).

9. *Pickering* v. *Board of Education,* 391 U.S. 563 (1968).

10. *Rackley* v. *School District No. 5, Orangeburg County, S.C.,* 258 F. Supp. 676 (D. S.C. 1966): *Shelton* v. *Tucker,* 364 U.S. 479 (1960); *Sweezy* v. *New Hampshire,* 354 U.S. 234 (1957).

11. *Keyishian* v. *Board of Regents of the University of State of New York,* 385 U.S. 589 (1967).

2. Ibid.; accord *Perry* v. *Sinderman,* 408 U.S. 593, 597-598 (1972).

13. See, generally, *Chicago* v. *Mosley,* 408 U.S. 92 (1972); *Cox* v. *Louisiana,* 379 U.S. 559 (1965).

14. See also *Elrod* v. *Burns,* 44 U.S.L.W. 5091 (June 28, 1976); *Ill. State Employees Union* v. *Lewis,* 473 F. 2d 561 (7 Cir. 1972), *cert. denied,* 410 U.S. 943 (1973).

15. *Ahern* v. *Board of Education of School District of Grand Island,* 327 F. Supp. 1391 (D. Neb. 1971).

16. *Clark* v. *Holmes,* 474 F. 2d 928 (7 Cir. 1972).

17. *Hetrick* v. *Martin,* 480 F. 2d 705 (6 Cir. 1973), *cert. denied,* 414 U.S. 1075 (1973).

18. *Keefe* v. *Geanakos,* 418 F. 2d 359 (1 Cir. 1969); *Parducci* v. *Rutland,* 316 F. Supp. 352 (M.D. Ala. 1970).

19. *Sterzing* v. *Ft. Bend Independent School District,* 376 F. Supp. 657 (S.D. Tex. 1973), *remanded,* 496 F.2d 92 (5 Cir. 1974).

20. *Keefe* v. *Geanakos*; *Parducci* v. *Rutland*; and *Mailloux* v. *Kiley,* 448 F. 2d 1242 (1 Cir. 1971), affirming 323 F. Supp. 1387 (D. Mass. 1971).

21. In 1972-73, 2556 Contracts had been negotiated involving 934, 794 teachers. *Negotiation Research Digest,* 7 (January 1974): 15.

22. *NLRB.* v. *Borg-Warner,* 356 U.S. 342 (1958); Joan Weitzman, *The Scope of Bargaining in Public Employment* (New York: Praeger, 1975), p. 72.

23. Weitzman, *Scope of Bargaining in Public Employment,* p. 87.

24. Dr. Frederick L. Hipp, executive secretary of the New Jersey Educational Association, quoted in *Educators Negotiating Service Newsletter,* November 1, 1975, p. 61.

25. *Educators Negotiating Service,* complete texts, January 15, 1975, pp. 3, 4.

26. Weitzman, *Scope of Bargaining in Public Employment,* pp. 200-213; Donald H. Wollett and Robert H. Chanin, *The Law and Practice of Teacher Negotiations* (Washington, D.C.: The Bureau of National Affairs, 1974), pp. 6:58-6:63.

27. Wollett and Chanin, *Law and Practice of Teacher Negotiations,*

pp. 1:9-1:13; Donald H. Wollett, "The Bargaining Process in the Public Sector: What is Bargainable?, *Oregon Law Review* 51 (Fall 1971): 177.

28. Weitzman, *Scope of Bargaining in Public Employment*, pp. 82-84.

29. Clyde W. Summers, "Public Employee Bargaining: A Political Perspective," *Yale Law Journal* 83 (May 1974): 1156.

30. Harry H. Wellington, and Ralph K. Winter, *The Unions and the Cities* (Washington, D.C.: The Brookings Institution, 1971), chaps. 1 and 9.

31. See, generally, *Fibreboard Paper Products Corp.* v. *NLRB*, 379 U.S. 203 (1964); see also Weitzman, *Scope of Bargaining in Public Employment*, pp. 72, 230, 236, 240-241.

32. Derek C. Bok and John T. Dunlop, *Labor and the American Community* (New York: Simon and Schuster, 1970), p. 327.

33. See for example, Mich. Stat. Ann. §17.455(1) et seq. (1975); New York Civil Service Law §200 et seq. (McKinney's 1973); Wisconsin Stat. Ann. §111.80 et seq. (1974).

34. Alaska Stat. §14.20.550 (1975).

35. Mass. Gen. Laws. Ann. c. 150-E, §6 (1975 Supp.).

36. See, for example, Mont. Rev. Code Ann. §59-1601 (1975 Cum. Supp.).

37. Cal. Government Code c. 10.7 §3540 et seq. (1975 Supp.); Me. Rev. Stat. Ann. tit. 26 §961 et seq. (Supp. 1975).

38. Cal. Gov. Code c. 10.7 §3543.2 (1975 Supp.).

39. Ibid.

40. Cal. Gov. Code c. 10.7 §3543.2 (1975 Supp.).

41. *Syracuse Teachers Association* v. *Board of Education,* 35 N.Y. 2d 743, 744 (1974); *Board of Education of Union Free School District No. 3 of the Town of Huntington* v. *Associated Teachers of Huntington,* 30 N.Y. 2d 122, 331 N.Y.S. 2d 17, 282 N.E. 2d 109 (1972); *Dunellen Board of Education* v. *Dunellen Education Association,* 64 N.J. 17, 311 A. 2d 737 (1973).

42. The results of this study, sponsored by the Academic Collective Bargaining Information Service, are reported in *Government Employment Relations Reporter,* No. 643 (February 9, 1976): D-1.

43. *West Hartford Education Association* v. *DeCourcy,* 295 A.2d 526 (1972); *In the Matter of Washoe County School District and the Washoe County Teachers Association,* Item #3, October 1971; *Hawaii State Teachers Association and Department of Education,* GERR No. 480 E-1 (1972).

44. *West Irondequoit Teachers Association* v. *Helsby,* 42 A.D. 2d

808, 346 N.Y.S. 2d 418 (1973), aff'd 35 N.Y. 2d 46(1974); *State College Area School District*, GERR no. 426 F-1 (1971); *NEA v. Board of Education of Shawnee Mission,* 512 P. 2d 426, 84 LRRM 2223 (1973).

45. *Yorktown Faculty Association v. Yorktown Central School District No. 2*, 7 PERB 3030 (1974).

46. *Government Employment Relations Reporter*, no. 643, D-1.

47. *Board of Education v. Rockaway Township Education Association*, 120 N.J. Super. 564, 295 A. 2d 380 (1972).

48. Ibid., 295 A. 2d, .382.

49. *Nickels v. Board of Education of Imlay City Community Schools*, File no. 1546, Lapper County Circuit Court, January 3, 1967, discussed in Weitzman, *Scope of Bargaining in Public Employment*, pp. 205-206.

50. *Government Employment Relations Reporter*, no. 643, D-1; *West Irondequoit Teachers Association v. Helsby*, 42 A.D. 2d 808, 346 N.Y.S. 2d 418 (1973).

51. *Government Employment Relations Reporter*, No. 643, D-1.

52. *Negotiation Research Digest*, 4, no. 8 (April 1971): 17.

53. A. Gray Thompson and Russel H. Zeimer, "Impact of Collective Bargaining on Curriculum-Instruction," *Research Report No. 1975-2* (Evanston, Ill.: National School Boards Association, 1975).

54. "Comment: Teacher Collective Bargaining—Who Runs the Schools?," *Fordham Urban Law Journal* 2 (Spring 1974): 505.

55. The account was taken from Ida Klaus, "The Evolution of a Collective Bargaining Relationship in Public Education: New York City's Changing Seven-Year History," *Michigan Law Review* 67 (March, 1969); 1033.

Chapter 7
The Public and Parents

1. *In Matter of Feldheim*, 8 Educ. Dept. Rptr. 136 (New York 1969).

2. Evelyn R. Sinaiko, . "Due Process Rights of Participation in Administrative Rule Making," *California Law Review* 63 (July 1975): 886, 889.

3. Ibid., pp. 889, 907 ff.

4. *Kramer v. Union Free School District No. 15*, 395 U.S. 621 (1969).

5. See *Owens v. School Committee of Boston*, 304 F. Supp. 1327 (D. Mass. 1969).

6. *Whitcomb* v. *Chavis*, 403 U.S. 124 (1971); *White* v. *Regester*, 412 U.S. 755 (1973); *Zimmer* v. *McKeithan,* 485 F. 2d 1297 (5 Cir. 1973); *City of Richmond* v. *U.S.*, 45 L. ed. 2d 245 (1975).

7. N.Y. Educ. Law §2590-c(6) (McKinney's 1969).

8. Melvin Zimet, *Decentralization and School Effectiveness* (New York: Teachers College Press, 1973), pp. 123-124.

9. LeRoy J. Peterson, Richard A. Rossmiller, and Marlin M. Volz, *The Law and Public School Operation* (New York: Harper & Row, 1969), pp. 237-250.

10. Laws of New York, Chapter 578 (1974).

11. *Pickering* v. *Board of Education,* 391 U.S. 563 (1968).

12. Mitchell J. Lindauer, "Government Employee Disclosures of Agency Wrongdoing: Protecting the Right to Blow the Whistle," *University of Chicago Law Review* 42 (Spring 1975): 530-561.

13. "Comment: The Right of the Press to Gather Information After *Branzburg* and *Pell*," *University of Pennsylvania Law Review* 124 (November 1975): 166-191; The Rights of the Public and the Press to Gather Information," *Harvard Law Review* 87 (May 1974):1505-1533.

14. *Grayned* v. *City of Rockford*, 408 U.S. 104 (1972).

15. *West Virginia Board of Education* v. *Barnette*, 319 U.S. 624 (1943).

16. *Baker* v. *Owen*, 395 F. Supp. 294 (M.D. N.C. 1975), *aff'd*, 46 L. Ed. 2d 137 (1975).

17. *Citizens for Parental Rights* v. *San Mateo Cty. Bd. of Ed.*, 124 Cal. Rptr, 68, 51 Cal. App. 3d 1 (Cal. App. 1975); *Cornwall* v. *State Board of Education,* 314 F. Supp. 340 (D. Md. 1969) *aff'd.*, 428 F.2d 471 (4 Cir. 1970), *cert. denied*, 400 U.S. 942 (1970).

18. *Citizens for Parental Right* v. *San Mateo Cty. Bd. of Ed.*

19. Ibid., 124 Cal. Rptr, p. 84.

20. *Hopkins* v. *Board of Education,* 29 Conn. Sup. 397, 289 A. 2d 914, 921 (1971).

21. *Citizens for Parental Rights* v. *San Mateo Cty. Bd. of Ed.,* 124 Cal. Rptr. p.84.

22. Ibid., 124 Cal. Rptr. pp. 91-92.

23. *Hopkins* v. *Board of Education*.

24. *Valent* v. *New Jersey State Board of Education,* 114 N.J. Super. 63, 274 A. 2d. 832 (1971).

25. See, for example, Ill. Ann. Stat. c. 122 §27-9.1 (1976 Supp.); Mich. Stat. Ann. §15-3789(3) (1975).

26. *Citizens for Parental Rights* v. *San Mateo Cty. Bd. of Ed.*

27. *Spence* v. *Bailey*, 465 F. 2d 797 (6 Cir. 1972); but compare *Sapp* v. *Renfroe* 511 F. 2d 172 (5 Cir. 1975).

28. *Mitchell* v. *McCall*, 273 Ala. 604, 143 So. 2d 629 (1962).

29. *State ex. rel. Kelley* v. *Ferguson*, 95 Neb. 63, 144 N.W. 1039 (1914).

30. *Hardwick* v. *Board of School Trustees*, 54 Cal. App. 696, 205 P. 49 (1921).

31. *School Board Dist. No. 18, Garvin County* v. *Thompson*, 103 P. 578 (1909).

32. *Morrow* v. *Wood*, 35 Wis. 59, (1894); *State* v. *Ferguson*, 144 N.W. 1039 (1914).

33. *State ex. rel. Andrews* v. *Webber*, 108 Ind. 31, 8 N.E. 708 (1886).

34. *State ex. rel. Shineman* v. *Board of Education*, 152 Neb. 644, 42 N.W. 2d 168 (1950); *Trustees of School* v. *People*, 87 Ill. 303, 29 Am. Rep. 55 (1877).

35. Such a statute was involved in *State ex. rel. Mueller* v. *Common Board of Joint School Dist. No. 2 of Princeton,* 208 Wis. 257, 242 N.W. 574 (1932).

36. *State ex. rel. Thayer* v. *School District of Nebraska City*, 99 Neb. 338, 156 . N.W. 641 (1916),

37. R.I. Gen. Laws Ann. §16-22-8 (1970).

38. Mass. Gen. Laws Ann. c. 71 §13 (1975 Cum. Supp.).

39. 395 U.S. 621 (1969).

40. *Eubank* v. *City of Richmond*, 226 U.S. 137 (1912); *Cusack Co.* v. *City of Chicago*, 242 U.S. 526 (1916); *Washington ex. rel. Seattle Title and Trust Co.* v. *Roberge*, 278 U.S. 116 (1928). The analysis which follows was strongly influenced by comments made in a private communication by Professor Frank I. Michelman.

41. *Eubank* v. *City of Richmond*.

42. *Guernsey* v. *Pitkin*, 32 Vt. 224, 76 Am. Dec. 171 (1859).

43. *Alexander* v. *Phillips*, 31 Ariz. 503, 254 P. 1056 (1927).

44. *Neilan* v. *Board of Directors of Independent School Dist. of Sioux City*, 200 Iowa 860, 205 N.W. 506 (1925).

45. *Wulff* v. *Inhabitants of Wakefield*, 221 Mass. 427, 109 N.E. 358 (1915).

46. *Rosenberg* v. *Board of Education of New York City*, 196 Misc. 542, 92 N.Y.S. 2d 344 (1949); also see *Todd* v. *Rochester Community Schools*, 200 N.W. 2d 90 (1972).

47. Peterson et al., *Law and Public School Operation*, p. 382.

48. *Isquith* v. *Levitt*, 137 N.Y.S. 2d 497 (1955).

49. *Sycamore Board of Education* v. *State*, 88 N.E. 412 (1909).

50. *Ackerman* v. *Rubin*, 35 Misc. 2d 707, 232 N.Y.S. 2d 112 (1962).

51. *Goss* v. *Lopez*, 419 U.S. 565 (1975).

52. *Pennsylvania Ass'n for Retarded Children* v. *Commonwealth*, 334 F. Supp. 1257 (E.D. Pa. 1971), *modified*, 343 F. Supp. 279 (E.D. Pa. 1972); *Mills* v. *Board of Education*, 343 F. Supp. 866 (D.D.C. 1972).

53. *Madera* v. *Board of Education*, 386 F. 2d 778 (2 Cir. 1967).

54. 20 U.S.C.A. 1232e (1976 Supp.); Cal. Educ. Code §10932 et seq. (West 1976 Supp.).

55. Don Davies, "The Emerging Third Force in Education," *Inequality in Education* no. 15 (November 1973): 5-22.

56. Ibid., pp. 9-10.

57. 20 U.S.C.A. 241g (1976 Supp.); 40 Fed. Reg. 11484, §116a.25 (1975).

58. See, for example, 20 U.S.C.A. §880(b)-1(E) (1976 Supp.) (bilingual education).

59. Cal. Educ. Code §5763 (1975); also districts are encouraged to involve parents in selecting instructional materials, Cal. Educ. Code §9462 (1975); Mass. Gen Laws Ann. c. 15 §1G and c. 28A §1(2) (1973).

60. N.Y. Educ. Law §2590-d (McKinney's 1969).

61. Fla. School Law §230.22(b) (West Supp. 1976).

62. Fla. School Law §228.165(3) (West Supp. 1976).

Chapter 8
State Control of Private Schools

1. Helen M. Jellison, ed., *State and Federal Laws Relating to Nonpublic Schools* (Washington, D.C.: Government Printing Office, 1975), p. 3; and, for additional data and information about private schools, see Daniel J. Sullivan, *Public Aid to Nonpublic Schools* (Lexington, Mass.: D.C. Heath, 1974), chap. 2; Otto F. Kraushaar, *American Nonpublic Schools* (Baltimore, Md.: Johns Hopkins University Press, 1972), chaps. 1-3.)

2. See, generally, Forest Chester Ensign, *Compulsory School Attendance and Child Labor* (New York: Arno Press and the *New York Times*, 1969).

3. David Tyack, "The Perils of Pluralism: The Background of the Pierce Case," *American Historical Review* 74 (October 1968): 74-98.

4. For an already somewhat dated compilation of state laws on pri-

vate education, see Jellison, ed., *State and Federal Laws Relating to Nonpublic Schools*.

5. Ky. Rev. Stat Ann. §156.160, 159.030 (1971, 1974 cum. supp.); Me. Rev. Stat. Ann. tit. 20, §102, 1281, 115, 911 (1975 Supp); N.H. Rev. Stat. Ann. §194:23b, 193:1 (1964); N.C. Gen. Stat. §115-225, 115-166 (1975); N.D. Cent. Code §15-34.1-03 (1975 Supp.); Pa. Stat. Ann. tit. 24 §2734, 13-1327 (1962 and 1975 Supp.); R.I. Gen. Laws Ann. §16-40-1, 16-19-1 (1969 and 1975 Supp.); S.C. Code Ann. §21-757 (1975 Supp.); S.D. Compiled Laws Ann. §13-4-1, 13-27-3 (1975); Wash. Rev. Code Ann. §28A.02.200, 28A.04.120, 28A.27010 (1970 and 1975 Supp.); W. Va. Code Ann. §178-2-6, 18-5-13, 18-8-1 (1971 and 1975 Supp.); Iowa Code Ann. §257.25, 299.2 (1972 and 1976 Supp.); Ala. Code tit. 52 §299 (1960); Alaska Stat. §14.07.020, 14.30.0-0 (1975); Idaho Code §33-119, 33-2-2 (1963); Mich. Stat. Ann. §15.1921, 15-3732 (1975); Mont. Rev. Code Ann. §75-7502, 75-6303 (1975 Supp.); Nev. Rev. Stat. tit. 34 §394.005 et seq., 392-070 (1975); N.J. Stat. Ann. §18A:69-1, 18A:69-2, 18A:38-25 (1968); Ohio Rev. Code Ann. §3301.076), 3321.04, 3321.07 (1972); Ore. Rev. Stat. §343.960, 339.030 (1975); Vt. Stat. Ann. tit. 16, §166, 1121 (1974); Md. Ann. Code art. 77 c.2 §12, c.6 §92 (1975); Ga. Code Ann. §32-818, 32-2104 (1969); Hawaii Rev. Stat. §298.6, 298.7 (1968); Kan. Stat. Ann. §72-1111 (1972); Neb. Rev. Stat. §79-1247.02, 79-201 (1971).

6. Mass. Gen. Laws Ann. c.76 §1 (1975 Supp.); Cal. Educ. Code §29081, 12154 (1975); Colo. Rev. Stat. §123-1-7, 123-20-5 (1964); Conn. Gen. Stat. Ann. §10-34, 10-184 (1973); New York Educ. Law §3601, 3210 (McKinney's 1969); La. Rev. Stat. Ann. §17-411, 17-221 (1976 Supp.); Okla. Stat. tit. 70, §3-104 (10), 10-105 (1975 Supp.); Tenn. Code Ann. §49-105 (19), 49-1708 (1966); Wyo. Stat. Ann. §21.1.191, 21.1-48 (1975 Supp.); Ariz. Rev. Stat. Ann. §15-321 (1975); Ark. Stat. Ann. §80-1502 (1960); Ill. Ann. Stat. §13-9, 26-1 (1962 and 1976 Supp.); Mo. Ann. Stat. §167.031 (1965); Del. Code Ann. §2703 (1970 Supp.) Fla. School Law §237.02 (1976 Supp.); Ind. Stat. Ann. §20-8,1-3-17 (1975); Minn. Stat. §120.10 (1976 Supp.); Texas Educ. Code Ann. §21.033 (1975 Supp.); Utah Code Ann. §53-24-1 (197); Va. Code §72-275.1 (1975 Cum. Supp.); Wisc. Stat. §118.15(1)(a) (1973).

7. See, for example, Ind. Stat. Ann. §20-8.1-3-17 (1975); and Minn. Stat. §120.10(2) (1960).

8, Kan. Stat. Ann. §72-1101 (1972); Me. Rev. Stat. Ann tit. 20, §1222 (1965); Neb. Rev. Stat. §79-213 (1971).

9. Texas Educ. Code Ann. §21.033 (1975 Supp.).

10. Idaho Code §33-118 (1963).

11. Mich. Stat. Ann. §15-3365(1) (1975).

12. N.J. Stat. Ann. §18A:6-1 (1968).

13. Iowa Code Ann. §257-25(8) (1976 Supp.).

14. Ala. Code tit. 52 §299 (1960); Alaska Stat. §14.30.010 (1975); Hawaii Rev. Stat. §297.2 (1975 Supp.); Ill. Ann. Stat. §33-1201 (1973); Iowa Code Ann. §257.30.257.25 (1976 Supp.); Kan. Stat. Ann. §72-1111 (1972); La. Rev. Stat. Ann. §17-411 (1976 Supp.); Me. Rev. Stat. Ann tit. 20 §59, 1281, 1751 (1975 Supp.); Mich. Comp. Laws Ann. §15.1923 (1975); Nev. Rev. Stat. §79-1233, 79-1701 (1973); N.C. Gen. Stat. §115.256 (1975); N.D. Cent. Code Laws Ann. §13-4-2, 13-42-2 (1975); Wash. Rev. Code Ann. §28A.02.200 (1970).

15. N.H. Rev. Stat. Ann. §186.11 (1964); Ohio Rev. Code Ann. §3301.7(D) (1972); Conn. Gen. Stat. Ann. §10.34 (1973).

16. *State* v. *Vaugn*, 44 N.J. 142, 207 A. 2d 537 (1965).

17. *Sheppard* v. *State*, 306 P. 2d 346 (1957); *Wright* v. *State*, 209 P. 179 (1922).

18. *People* v. *Levinsen*, 404 Ill. 574, 90 N.E. 2d 213, 215 (1950).

19. *State* v. *Counort*, 69 Wash. 361, 124 P. 910 (1912); and see *State* v. *Lowry*, 191 Kan. 962, 383 P. 2d 962 (1963).

20. *State* v. *Cournot*, 124 P., p. 912.

21. *State* v. *Hoyt*, 84 N.H. 38, 146 A. 170 (1929).

22. *State* v. *Peterman*, 32 Ind. App. 665, 70 N.E. 550 (1904).

23. Ibid., 70 N.E., p. 551.

24. Ibid., 70 N.E., p. 550.

25. See fig. 8-1 in text.

26. Wash. Rev. Code Ann. §28A.27.010 (1975 Supp.).

27. *State* v. *Counort*.

28. *Rice* v. *Commonwealth*, 188 Va. 224, 49 S.E. 2d 342 (1948).

29. Ibid., 49 S.E. 2d, p. 348.

30. Ibid.: *Commonwealth* v. *Renfrew*, 332 Mass. 492, 126 N.E. 2d 109 (1955).

31. Cal. Educ. Code §12155 (1975).

32. *In re Shinn*, 195 CA 2d 165, 16 Cal. Rptr. 165 (1961); see also *T.A.F.* v. *Duval County*, 273 So. 2d 15 (1963).

33. *In re Meyers*, 119 N.Y.S. 2d 98 (1953); *People* v. *Turner*, 227 A.D. 317, 98 N.Y.S. 2d 886 (1950).

34. *State* v. *Massa*, 95 N.J. Super. 382, 231, A. 2d 252 (1967); *Stephans* v. *Bongart*, 15 N.J.M. 80, 189 A. 131 (1937).

35. *State* v. *Massa*, 231 A. 2d, p. 257.

36. See, generally, *People* v. *Levinson; State* v. *Peterman; Wright* v.

State; State v. *Lowery; In re Meyers; People* v. *Turner; State* v. *Massa; Stephans* v. *Bongart*.

37. See, for example, *State* v. *Peterman*.

38. *State* v. *Massa; State* v. *Peterman*.

39. *State* v. *Lowery*.

40. *Stephans* v. *Bongart*.

41. *People* v. *Donner*, 199 Misc. 643, 99 N.Y.S. 2d 830, *aff'd*, 278 A.D. 704, 103 N.Y.S. 2d 757, *aff'd*, 302 N.Y. 857, 100 N.E. 2d 48, *appeal dismissed*, 342 U.S. 884 (1951); *Auster* v. *Weberman*, 198 Misc. 1055, 100 N.Y.S. 2d 60, *aff'd*, 278 A.D. 656, 102 N.Y.S. 2d 418, *aff'd*, 302 N.Y. 855, 100 N.E. 47, *appeal dismissed* 342 U.S. 884, *aff'd*, 278 A.D. 784, 104 N.Y.S. 2d 65 (1951).

42. *Packer Collegiate Institute* v. *The University of the State of New York*, 298 N.Y. 184, 81 N.E. 2d 80 (1948).

43. Ibid., p. 298 N.Y., pp. 191-192.

44. Kenneth Culp Davis, *Administrative Law Text*, 3d ed. (St. Paul, Minn.: West, 1972), pp. 43, 51.

45. Ibid., pp. 184-186.

46. See, generally, Thomas I. Emerson, *The System of Freedom of Expression* (New York: Random House, Vintage Books, 1970), p. 506.

47. Arthur R. Block, "Compulsory School Attendance Laws: Limitations on Their Use Against Children in Non-Public Schools," (Cambridge, Mass.: unpublished memorandum, December 1972), p. 20c.

48. *Freedman* v. *Maryland*, 380 U.S. 51 (1965); *Blount* v. *Rizzi*, 400 U.S. 410 (1971).

49. Stephen Arons, "The Separation of School and State: *Pierce* Reconsidered," *Harvard Educational Review* 46 (February 1976):76.

50. See, for example, *Cleveland Board of Education* v. *LaFleur*, 414 U.S. 632 (1974).

51. See Note 14.

52. See, generally, Donald A. Erickson, "Showdown at an Amish Schoolhouse: A Description and Analysis of the Iowa Controversy," in Donald A. Erickson, ed., *Public Controls for Nonpublic Schools* (Chicago: University of Chicago Press, 1969), p. 15.

53. *Yates* v. *United States*, 354 U.S. 298 (1957); *Brandenburg* v. *Ohio*, 395 U.S. 444 (1969).

54. *Runyon* v. *McCary*, 44 U.S.L.W. 5034, 5039 (1976).

55. Mich. Stat. Ann. §15-3365(1) (1975).

56. *Commonwealth* v. *Roberts*, 159 Mass. 372, 34 N.E. 402, 403 (1893); *State* v. *Peterman*, 70 N.E., p. 550.

Chapter 9
Conclusions and Policy Recommendations

1. 20 U.S.C.A. §331 (1976 Supp.)

2. Quoted in Joseph M. Cronin, "The Federal Takeover: Should the Junior Partner Run the Firm?" *Phi Delta Kappan* 57, no. 8 (April 1976): 499.

3. Based on Fred R. Eichelman, "The Government as Textbook Writer: A Case History," *Phi Delta Kappan*, 57, no. 7 (March 1976): 456.

4. See, generally, Byron G. Massialas, "American Government, We Are the Greatest," in C. Benjamin Cox and Byron G. Massialas, eds., *Social Studies in the United States* (New York: Harcourt, Brace & World, 1967), p. 178; Robert J. Goldstein, "Elementary School Curriculum and Political Socialization," in Byron G. Massialas, ed., *Political Youth, Traditional Schools*, (Englewood Cliffs, N.J.: Prentice-Hall, 1972), p. 17; James P. Shaver, "Reflective Thinking, Values and Social Studies Textbooks," *School Review* 73 (Autumn 1965): 226; Frederick R. Smith and John J. Patrick, "Civics," in Cox and Massialas, eds., *Social Studies in the United States*, p. 105; Bruce R. Joyce, "The Primary Grades," in ibid., p. 15.

5. George Z. F. Bereday and Bonnie B. Stretch, "Political Education in the U.S.A. and the U.S.S.R.," *Comparative Education Review* 7 (June 1963): 9.

6. M. Kent Jennings, "Correlates of the Social Studies Curriculum," in C. Cox and Massialas, eds., *Social Studies in the United States*, p. 306.

7. Sidney Verba and Norman H. Nie, *Participation in America* (New York: Harper& Row, 1972), pt. I, passim.

8, Ibid., chap. 13.

9. See, generally, Charles Hamilton, "Race and Education: A Search for Legitimacy," *Harvard Educational Review* 38 (Fall 1968): 669.

10. Cal. Government Code §3547 (1976 Supp.).

11. The idea is taken from Tyll van Geel, "Judicial Reform of the Political Education Program of the Public Schools: On Fairness, Vouchers, and Academic Freedom," Rochester, N.Y., unpublished manuscript, January 1976: 25-37.

12. Hannah N. Geffert, Robert J. Harper II, and Daniel M. Schember, "Dealing with Bias in Textbooks and Educational Material Used in the Public Schools: A Model Statute," (Washington, D.C., Lawyers' Committee for Civil Rights Under Law, n.d. (unpublished paper).

13. *Education U.S.A.*, vol. 18, no. 24 (February 9, 1976): 138.

14. Geffert et al., "Selecting Educational Material for Use in the Public School: A Model Statute."

15. Much has been written on the concept of educational vouchers: Milton Friedman, "The Role of Government in Education," in *Capitalism and Freedom* (Chicago: University of Chicago Press, 1962), p. 85; E.G. West, *Education and the State*, 2d ed. (London: Institute of Economic Affairs, 1970); Center for the Study of Public Policy, *Education Vouchers*, Cambridge, Mass., 1970 (processed); John E. Coons and Stephan Sugarman, "Family Choice in Education: A Model State System for Vouchers," *California Law Review* 59 (March 1971): 321; Stephen Arons, "Equity, Option, and Vouchers," *Teachers College Record* 72 (February 1971): 337; Stephen D. Sugarman, "Family Choice: The Next Step in the Quest for Equal Educational Opportunity," *Law and Contemporary Problems* 38 (Winter-Spring 1974): 513.

16. In *Norwood* v. *Harrison*, 413 U.S. 455 (1973) the Supreme Court voided a law that provided free textbooks to students in private schools that segregated on the basis of race. Also see *Gonzales* v. *Fairfax-Brewster School Inc.*, 363 F. Supp. 1200 (E.D. Va. 1973), *cert. granted* 44 U.S. L.W. 3279 (1975), *aff'd sub nom. Runyon* v. *McCary*, 44 U.S.L.W. 5034 (1976).

Bibliography

Books

Altshuler, Alan A. *Community Control*. New York: Pegasus, 1970.

Banfield, Edward C., and Wilson, James Q. *City Politics*. New York: Vintage Books, 1963.

Barker, Ernest. *Greek Political Theory*. London: Methuen, 1970.

Bickel, Alexander M. *The Least Dangerous Branch*. Indianapolis: Bobbs-Merrill, 1962.

_____. *The Supreme Court and the Idea of Progress,* Harper Torchbook ed. New York: Harper & Row, 1970.

Bok, Derek C., and Dunlop, John T. *Labor and the American Community*. New York: Simon and Schuster, 1970.

Boll, Eleanor, and Bossard, James. *The Sociology of Child Development,* 3rd ed. New York: Harper, 1960.

Bolmeier, Edward C. *The School in the Legal Structure*, 2d ed. Cincinnati: W. H. Anderson, 1973.

Bolmeier, Edward C., and Fulbright, Evelyn R. *Courts and the Curriculum*. Cincinnati: W. H. Anderson, 1964.

Campbell, Roald F., and Mazzoni, Tim B. Jr. *State Policy Making for the Public Schools*. Berkeley, Cal.: McCutchan Publishing, 1976.

Chanin, Robert H., and Wollett, Donald H. *The Law and Practice of Teacher Negotiations*. Washington, D.C.: Bureau of National Affairs, 1974.

Childs, John L. *Education and Morals*. New York: Appleton-Century-Crofts, 1950.

Coons, John E.; Clune, William H. III; and Sugarman, Stephan D. *Private Wealth and Public Education*. Cambridge, Mass.: Harvard University Press, Belknap Press, 1970.

Cox, Archibald. *The Warren Court*. Cambridge, Mass.: Harvard University Press, 1968.

Cronin, Joseph M. *The Control of Urban Schools*. New York: Free Press, 1973.

Dahl, Robert. *After the Revolution?* New Haven: Yale University Press, 1970.

Davis, Kenneth Culp. *Administrative Law Text*. 3rd ed. St. Paul, Minn.: West Publishing, 1973.

De Tocqueville, Alexis. *Democracy in America*, ed. Phillips Bradley. New York: Alfred A. Knopf, 1956.

Emerson, Thomas I. *The System of Freedom of Expression*. New York: Random House, Vintage Books, 1970.

Ensign, Forest Chester. *Compulsory School Attendance and Child Labor*. New York: Arno Press and the *New York Times*, 1969.

Fein, Leonard J. *The Ecology of the Public Schools*. New York: Pegasus, 1971.

Grubb, W. Norton, and Michelson, Stephan. *States and Schools*. Lexington, Mass.: D.C. Heath, 1974.

Hand, Learned. *The Bill of Rights*. New York: Atheneum, 1972.

Horner, V., and John, V. *Early Childhood Bilingual Education Project*. New York: Modern Language Association, 1971.

Hughes, John F. and Anne O. *Equal Education*. Bloomington: Indiana University Press, 1972.

Jellison, Helen M., ed., *State and Federal Laws Relating to Nonpublic Schools*. Washington, D.C.: Government Printing Office, 1975.

Katz, Michael B. *Class, Bureaucracy, and Schools*. New York: Praeger, 1975.

Kirp, David L., and Yudof, Mark G. *Educational Policy and the Law*. Berkeley, Cal.: McCutchan Publishing, 1974.

Kirst, Michael W., and Wirt, Fredrick M. *The Political Web of American Schools*. Boston: Little, Brown, 1972.

Kraushaar, Otto F. *American Nonpublic Schools*. Baltimore, Md.: Johns Hopkins University Press, 1972.

Kurland, Phillip B. *Politics, The Constitution, and the Warren Court*. Chicago: University of Chicago Press, 1970.

Levy, Frank; Meltsher, Arnold J.; and Wildavsky, Aaron. *Urban Outcomes*. Berkeley, Cal.: University of California Press, 1974.

MacCann, D., and Woodard, G. *The Black American in Books for Children: Readings in Racism*. Metuchen, N.J.: Scarecrow Press, 1972.

McCloskey, Robert G. *The American Supreme Court*. Chicago: University of Chicago Press, 1960.

————. *The Modern Supreme Court*. Cambridge, Mass.: Harvard University Press, 1972.

Mieklejohn, Alexander. *Political Freedom*. New York: Harper & Brothers, 1960.

Orfield, Gary. *The Reconstruction of Southern Education*. New York: Wiley-Interscience, 1969.

Peterson, LeRoy J.; Rosmiller, Richard A.; and Volz, Marlin M. *The Law and Public Education*. New York: Harper & Row, 1969.

Plato, *Republic*. In Edith Hamilton and Huntington Cairns, eds., *Plato: The Collected Dialogues*, Bollingen Series LXXI, p. 575. New York: Pantheon Books, 1961.

Rawls, John. *A Theory of Justice*. Cambridge, Mass.: Harvard University Press, 1971.

Reischauer, R., and Hartman, R. *Reforming School Finance*. Washington, D.C.: Brookings Institution, 1973.

Shapiro, Martin. *Law and Politics in the Supreme Court*. New York: Free Press of Glencoe, 1964.

Sullivan, Daniel J. *Public Aid to Nonpublic Schools*. Lexington, Mass.: D.C. Heath, 1974.

Tiedt, Sidney W. *The Role Of the Federal Government in Education*. New York: Oxford University Press, 1966.

Verba, Sidney, and Nie, Norman H. *Participation in America*. New York: Harper & Row, 1972.

Wellington, Harry H., and Winter, Ralph K. *The Unions and the Cities*. Washington, D.C.: Brookings Institution, 1971.

West, E.G. *Education and the State*, 2d ed. London: Institute of Economic Affairs, 1970.

Wirt, Fredrick M. *Politics of Southern Equality: Law and Social Change in a Mississippi County*. Chicago: Aldine, 1970.

Zimet, Melvin. *Decentralization and School Effectiveness*. New York: Teachers College Press, 1973.

Articles

Amyx, Carol. "Comment: Sex Discrimination: The Textbook Case." *California Law Review* 62 (July-September 1974):1312-1343.

Arons, Stephen. "Equity, Option, and Vouchers." *Teachers College Record* 72 (February 1971):337-363.

_____. "The Separation of School and State: *Pierce* Reconsidered." *Harvard Educational Review* 46 (February 1976):76-104.

Bell, Derrick A. "Waiting on the Promise of *Brown*." *Law and Contemporary Problems* 39 (Spring 1975):341-373.

Bereday, George S.F., and Stretch, Bonnie B. "Political Education in the U.S.A. and the U.S.S.R." *Comparative Education Review* 7 (June 1963):9-16.

Boyd, William. "The Public, the Professionals, and Educational Policymaking: Who Governs." *Teachers College Record* 77 (May 1976): 539-577.

Browning, R. Stephan, and Costello, Jack, Jr. "Title I: More of the Same?" *Inequality in Education* 17 (June 1974):23-45.

Budoff, Milton. "Engendering Change in Special Education Practices." *Harvard Educational Review* 45 (November 1975): 507-526.

Cohen, David K., and Murphy, Jerome T. "Accountability in Education—The Michigan Experience." *The Public Interest* 36 (Summer 1974):53-81.

Cohen, David K., and van Geel, Tyll. "The Public Education." In Samuel H. Beer and Richard E. Barringer, eds., *The State and the Poor*. Cambridge, Mass.: Winthrop Publishers, 1970: 231-258.

"Comment, Alternative Schools for Minority Students: The Constitution, The Civil Rights Act, and the Berkeley Experiment." *California Law Review* 61 (May 1973):858-918.

"Comment, Implementing Title IX: The HEW Regulations." *University of Pennsylvania Law Review* 124 (January 1976):806-846.

"Comment: Teacher Collective Bargaining—Who Runs the Schools?" *Fordham Urban Law Journal* 2 (Spring 1974):505-562.

"Comment: The Right of the Press to Gather Information after *Branzburg* and *Pell*." *University of Pennsylvania Law Review* 124 (November 1975):166-191.

Coons, John E., and Sugarman, Stephan. "Family Choice in Education: A Model State System for Vouchers." *California Law Review* 59 (March 1971):321-438.

Cronin, Joseph M. "The Federal Takeover: Should the Junior Partner Run the Firm?" *Phi Delta Kappan* 57 (April 1976): 499-501.

Davies, Don. "The Emerging Third Force in Education." *Inequality in Education* 15 (November 1973):5-22.

"Developments in the Law—Equal Protection." *Harvard Law Review* 82 (March 1969):1065-1192.

Eichelman, Fred R. "The Government as Textbook Writer: A Case History." *Phi Delta Kappan* 57 (March 1976):456-458.

Ely, John Hart. "Legislative and Administrative Motivation." *Yale Law Journal* 79 (June 1970):1205-1341.

Erickson, Donald A. "Showdown at an Amish Schoolhouse: A Description and Analysis of the Iowa Controversy.: In Donald A. Erickson, ed., *Public Controls of Nonpublic Schools*. Chicago: University of Chicago Press, 1969, pp. 15-59.

Flanagan, Robert L. "Note: The Right of Handicapped Children to an Education: The Phoenix of *Rodriguez*." *Cornell Law Review* 59 (March 1974):519-545.

Frantz, Laurent B. "The First Amendment in the Balance." *Yale Law Journal* 71 (July 1962):1424-1450.

Friedman, Milton. "The Role of Government in Education." In *Capitalism and Freedom*. Chicago: University of Chicago Press, 1962, pp. 85-107.

Gallagher, James J. "Phenomenal Growth and New Problems Characterize Special Education." *Phi Delta Kappan* 55 (April 1974):516-520.

Glazer, Nathan. "Towards an Imperial Judiciary." *The Public Interest* 41 (Fall 1975):104-123.

Goldstein, Robert J. "Elementary School Curriculum and Political Socialization." In Byron G. Massialas, ed., *Political Youth, Traditional Schools*. Englewood Cliffs, N.J.: Prentice-Hall, 1972, pp. 14-33.

Grubb, W. Norton and Lazerson, Marvin. "Rally 'Round the Workplace: Continuities and Fallacies in Career Education." *Harvard Educational Review* 45 (November 1975):451-474.

Gunther, Gerald. "Foreword: In Search of Evolving Doctrine on a Changing Court." *Harvard Law Review* 86 (November 1972):1-48.

Hamilton, Charles V. "Race and Education: A Search for Legitimacy." *Harvard Educational Review* 38 (Fall 1968):669-684.

Hazard, William R. "Courts in the Saddle: School Board Out." *Phi Delta Kappan* (December 1974):259-261.

Herr, Stanley. "Retarded Children and the Law." *Syracuse Law Review* 23 (Fall 1972): 995-1035.

House, Ernest R.; Rivers, Wendell; and Stufflebeam, Daniel L. "A Counter-Response to Kearney, Donovan, and Fisher." *Phi Delta Kappan* 56 (September 1974):19.

House, Ernest R.: Rivers, Wendell; and Stufflebeam, Daniel L. "An Assessment of the Michigan Accountability System." *Phi Delta Kappan* 55 (June 1974):663-669.

Iannaccone, Laurence. "The Politics of Federal Aid to Education in Massachusetts." In Joel S. Berke and Michael W. Kirst, *Federal Aid to Education*. Lexington, Mass.: D.C. Heath, 1972, pp. 193-233.

Jennings, M. Kent. "Correlates of the Social Studies Curriculum." In C. Benjamin Cox and Byron G. Massialas, eds., *Social Studies in the United States*. New York: Harcourt, Brace and World, 1967, pp. 289-305.

Joyce, Bruce R. "The Primary Grades." In C. Benamin Cox and Byron G. Massialas, eds., *Social Studies in the United States*. New York: Harcourt, Brace and World, 1967, pp. 15-36.

Karst, Kenneth L. "California, *Serrano* v. *Priest*'s Inputs and Outputs." *Law and Contemporary Problems* 38 (Winter-Spring 1974):333-349.

Katz, Jay. "The Right to Treatment—An Enchanting Legal Fiction?" *University of Chicago Law Review* 36 (Summer 1969):755-783.

Kearney, C. Phillips; Donovan, David L.; and Fisher, Thomas H. "In

Defense of Michigan's Accountability Program." *Phi Delta Kappan* 56 (September 1974):14-19.

Kirp, David L. "Schools as Sorters: The Constitutional and Policy Implications of Student Classification." *University of Pennsylvania Law Review* 121 (April 1973):705-797.

Kirst, Michael W. "The Growth of Federal Influence in Education." In C. Wayne Gordon, ed., *Uses of the Sociology of Education*. (The Seventh-Third Yearbook of the National Soceity for the Study of Education, Part II). Chicago: National Society for the Study of Education, 1974, pp. 448-477.

————. "The Politics of Federal Aid to Education in California." In Joel S. Berke and Michael W. Kirst, *Federal Aid to Education*. Lexington, Mass.: D. C. Heath and Co., 1972, pp. 77-130.

Klaus, Ida. "The Evolution of a Collective Bargaining Relationship in Public Education: New York City's Changing Seven-Year History." *Michigan Law Review* 67 (March 1969):1033-1066.

Levin, Betsy, and Moise, Phillip. "School Desegregation Litigation in the Seventies and the Use of Social Science Evidence: An Annotated Guide." *Law and Contemporary Problems* 39 (Winter 1975):50-133.

Lindauer, Mitchell J. "Government Employee Disclosures of Agency Wrongdoing: Protecting the Right to Blow the Whistle." *University of Chicago Law Review* 42 (Spring 1975):530-561.

McLaughlin, Milbery Wallin. "Implementation of ESEA Title I: A Problem of Compliance." *Teachers College Record* 77 (February 1976):397-415.

Massialas, Byron G. "American Government, We Are the Greatest." In C. Benjamin Cox and Byron G. Massialas, eds., *Social Studies in the United States*. New York: Harcourt, Brace & World, 1967, pp. 167-195.

Members of Harvard Graduate School of Education Seminar. "Quality Control for Instructional Materials: Legislative Mandates of Learner Verification and Implications for Public Education." *Harvard Journal on Legislation* 12 (June 1975):511-562.

Michelman, Frank I. "In Pursuit of Constitutional Welfare Rights: One View of Rawls's Theory of Justice." *University of Pennsylvania Law Review* 121 (May 1973):962-1019.

Mill, J.S. "On Liberty." In *Utilitarianism, Liberty, and Representative Government*. Everyman's Library Edition. New York: J.M. Dent & Sons, n.d.

————. "On Representative Government." In *Utilitarianism, Liberty, and Representative Government.* Everyman's Library Edition. New York: J.M. Dent & Sons, n.d.

Milofsky, Carl D. "Why Special Education Isn't Special." *Harvard Educational Review* 44 (November 1974):437-458.

Molina, John. "ESEA Title VII Bilingual Education: State of the Art." *Linguistic Reporter* 15 (November 1973):4.

Murphy, Jerome T. "Title I of ESEA: The Politics of Implementing Federal Education Reform." *Harvard Educational Review* 41 (February 1971):35-63.

Neiman, Tanya. "Comment: Teaching Woman Her Place: The Role of Public Education in the Development of Sex Roles." *Hastings Law Journal* 24 (May 1973):1191-1225.

"Note, 'The Courts,' HEW, and Southern School Desegregation." *Yale Law Journal* 77 (December 1967):321-365.

"Notes: Aliens' Right to Teach: Political Socialization and the Public Schools." *Yale Law Journal* 85 (November 1975):90-111.

Nowak, John E. "Realigning the Standards of Review Under the Equal Protection Guarantee—Prohibited, Neutral, and Permissive Classifications." *Georgetown Law Journal* 62 (March 1974):1071-1122.

Olafson, Fredrick A. "Teaching About Religion: Some Reservations." In Theodore R. Sizer, ed., *Religion and Public Education.* Boston: Houghton Mifflin, 1967, pp. 84-95.

Orfield, Gary. "How to Make Desegregation Work: The Adaptation of Schools to Their Newly-Integrated Student Bodies." *Law and Contemporary Problems* 39 (Spring 1975):314-340.

Peterson, Paul E. "The Politics of American Education." In F.N. Kerlinger and J.B. Carroll, eds., *Review of Research in Education,* 2, Itasco, Ill.: F. E. Peacock, 1974, pp. 348-386.

Porter, David O., and Warner, David C. "How Effective Are Grantor Controls?" In Kenneth E. Boulding, Martin Pfaff, and Anita Pfaff, eds., *Tax Transfer in an Urbanized Economy.* Belmont, Cal.: Wadsworth Publishing, 1973, pp. 276-302.

Read, Frank T. "Judicial Evolution of the Law of School Integration Since *Brown* v. *Board of Education.*" *Law and Contemporary Problems* 39 (Winter 1975):7-49.

Scribner, Jay D. "The Politics of Federal Aid to Education in Michigan." In Joel S. Berke and Michael W. Kirst, *Federal Aid to Education.* Lexington, Mass.: D.C. Heath, 1972, pp. 131-192.

Shaver, James P. "Reflective Thinking, Values, and Social Studies Textbooks," *School Review* 73 (Autumn 1965):226-257.

Sinaiko, Evelyn R. "Due Process Rights of Participation in Administrative Rule Making." *California Law Review* 63 (July 1975):886-925.

Smith, Frederick R., and Patrick, John J. "Civics." In C. Benjamin Cox and Byron G. Massalas, eds., *Social Studies in the United States*. New York: Harcourt, Brace and World, 1967, pp. 105-127.

Sugarman, Stephan D. "Family Choice: The Next Stop in the Quest for Equal Educational Opportunity." *Law and Contemporary Problems* 38 (Winter-Spring 1974):513-565.

Summers, Clyde W. "Public Employee Bargaining: A Political Perspective." *Yale Law Journal* 83 (May 1974):1156-1200.

"The Rights of the Public and the Press to Gather Information." *Harvard Law Review* 87 (May 1974):1505-1533.

"The Supreme Court, 1974 Term." *Harvard Law Review* 89 (November 1975):47-281.

Timpane, P. Michael. "Federal Aid to Schools: Its Limited Future." *Law and Contemporary Problems* 38 (Winter-Spring 1974):493-512.

Tyack, David. "The Perils of Pluralism: The Background of the Pierce Case." *American Historical Review* 74 (October 1968):74-98.

Weber, George. "The Case Against *Man: A Course of Study.*" *Phi Delta Kappan* 57 (October 1975):81-82.

Weinberg, Meyer. "The Relationship Between School Desegregation and Academic Achievement: A Review of the Research." *Law and Contemporary Problems* 39 (Spring 1975):241-270.

Weintraub, Fredrick J., and Abeson, Alan. "New Education Policies for the Handicapped: The Quiet Revolution." *Phi Delta Kappan* 55 (April 1974):526-529.

Wirt, Fredrick M., with assistance of Cresswell, Anthony M., and Irwin, Paul M. "The Politics of Federal Aid to Education in New York." In Joel S. Berke and Michael W. Kirst, *Federal Aid to Education*. Lexington, Mass.: D.C. Heath, 1972, pp. 325-375.

Wollett, Donald H. "The Bargaining Process in the Public Sectors: What is Bargainable?" *Oregon Law Review* 51 (Fall 1971): 177-182.

Reports

Cain, Nancy Ellen; Hensley, Gene; and Jones, C.D., "Questions and Answers: The Education of Exceptional Children." Report no. 73. Denver, Colo: Education and Commission of the States (September 1975).

Center for the Study of Public Policy, *Education Vouchers*. Cambridge, Mass. 1970.

Children's Defense Fund of the Washington Research Project, Inc., *Children Out of School*. Cambridge, Mass.: Children's Defense Fund, 1974.

Clasby, Miriam; Webster, Maureen, and White, Naomi. *Laws, Tests, and Schooling*. Syracuse, N.Y.: Educational Policy Research Center, October 1973.

New York Board of Regents, Position Paper No. 14. Quoted in Division of Curriculum Development, "Reviewing Curriculum for Sexism." Albany, N.Y.: N.Y. State Education Department, 1975 (booklet).

"Selected Curriculum Review and Textbook Selection Provisions Contained in Negotiation Agreements," *Negotiation Research Digest* 4 (March 1971):40-45.

Thompson, A. Gray, and Zeimer, Russel H. "Impact of Collective Bargaining on Curriculum-Instruction." *Research Report No. 1975-2*. Evanston, Ill.: National School Boards Association, 1975.

Title I of ESEA, *Is it Helping Poor Children?* (A Report by the Washington Research Project of the Southern Center for Studies in the Public Policy and the NAACP Legal Defense and Educational Fund, Inc., 1969.)

Weitzman, Lenore J., and Rizzo, Diane. "Biased Textbooks." Washington, D.C.: National Foundation for the Improvement of Education, 1974 (pamphlet).

Congressional Documents

U.S. Congress, House, H.R. Rep. no. 93-805 on the Educational Amendments of 1974. 93rd Congress, 2d Sess., 1974, reprinted in *U.S. Congressional and Administrative News* 3 St. Paul: West Publishing, 1975, p. 4093.

U.S. Congress, House, Science Curriculum Implementation Review Group, *National Science Foundation Curriculum Development and Implementation for Pre-College Science Education*, A Report Prepared for the House Committee on Science and Technology, 94th Cong., 1st Sess., November 1975.

U.S. Congress, Senate, Select Committee on Equal Education Opportunity. *Toward Equal Educational Opportunity*, S. Rep. no. 92-000, 92nd Congress, 2d Sess., (1970).

U.S. Congress, Senate, Select Committee on Equal Educational Opportunity. of the Senate, Hearings before the Senate Select Committee on *Equal Education Opportunity*, 91st Congress, 2d Sess. (1970).

U.S. Public Documents

Controller General of the United States. "Administration of the Science Education Project 'Man: A Course of Study.'" In U.S. Congress, House Committee on Science and Technology, *National Science Foundation Curriculum Development and Implementation for Pre-College Science Education.* 94th Congress, 1st Sess., November 1975.

Controller General of the United States. *Assessment of Reading Activities Funded Under the Federal Program of Aid for Educationally Deprived Children.* December 12, 1975.

National Advisory Council on the Education of Disadvantaged Children. *1975 Annual Report to the President and the Congress.* Washington, D.C.: 1975.

Science Curriculum Review Team. "Pre-College Science Curriculum Activities of the National Science Foundation." In U.S. Congress, House, Committee on Science and Technology, *National Science Foundation Curriculum Development and Implementation for Pre-College Science Education.* 94th Congress, 1st Sess., November 1975.

U.S. Bureau of the Census. *Census of Population: 1970. American Indians.* PC(2)-1F (Washington, D.C.: Government Printing Office, June 1973).

U.S. Bureau of the Census. *Census of Population: 1970. Japanese, Chinese, and Filipinos in the United States.* PC(2)-1G (Washington, D.C.: Government Printing Office, July 1973).

U.S. Bureau of the Census. *Census of Population: 1970. National Origin and Language.* PC(2)-1A (Washington, D.C.: Government Printing Office, June 1973).

U.S. Bureau of the Census. *Current Population Reports. Persons of Spanish Origin in the United States.* PC(2)-1C (Washington, D.C.: Government Printing Office, June 1973).

U.S. Commission on Civil Rights. *A Better Chance to Learn: Bilingual-Bicultural Education.* Clearinghouse Publication 51, May 1975.

U.S. Commission on Civil Rights. *The Excluded Student: Education Practices Affecting Mexican-Americans in the Southwest.* (Washington, D.C.: Government Printing Office, 1972).

Newspapers and Newsletters

Education U.S.A. February 9, 1976, p. 138.
Education U.S.A. March 15, 1976, p. 173.

Government Employment Relations Reporter No. 643, February 9, 1976, pp. D-1 - D-11.

Hipp, Dr. Frederick L. Quoted in *Educators Negotiating Service Newsletter* November 1, 1975, p. 61.

"Negotiation Agreements: Pupil Testing Procedures and Programs," *Negotiation Research Digest* 4, no. 8, April 1971, pp. 17-19.

New York Times. Tuesday, March 2, 1976, p. 14.

Rochester Democrat and Chronicle. March 27, 1976, p. 5A.

Local Public Document

San Francisco Unified School District, *Bilingual Education in the San Francisco Unified School District 1* (November 1, 1967), Appendix at 61 *Lau* v. *Nichols*, 414 U.S. 563 (1974).

Unpublished Materials

Block, Arthur R. "Compulsory School Attendance Laws: Limitations on Their Use Against Children in Non-Public Schools" (Cambridge, Mass., December 1972).

Block, Arthur, and van Geel, Tyll. "State of Arizona Curriculum Law." In "Authority to Control the School Curriculum: An Assessment of Rights in Conflict," by Tyll van Geel with assistance of Arthur Block, November 1975.

Britton, Gwyneth E. "Why Jane Can't Win: Sex Stereotyping and Career Role Assignments in Reading Materials." ERIC, ED 092-919, May 1974.

Clune, Daniel A., and Shelton, Dinah. "The Politics of Morality: A History of California's Guidelines for Moral Instruction." Childhood and Government Project, University of California, Berkeley.

Geffert, Hannah N.; Harper, Robert J. II; and Schember, Daniel M. "Dealing with Bias in Textbooks and Educational Material Used in the Public Schools: A Model Statute." Washington, D.C.: Lawyers' Committee for Civil Rights Under Law, n.d.

Geffert, Hannah N.; Harper, Robert J. II; and Schember, Daniel M. "Selecting Educational Material for Use in the Public School: A Model Statute." Washington, D.C.: Lawyers' Committee for Civil Rights Under Law, n.d.

Gerry, Martin H., Statement of, Dept. Dir., Office for Civil Rights, Before General Subcommittee on Education, Committee on Education and Labor, March 12, 1974.

Jay, W. "Sex Stereotyping in Selected Mathematics Textbooks for Grades Two, Four, and Six." Dissertation, University of Oregon, 1973.

Land, J., "Sex Role Stereotyping in Elementary School Readers, Grades 1-6, Adopted by the State of Indiana for the Years 1973-1978." Dissertation, Ball State University, 1974.

Schlessinger, F.R., et al., 'A Survey of Science Teaching in Public Schools of the United States." Columbus, Ohio: Center for Science and Mathematics Education, Ohio State University, 1971.

van Geel, Tyll. "Evaluation and Federalism." Special Qualifying Paper, Harvard Graduate School of Education, April 1970.

van Geel, Tyll. "Judicial Reform of the Political Education Program of the Public Schools: On Fairness, Vouchers, and Academic Freedom." Rochester, N.Y., January 1976.

Cases

Ackerman v. *Rubin*. 35 Misc. 2d 707, 231 N.Y.S.2d 112 (1962).

Acorn Auto Driving School v. *Board of Education,* 187 N.E. 2d 722 (1963).

Ahern v. *Board of Education of School District of Grand Island,* 327 F. Supp. 1391 (D. Neb. 1971).

Alexander v. *Phillips,* 31 Ariz. 503, 245 P. 1056 (1927).

Alvin Independent School District v. *Cooper,* 404 S.W.2d 76 (1966).

Andrews v. *Drew Municipal Separate School District,* 507 F.2d 611 (6 Cir. 1975).

Augustus v. *School Board of Escamba County,* 507 F.2d 152 (5 Cir. 1975).

Auster v. *Weberman,* 198 Misc. 1055, 100 N.Y.S.2d 60, *aff'd,* 278 A.D. 656, 102 N.Y.S.2d 418, *aff'd,* 302 N.Y. 855, 100 N.E. 47, *appeal dismissed,* 342 U.S. 884, *aff'd,* 278 A.D. 784, 104 N.Y.S.2d 65 (1951).

Baker v. *Owen,* 395 F. Supp. 294 (M.D. N.C. 1975), *affd,* 46 L. Ed. 2d 137 (1975).

Blaine v. *Board of Education,* 502 P.2d 643 (1972).

Blount v. *Rizzi,* 400 U.S. 410 (1971).

Board of Directors v. *Green,* 259 Iowa 1260, 147 N.W.2d 854 (1967).

Board of Education v. *Allen* 392 U.S. 236 (1968).

Board of Education v. *Bentley*, 383 S.W.2d 677 (1964).

Board of Education v. *Rockaway Township Education Association*, 120 N.J. Super. 564, 295 A.2d 380 (1972).

Board of Education, Levittown Union Free School District, Nassau County v. *Nyquist*, No. 8208/74 (Supreme Court, Nassau County, N.Y.)

Board of Education of Sycamore ex. rel. Wickham v. *State*, 80 Ohio St. 133, 88 N.E. 412 (1909).

Board of Education of Topeka v. *Welch*, 51 Kan. 792, 33 P. 654 (1893).

Board of Education of Union Free School District No. 3 of the Town of Huntington v. *Associated Teachers of Huntington*, 30 N.Y.2d 122, 331 N.Y.S. 2d 17, 282 N.E. 2d 109 (1972).

Board of Public Instruction of Taylor County, Fla. v. *Finch*, 414 F.2d 1068 (5 Cir. 1969).

Bond v. *Public Schools of Ann Arbor School District*, 383 Mich. 693, 178 N.W.2d 484 (1970).

Brandenburg v. *Ohio*, 395 U.S. 444 (1969).

Brown v. *Board of Education*, 347 U.S. 483 (1954).

Brusca v. *State Board of Education*, 332 F. Supp. 275 (E.D. Mo. 1971), *aff'd mem.*, 405 U.S. 1050 (1972).

Caldwell v. *Craighead*, 432 F.2d 213 (6 Cir. 1970), cert. denied, 402 U.S. 953 (1971).

Carpio v. *Tucson*, 21 Ariz. App. 241, 517 P.2d 1288 (1974).

Carrollton-Farmers Branch Independent School Dist. v. *Knight*, 418 S.W.2d 535 (1967).

Chicago v. *Mosley*, 408 U.S. 92 (1972).

Citizens for Parental Rights v. *San Mateo Cty. Bd. of Ed.*, 124 Cal. Rptr. 68, 51 Cal. App. 3d 1 (Cal. App. 1975).

City of Richmond v. *U.S.*, 45L.ed. 2d 245 (1975).

Clark v. *Holmes*, 474 F.2d 928 (7 Cir. 1972).

Cleveland Board of Education v. *La Fleur*, 414 U.S. 632 (1974).

Cole v. *Richardson*, 405 U.S. 676 (1972).

Committee for Public Education and Religious Liberty v. *Nyquist*, 413 U.S. 756 (1973).

Commonwealth v. *Renfrew*, 332 Mass. 492, 126 N.E.2d 109 (1955).

Commonwealth v. *Roberts*, 159 Mass. 372, 34 N.E. 402, (1893).

Connell v. *Higginbotham*, 403 U.S. 207 (1971).

Consolidated Edison Co. v. *NLRB*, 305 U.S. 197 (1938).

Corn Prod. Co. v. *Department of Health, Education, and Welfare*, 427 F.2d 511 (3 Cir. 1970).

Cornwell v. *State Board of Education*, 314 F. Supp. 340 (D. Md. 1969), *aff'd.*, 428 F.2d 471 (4 Cir. 1970), *cert. denied*, 400 U.S. 942 (1970).

Cox v. *Louisiana*, 379 U.S. 559 (1965).

Cross v. *Trustees of Walton Graded School*, 129 Ky. 35, 100 S.W. 346 (1908).

Daniel v. *Waters*, 515 F.2d 485 (6 Cir. 1975).

Dritt v. *Snodgrass*, 66 Mo. 286 (1877).

Dunellen Board of Education v. *Dunellen Education Association*, 64 N.J. 17, 311 A.2d 737 (1973).

Ehert v. *School District of Borough of Kulpmont*, 333 Pa. 518, 5 A.2d 188 (1939).

Elrod v. *Burns*, 44 U.S.L.W. 5091 (June 28, 1976).

Engle v. *Vitale*, 370 U.S. 421 (1962).

Epperson v. *Arkansas*, 393 U.S. 97 (1968).

Eubank v. *City of Richmond*, 266 U.S. 137 (1912).

Everson v. *Board of Education*, 330 U.S. 1 (1947).

FPC v. *Florida Power & Light Co.*, 404 U.S. 453 (1972).

F.S. Royster Guano Co. v. *Virginia*, 253 U.S. 412 (1920).

Farrington v. *Tokushige*, 273 U.S. 284 (1926).

Fiberboard Paper Products Corp. v. *NLRB.*, 379 U.S. 203 (1964).

Frederick L. v. *Thomas et al.*, Memorandum and Order Dated Jan. 7, 1976, Civ. Action No. 74-42 (E.D. D.C. Pa. 1976).

Freedman v. *Maryland*, 380 U.S. 51 (1965).

Gonzales v. *Fairfax-Brewster School Inc.*, 363 F. Supp. 1200 (E.D. Va. 1973), *cert. granted* 44 U.S.L.W. 3279 (1975), *aff'd sub nom.*, *Runyon* v. *McCrary*, 44 U.S.L.W. 5034 (1976).

Goss v. *Lopez*, 419 U.S. 565 (1975).

Graham v. *Richardson*, 403 U.S. 365 (1971).

Graves v. *Walton Cty. Bd. Ed.*, 300 F. Supp. 188 (D.C. Ga.) *affd*, 410 F.2d 1152 (5 Cir. 1968).

Grayned v. *City of Rockford*, 408 U.S. 104 (1972).

Green v. *County School Board*, 391 U.S. 430 (1968).

Griffin v. *Illinois*, 351 U.S. 12 (1956).

Guernsey v. *Pitkin*, 32 Vt. 224, 76 Am. Dec. 171 (1859).

Hamer v. *Board of Education*, 292 N.E.2d 569 (1973).

Hardwick v. *Board of School Trustees*, 54 Cal. App. 696, 205 P. 49 (1921).

Harper v. *Virginia Board of Elections*, 383 U.S. 663 (1966).

Hart v. *Community School Board*, 383 F. Supp. 699, (E.D. N.Y. 1974), *aff'd*, 512 F.2d 37 (2 Cir. 1975).

Hawaii State Teachers Association and Department of Education, reported in *Government Employment Relations Reporter* no. 480, E-1 (1972).

Helvering v. *Davis*, 301 U.S. 619 (1937).

Hetrick v. *Martin*, 480 F.2d 705 (6 Cir. 1973), *cert. denied*, 414 U.S. 1075 (1973).

Hobbs v. *Germany*, 94 Misc. 469, 49 So. 515 (1909).

Hobson v. *Hansen*, 269 F. Supp. 401 (D.D.C. 1967), *aff'd sub. nom.*, *Smuck* v. *Hobson* 408 F.2d 175 (D.C. Cir. 1969) (en banc).

Hopkins v. *Board of Education*, 29 Conn. Sup. 397, 289 A. 2d 914 (1971).

Illinois Department of Public Welfare v. *Haas*, 15 Ill.2d 204, 154 N.E. 2d 265 (1958).

In Matter of Feldheim, 8 Educ. Dept. Rptr. 136 (New York 1969).

In re Meyers, 119 N.Y.S. 2d 98 (1953).

In re Shinn, 195 CA 2d 165, 16 Cal. Rptr. 165 (1961).

Isquith v. *Levitt*, 285 A.D. 833, 137 N.Y.S.2d 497 (1955).

Jackson v. *Godwin*, 400 F.2d 529 (5 Cir. 1968).

James v. *Board of Education,* 461 F.2d 566 (2 Cir. 1972) *cert. denied* 409 U.S. 1042 (1972).

Johnson v. *Joint School District*, 95 Idaho 317, 508 P.2d 547 (1973).

Jones v. *Board of Trustees of Culver City School District,* 8 Cal. App. 2d 146, 47 P.2d 804 (1935).

Keefe v. *Geanakos*, 418 F.2d 359 (1 Cir. 1969).

Kelley v. *Johnson*, 44 U.S.L.W. 4469 (April 5, 1976).

Keyishian v. *Board of Regents of the University of State of New York,* 385 U.S. 589 (1967).

Kissick v. *Garland Independent School District,* 330 S.W.2d 708 (1959).

Knight v. *Board of Education of City of New York*, 48 F.R.D. 108 (E.D. N.Y. 1969); and also 48 F.R.D. 115 (E.D. N.Y. 1969).

Korematsu v. *United States*, 323 U.S. 214 (1944).

Kramer v. *Union Free School District No. 15*, 395 U.S. 621 (1969).

Lapolla v. *Dullaghan*, 63 Misc. 2d 157, 313 N.Y.S. 2d 435 (1970).

Larry P. v. *Riles*, 343 F. Supp. 1306 (N.D. Cal. 1972).

Lau v. *Nichols*, 483 F.2d 791 (9 Cir. 1973) (en banc).

Lau v. *Nichols*, 414 U.S. 563 (1974).

Lehman v. *City of Shaker Heights*, 418 U.S. 298 (1974).

Lemon v. *Bossier Parish School Board*, 444 F.2d 1400 (5 Cir. 1971).

Lemon v. *Kurtzmann*, 403 U.S. 602 (1971).

Leonard v. *School Committee*, 349 Mass. 704, 212 N.E.2d 468 (1965).

McCollum v. *Board of Education*, 333 U.S. 203 (1948).

McDonald v. *Board of Election Commissioners*, 394 U.S. 802 (1969).

McGowan v. *Maryland*, 366 U.S. 420 (1961).

McLeon v. *State ex. rel. Colmer*, 154 Miss. 468, 122 So. 737 (1929).

Maddox v. *Neal*, 45 Ark. 121 (1885).

Madera v. *Board of Education*, 386 F.2d 778 (2 Cir. 1967).

Magnum v. *Keith*, 147 Ga. 603, 95 S.E. 1 (1918).

March v. *Earle*, 24 F. Supp. 385 (D.C. Pa. 1938).

Matter of Hilary M. 73 Misc. 2d 513, 342 N.Y.S. 2d 12 (1972).

Matter of Peter H. 66 Misc. 2d 1097, 323 N.Y.S.2d 302 (1971).

Matter of Richard C. 75 Misc. 2d 517, 348 N.Y.S. 2d 42 (1973).

Meek v. *Pittenger*, 95 S. Ct. 1753 (1975).

Melton v. *Young*, 465 F.2d 1332 (6 Cir 1972).

Memorandum Opinion re Intended Decision, *Serrano* v. *Priest,* Civil no. 938,254 (Cal. Super. Ct., April 10, 1971).

Meyer v. *Nebraska*, 262 U.S. 390 (1923).

Miller v. *School District No. 2, Clarendon Cty., S.C.,* 256 F. Supp. 370 (S.C. 1966).

Mills v. *Board of Education*, 348 F. Supp. 866 (D.D.C. 1972).

Mitchell v. *McCall*, 273 Ala. 604, 143 So. 2d 629 (1962).

Morning v. *Family Publications Service Co.,* 411 U.S. 356 (1973).

Morris v. *Vandiver*, 164 Miss. 476, 154 So. 228 (1933).

Morrow v. *Wood*, 35 Wis. 59 (1874).

Murphy v. *Pocatello School District no. 25.* 94 Idaho 32, 480 P.2d 878 (1971).

Myers Publishing Co. v. *White River School Township,* 28 Ind. App. 91, 62 N.E. 66 (1901).

NEA v. *Board of Education of Shawnee Mission*, 512 P.2d 426, 84 LRRM 2223 (1973).

Neilan v. *Board of Directors of Independent School District of Sioux City*, 200 Iowa 860, 205 N.W. 506 (1925).

Neuhaus v. *Federico*, 505 P. 2d 939 (1973).

New Rider v. *Board of Education of Independent School District No. 1, Oklahoma,* 480 F. 2d 693 (10 Cir. 1973), *cert. denied,* 414 U.S. 1097 (1973).

Nickels v. *Board of Education of Imlay City Community Schools,* file no. 1546, Lapper County Circuit Court, January 3, 1967. Discussed in Joan Weitzman, *The Scope of Bargaining in Public Employment,* New York: Praeger, 1975, pp. 205-206.

Nistad v. *Board of Education of City of New York,* 61 Misc. 2d 60, 304 N.Y.S. 2d 971 (1969).

NLRB v. *Borg-Warner,* 356 U.S. 342 (1958).

Norwood v. *Harrison,* 413 U.S. 455 (1973).

Nutt v. *Board of Education,* 128 Kan. 507, 278 P. 1065 (1929).

Ordway v. *Hargraves,* 323 F. Supp. 1155 (D. Mass. 1971).

Owens v. *School Committee of Boston,* 304 F. Supp. 1327 (D. Mass. 1969).

Packer Collegiate Institute v. *The University of the State of New York,* 298 N.Y. 184, 81 N.E. 2d 80 (1948).

Parducci v. *Rutland,* 316 F. Supp. 352 (M.D. Ala. 1970).

Parrish v. *Moss,* 200 Misc. 375, 106 N.Y.S. 2d 577 (1951), *aff'd,* 279 A.D. 608, 107 N.Y.S. 2d 580 (1951).

Paulson v. *Minidonka County School District,* 93 Idaho 469, 463 P. 2d 935 (1970).

Pennsylvania Association for Retarded Children v. *Commonwealth,* 334 F. Supp. 1257 (E.D. Pa. 1971), *modified,* 343 F. Supp. 279 (E.D. Pa. 1972).

People v. *Donner,* 199 Misc. 643, 99 N.Y.S. 2d 830, *aff'd,* 278 A.D. 704, 103 N.Y.S. 2d 757, *aff'd,* 302 N.Y. 857, 100 N.E. 2d 48, *appeal dismissed,* 342 U.S. 884 (1951).

People v. *Levinsen,* 404 Ill. 574, 90 N.E. 2d 213 (1950).

People v. *School Board,* 161 N.Y. 598, 56 N.E. 81 (1900).

People v. *Turner,* 227 A.D. 317, 98 N.Y.S. 2d 886 (1950).

Permeter v. *Young,* 31 So. 2d 387 (1947).

Perry v. *Sinderman,* 408 U.S. 593 (1972).

Pickering v. *Board of Education,* 391 U.S. 563 (1968).

Pierce v. *Society of Sisters,* 268 U.S. 510 (1925).

Piper v. *Big Pine School District of Inyo County,* 193 C. 664, 226 P. 926 (1924).

Presidents Council, Dis. No. 25 v. *Community School Board No. 25,* 457 F. 2d 289 (2 Cir. 1972).

Rackley v. *School District No. 5, Orangeburg County, S.C.,* 258 F. Supp, 676 (D. S.C. 1966).

Realy v. *Caine,* 16 A.D. 2d 976, 230 N.Y.S. 2d 453 (1962).

Rice v. *Commonwealth,* 188 Va. 224, 49 S.E.2d 342 (1948).

Robinson v. *Cahill*, 118 N.J. Super. 223, 287A.2d 187 (1972), *modified and aff'd on other grounds*, 62 N.J. 473, 303 A. 2d 273 (1973).

Rosenberg v. *Board of Education of City of New York*, 196 Misc. 542, 92 N.Y.S. 2d 344 (1949).

Russo v. *Central School District No. 1*, 469 F. 2d 623 (2 Cir. 1972) *cert. denied*, 411 U.S. 932 (1973).

San Antonio Independent School District v. *Rodriguez*, 411 U.S. 1 (1973).

Sapp v. *Renfroe* 511 F. 2d 172 (5 Cir. 1975).

School Board Dist. No. 18, Garvin County v. *Thompson*, 103 P. 578 (1909).

School District of Abington v. *Schempp*, 374 U.S. 203 (1963).

Scott v. *Board of Education of Union Free School District No. 17*, Hicksville, 61 Misc. 2d 333, 305 N.Y.S. 2d 601 (1969).

Serrano v. *Priest*, 5 Cal 3d 584, 487 P. 2d 1241, 96 Cal. Rptr. 601 (1971).

Shapiro v. *Thompson*, 394 U.S. 618 (1969).

Shelton v. *Tucker*, 364 U.S. 479 (1960).

Sheppard v. *State*, 306 P.2d 346 (1957).

Smith v. *St. Tammany Parish School Bd.*, 448 F. 2d 414 (5 Cir. 1971).

Special School Dist. No. 65 v. *Bangs*, 144 Ark. 34, 221 S.W. 1060 (1920).

Spence v. *Bailey*, 465 F. 2d 797 (6 Cir. 1972).

Starkey v. *Board of Education*, 14 Utah 2d 227, 381 P. 2d 718 (1963).

State v. *Avoyelles Parish School Board*, 147 So. 2d 729 (1962).

State v. *Counort*. 69 Wash. 361, 124 P. 910 (1912).

State v. *Ferguson*, 144 N.W. 1039 (1914).

State v. *Ghrist*, 222 Iowa 1069, 270 N.W. 376 (1936).

State v. *Hoyt*, 84 N.Y. 38, 146 A. 170 (1929).

State v. *Lowry*, 191 Kan. 962, 383 P. 2d 962 (1963).

State v. *Massa*, 95 N.J. Super. 382, 231 A. 2d 252 (1967).

State v. *Peterman*, 32 Ind. App. 665, 70 N.E. 550 (1904).

State v. *Vaughn*, 44 N.J. 142, 207 A. 2d 537 (1965).

State College Area School District, reported in *Government Employment Relations Reporter*, No. 426, F-1 (1971).

State ex. rel. Andrews v. *Webber*, 108 Ind. 31, 8 N.E. 708 (1886).

State ex. rel. Barker v. *Stevenson*, 27 Ohio Op. 2d 223, 189 N.E. 2d 181 (1962).

State ex. rel. Brewton v. *Board of Education of St. Louis*, 361 Mo. 86, 233 S.W. 2d 697 (1950).

State ex. rel. Clark v. *Osborne*. 24 Mo. App. 309 (1887).

State ex. rel Idle v. *Chamberlin*, 12 Ohio Misc. 44, 175 N.E. 2d 539 (1961).

State ex. rel. Kelley v. *Ferguson*, 95 Neb. 63, 144 N.W. 1039 (1914).

State ex. rel. Mueller v. *Common Board of Joint School Dis. No. 2 of Princeton*, 208 Wis. 257, 242 N.W. 574 (1932).

State ex. rel. Shineman v. *Board of Education,* 152 Neb. 644, 42 N.W. 2d 168 (1950).

State ex. rel. Thayer v. *School District of Nebraska City*, 99 Neb. 338, 156 N.W. 641 (1916).

Stephens v. *Bongart*, 189 A. 131, 15 N.J. Misc. 80 (1937).

Sterzing v. *Ft. Bend Independent School District*, 376 F. Supp. 657 (S.D. Tex. 1973), *remanded,* 496 F.2d 92 (5 Cir. 1974).

Steward Machine Co. v. *Davis*, 301 U.S. 548 (1937).

Sweezy v. *New Hampshire*, 354 U.S. 234 (1957).

Sycamore Board of Education v. *State*, 88 N.E. 412 (1909).

Syracuse Teachers Association v. *Board of Education,* 35 N.Y. 2d 743 (1974).

T.A.F. v. *Duval County*, 273 So. 2d 15 (1973).

Talbot v *Board of Education of New York*, 171 Misc. 974, 14 N.Y.S. 2d 340 (1939).

Tate v. *Board of Education of Jonesboro, Ark., Special School District*, 453 F. 2d 975 (8 Cir. 1972).

Tinker v. *Des Moines Independent Community School District*, 393 U.S. 503 (1969).

Todd v. *Rochester Community Schools,*, 200 N.W. 2d 90 (1972).

Trustees of School v. *People*, 87 Ill. 303, 29 Am. Rep. 55 (1877).

United States v. *Butler*, 297 U.S. 1 (1936).

Valent v. *New Jersey State Board of Education,* 114 N.J. Super. 63, 274 A. 2d 832 (1971).

Wagner v. *Royal*, 78 P. 1094 (1904).

Ward v. *Flood*, 48 C. 36, 17 Am. R. 405 (1874).

West Hartford Education Association v. *DeCourcy*, 295 A. 2d 526 (1972).

West Irondequoit Teachers Association v. *Helsby*, 42 A.D. 2d 808, 346 N.Y.S.2d 418 (1973), *affd*, 35 N.Y.2d 46 (1974).

West Virginia Board of Education v. *Barnette*, 319 U.S. 624 (1943).

Whitcomb v. *Chavis*, 403 U.S. 124 (1971).

White v. *Regester*, 412 U.S. 755 (1973).

Wisconsin v. *Yoder*, 406 U.S. 205 (1972).

Wright v. *Houston Independent School District,* 486 F. 2d 137 (5 Cir. 1973), *cert. denied*, 417 U.S. 969 (1974).

Wright v. *State*, 209 P. 179 (1922).

Wulff v. *Inhabitants of Wakefield*, 221 Mass. 427, 109 N.E. 358 (1915).

Yates v. *United States*, 354 U.S. 298 (1957).

Yorktown Faculty Association v. *Yorktown Central School District No. 2*, 7 PERB 3030 (N.Y. 1974).

Young v. *Trustees of Fountain Grade School*, 64 S.C. 131, 41 So. 824 (1902).

Zeller v. *Donegal School District Board of Education*, 517 F. 2d 600 (3 Cir. 1975) (en banc).

Zimmer v. *McKeithan*, 485 F.2d 1297 (5 Cir. 1973).

Index

Index

abuse of discretion. *See* discretion, abuse of
academic freedom, 27-28, 120-123
accountability, 85-88
acculturation, 29-35
advisory committees (councils), 150-152
aliens, 27
alternative schools, 94
Alum Rock Union School District, 94
American Association of School Administrators, 125
Amish, 18, 157, 166
anti-Semitism, 133, 148
Arizona, 79, 85, 91, 110, 177
arm bands, black, 27, 28. *See also* free speech
athletics, 60-62, 83, 113, 142
authority (principles for allocating), ix, 7-12, 175

bargaining. *See* collective bargaining
behavior problems, 35
bias in educational materials, 148, 174, 180, 182
Bible, 21, 162
bicultural education, 4, 41, 91
bilingual education, 4, 35-36, 41, 55-57, 91-93, 110
black history, 41, 83
block grants, 70-71, 177
Board of Education. *See* School Boards; State Board of Education
Bok, Derek, 127
"Book of Genesis," 21
Brown v. *Board of Education*, 39, 40, 41
bureaucracy (federal and state agencies), 3, 45, 170
Burger, Chief Justice, 17

California, 78, 82, 83, 84, 89, 90, 93, 94, 99-104, 115, 129, 150, 161, 179

career education, 70, 88, 94
Cavalier Commonwealth, 175
centralization, 1-2, 73-83, 86, 151, 176-177
Chemical Study, 67
chief state school officer (Commissioner of, State Superintendent of), 1, 75, 76, 77, 79, 82-83
Childs, John, 22
Chinese-speaking students, 52
citizenship training. *See* political education
Civil Rights Act of 1964, 36, 44, 51-57
classification of pupils, 37, 41, 74-75, 88-89, 112, 148-149
class size, 6, 130
collective bargaining, 123-135
collective bargaining contracts, 133
Communism, 19, 24, 27, 83, 167, 174
compensatory education, 41, 179. *See also* Title I, ESEA
compulsory education, 18, 153, 155-157, 158
Congress. *See* U.S. Congress
constitutionally required curriculum, 42, 172
corporal punishment, 140, 157
counseling, 60, 83, 150
course of study, 109, 113, 155, 167
courses, 74, 77, 83, 113, 140-144, 155, 175
courts, role of, 32, 36, 38, 41, 56, 97, 108, 111, 113, 115, 129, 170, 172
curricular committees, 133
curriculum, ix, 36, 41, 42, 74, 78, 83, 109, 117, 133, 155, 157, 167, 174
curriculum development, 66-70

Darwin (evolution), 20-22
decentralization, 151. *See also* centralization
delegation of authority, scope of, 109, 112, 117, 145, 151, 163, 173, 182
discretion, abuse of, 74, 111, 113-115, 148, 163

245

discrimination, 24, 29, 30, 33, 36-37, 38-39, 55, 83, 120-121
due process, 35, 89, 108, 122-123, 149-150, 164, 183-184
Dunlop, John, 127

Educational Development Center, 69
educational materials. *See* instructional materials
educationally disadvantaged, 45-51
Elementary and Secondary Education Act of 1965, 43, 45-51, 94
English, 4, 29, 35, 52-53, 74, 91, 167, 168
English-as-a-second-language, 55
Epperson v. *Arkansas*, 20, 24, 30
equal protection, 24-26, 29, 30, 33-34, 36, 37, 40, 99, 107, 108, 120-121, 141, 145
establishment of religion, 20, 140
ethnic studies, 34, 41, 83
exclusion of political materials, 24, 33
exclusion of students, 35, 37, 62, 88, 97-98, 111, 114-115
exemptions from courses, 22, 141, 142-143, 180
experimental programs, 93
extracurricular activities, 60, 98, 113, 114

fairness, duty of, 180-182
Farrington v. *Tokushige*, 18, 168
federal aid, 43-44, 52, 57, 70-71, 91, 94, 169-170, 177
federal control, 171. *See also* Title I; Title VI; Title IX; U.S. Congress; U.S. Department of Health, Education and Welfare; U.S. Office of Civil Rights; U.S. Office of Education
fees, 98-99
finance, educational, schools, 38-39, 99-108, 184
First Amendment, 28, 63, 120, 121, 139, 167-168
fishbowl bargaining, 179
flag salute (pledge to the flag), 23, 27

Florida, 84, 85, 87, 152
Ford, Gerald A., U.S. President, 71, 177
foreign language instruction, 30, 41, 91, 144, 167
Fourteenth Amendment, 25, 29, 64, 99, 144
freedom of information, 138, 178
free exercise of religion, 18, 31, 141, 142, 165, 167, 168
free speech, 19, 23, 24, 28, 32, 63, 120, 139, 164, 165, 167
  prior restraint, 164
functional exclusion of students, 35-37, 38

Goss v. *Lopez*, 149, 150
grade structure, 148
grading pupils, 148
graduation requirements, 76-77, 85
grants-in-aid, 70-71, 91, 94-95, 169-170, 177. *See also* Federal aid

hair and dress codes, 31, 62, 111, 113, 114
Hamer v. *Board of Education*, 99
handicapped children, 36-37, 88-91, 98, 112, 150, 172, 176
Harvard Project Physics, 66
health courses, 141, 174
home economics, 30-31, 41, 57, 142, 143, 147
home instruction, 159-162, 165-166

individualized instruction, 113
instructional materials, 31, 41, 63-66, 80-83, 121-122, 133, 148, 180-183
integration, 40-41
Introductory Physical Science, 67

kindergarten, 109, 113, 143, 148
Kramer v. *Union Free School District No. 1*, 144

Lau v. *Nichols*, 53, 58, 59
Lawyers' Committee for Civil Rights Under Law, 148, 182, 183

learner verification, 84
learning disabilities, 36, 172
licensing, private schools, 153-154, 158, 163-165
Little Black Sambo, 33
local control, 2, 74-75, 86, 90, 96, 169, 173, 176
loyalty oath, 27, 120

Man: A Course of Study, 66, 68, 69, 137
Man-Made World, 68
married students, 114-115. *See also* students
Marx, Karl (Marxism), 19, 27, 167
Massachusetts, 90, 92, 93, 95, 144, 161, 182
mentally retarded children, 35, 37, 88-91, 150, 172
Merchant of Venice, The, 113, 148
methods of instruction, 35, 41, 55, 74, 113, 115, 147
Mexican-Americans, 5, 41
Michigan, 85-86, 98, 157
Mill, J.S., 22
minimally adequate education, 19, 35-41, 38, 39, 85, 104-105, 107, 112, 115
More Effective Schools Plan, 134
multi-party bargaining, 179

National Association of Secondary School Principals, 125
National Defense Education Act, 43
National Educational Association, 133
National School Boards Association, 133
National Science Foundation, 66-70
negotiations, 123-135
New Jersey, 104, 129, 130, 141, 157, 158, 162
New York, 84, 85, 89, 95, 98, 106-108, 112, 114, 115, 119, 129, 138, 151, 162, 163, 178
New York City, 134, 151
Nickels v. *Board of Education of Imlay City Community Schools*, 132

non-English-speaking students, 4, 29, 30, 35-36, 41, 52-57, 176
non-graded instruction, 148

Oliver Twist, 113, 148
Othello, 33

parent advisory councils, 150-152
parents, 19, 89, 92, 114, 139-151, 158, 162, 165, 167, 173-174, 182-183
participation, 137, 139, 144, 148, 176, 182
Pennsylvania Education Secretary, 172
Physical Science Study Committee, 66
Pierce v. *Society of Sisters*, 18, 139-140, 163, 173
Pittenger, John, 172
Plato, 18
policymaking system, 2, 13-16
political education (social studies), 74, 79, 83, 174-175, 180-182
prayers. *See* establishment of religion
pregnancy, 32, 62, 114
private groups, 145-147, 151
private schools, 18, 112, 153-167, 173-174
    certified teacher, 157, 161, 166
    definition, 159-160
    equivalence, 162. *See also* home instruction
    licensing, 163
    prior approval, 160
    registration, 153-154, 163
professionals, control by, 117-135, 176
promotion of pupils, 148
proportional representation, 138, 178
protest, 120, 139. *See also* free speech
public disclosure of bargaining positions, 179
pupils, classification. *See* classification of pupils

racial discrimination, 32-35, 37, 39-41. *See also* discrimination
racially biased materials, 32-35, 41, 63 *passim*, 157, 167, 172
Rafferty, Max, 80

records, permanent access to, 149, 150
reform, 177-186
religion, 20-21. *See also* establishment of religion; free exercise of religion; secular education
representation, 138, 178
Republic, The, 18
Reserve Officer Training Corps, 22, 142
right to an education, 97 *passim*
Riles, Wilson, 94
Robinson v. *Cahill*, 104-106

San Antonio Independent School District v. *Rodriguez*, 101-102
school boards (local districts), 63, 74, 109, 110, 117, 137, 144, 169
school finance, 38, 99, 108, 184
school program, ix, 41, 74, 78, 83, 88, 91, 109, 113, 133, 155
Science, A Process Approach, 67
scope of negotiations, 124-132, 178-179
secular education, 21, 42, 174
segregation, 39, 49, 98
Serrano v. *Priest*, 99-104
sex education, 59, 83, 140-142, 174
sexual discrimination, 30, 57-63, 63-66, 83-84. *See also* discrimination
sexual roles, 30
sexually biased materials, 31, 63-66, 83, 84, 172. *See also* discrimination; instructional materials
Shanker, Albert, 124
shop (industrial arts), 20, 31, 57
socialization. *See* acculturation
special education. *See* handicapped children
standards of review, 25, 29, 30, 34, 37, 39, 99, 100, 102, 107, 108, 145. *See also* equal protection
state aid for private schools, 20, 173
state board of education, 1, 75, 76, 77, 82-83, 110, 157, 163
state control, 86, 153. *See also* chief state school officer; local control; state board of education; state department of education; state legislatures
state department of education, 1, 92, 94-95
state legislatures, 1, 73, 88, 95
state textbook selection, 73, 76, 77, 78, 80-83, 84, 174-175, 177, 183
statewide assessment, 85-88
students, 28, 31, 32, 35, 39-41, 62, 111, 142-143, 144, 148
subdelegation of authority, 118
substantial evidence, 56
Summers, Clyde, 126
superintendent, local, 118, 119, 173
Supreme Court, 17, 36, 39, 53, 149, 164

Talmud, The, 162
teachers, 27, 37, 63, 93, 119, 120, 173, 182, 183
teachers, free speech, 27, 120, 139, 167
teachers, pregnant, 32
tests (standardized, I.Q.), 37, 41, 59, 76-77, 85, 89, 90, 152
textbooks, 31, 41, 63 *passim*, 73, 76, 78-83, 98-99, 108, 109, 113, 129, 133-134, 148, 157, 168, 174-175, 177, 182, 183. *See also* state textbook selection
Tinker v. *Des Moines Independent School District*, 28
Title I, ESEA, 43, 45-51, 94-95, 151
Title VI, Civil Rights Act of 1964, 44, 51-57, 63-66, 91, 171, 172
Title IX, Education Amendments 1972, 44, 57-63, 63-66, 172
tracking, 37, 88, 148

ultra vires, 109-110, 118, 130-131
unions, 123-135, 173
U.S. Commission on Civil Rights, 55
U.S. Congress, 44-45, 53, 58-59, 63-64, 71, 91
U.S. Department of Health, Education, and Welfare, 45, 51-66
U.S. Office of Civil Rights, 5, 7, 51, 57, 63, 171

U.S. Office of Education, 43, 45-51
United States v. *Butler*, 44-45

Vietnam Moritorium Day, 114
Virginia, 78, 161, 174-175, 177
Virginia History and Government
    Textbook Commission, 175
vocational education, 41, 43, 57, 70, 83,
    88
vote, right to, 138, 144-145

vouchers, 89, 93, 112, 184-186

Warren, Earl, 17
wealth discrimination, 38-39, 100. *See
    also* discrimination
Wellington, Harry, 126
West Virginia Board of Education v.
    Barnette, 23, 140, 167
Winter, Ralph, 126
Wisconsin v. *Yoder*, 18, 166

About the Author

Tyll van Geel, is Assistant Professor of Education at the College of Education, University of Rochester. He attended Princeton University, Northwestern University School of Law, where he received the J.D. degree, and the Harvard Graduate School of Education where he received the Ed.D. in 1972. Before turning his attention to education Professor van Geel worked as an attorney with the Civil Aeronautics Board in Washington, D.C. He has contributed articles and chapters to several journals and books on such issues as the constitutional rights of students, the role of the courts in educational policy-making, educational finance, federal aid to education, law and the school curriculum, and social philosophy and educational policy. In 1975 Professor van Geel was awarded a Spencer Fellowship by the National Academy of Education.